About the editor

David Francis is Senior Lecturer in the Department of Peace Studies at the University of Bradford, where he established and directs the Africa Centre for Peace and Conflict Studies. He has published extensively on the economics and politics of security in Africa. He is the author of *Uniting Africa: Building Regional Peace and Security Systems* (2006).

DAVID J. FRANCIS | editor

Peace and conflict in Africa

Zed Books

LONDON | NEW YORK

Peace and Conflict in Africa was first published in 2008 by Zed Books Ltd, 7 Cynthia Street, London N1 9JF, UK and Room 400, 175 Fifth Avenue, New York, NY 10010, USA

www.zedbooks.co.uk

Set in OurType Arnhem and Futura Bold by Ewan Smith, London
Cover designed by Andrew Corbett
Printed and bound in Malta by Gutenberg Press Ltd

Distributed in the USA exclusively by Palgrave Macmillan, a division of St Martin's Press, LLC, 175 Fifth Avenue, New York, NY 10010

A catalogue record for this book is available from the British Library
Library of Congress Cataloging in Publication Data available

ISBN 978 1 84277 953 8 hb
ISBN 978 1 84277 954 5 pb

Contents

Tables and figures

Tables

Figures

Acknowledgements

The contributors to this book provided an interesting and stimulating forum to engage with some of the critical issues pertinent to the understanding and appreciation of peace and conflict in Africa, in particular the challenge of agreeing on what constitutes a 'distinctive African interpretation and construction' of peace and conflict. Therefore, my sincere thanks and appreciation to all the contributors for this interesting and engaging opportunity. Without doubt, putting together an edited volume demands a lot of quality time, attention and focus from busy academics. But the editorial and technical aspects of this book were made easier by the remarkable support and expertise of Grace Maina, the John Ferguson Research Assistant, and Leslie Shyllon and David Yambasu, Research Assistants, in the Africa Centre. We appreciate with thanks their support. We also acknowledge with thanks the encouragement and support of Ellen McKinlay, the commissioning editor, and her colleagues at Zed Books.

About the authors

David J. Francis is the UNESCO Chair of African Peace and Conflict Studies and Senior Lecturer in the Department of Peace Studies at the University of Bradford.

Dr Tim Murithi is a Senior Research Fellow at the Centre for International Co-operation and Security in the Department of Peace Studies at the University of Bradford.

Dr Isaac O. Albert is Senior Lecturer and the Director of the Institute of African Studies at Ibadan University in Nigeria.

Dr João Gomes Porto is Lecturer in Peace Studies in the Department of Peace Studies and head of the African Regional Institutions Cluster Programme in the Africa Centre for Peace and Conflict Studies at the University of Bradford.

Dr Kenneth C. Omeje is a Lecturer in African Peace and Conflict Studies in the Department of Peace Studies and joint head of the Human Security Cluster Programme in the Africa Centre for Peace and Conflict Studies at the University of Bradford.

Professor Nana K. Poku is the John Ferguson Chair of African Studies in the Africa Centre for Peace and Conflict Studies and Director of Research in the Department of Peace Studies at the University of Bradford.

Dr Tony Karbo is Programme Manager for the University for Peace Africa Programme in Addis Ababa, Ethiopia, and Associate Lecturer in the Institute for Peace Leadership and Governance at Africa University in Zimbabwe.

Professor Jannie Malan is a Senior Research Fellow at ACCORD in South Africa and editor of the *African Journal of Conflict Resolution*.

Dr Belachew Gebrewold is Lecturer in African International Relations in the School of Political Science and Sociology at the University of Innsbruck in Austria.

Professor Mohamed Salih is Chair of Politics of Development at the Institute of Social Studies in The Hague and at the Department of Political Science at the University of Leiden in the Netherlands.

Dr Jim Whitman is Lecturer in Peace Studies at the University of Bradford and has directed both the Department of Peace Studies undergraduate and postgraduate degree programmes.

Abbreviations

ACCORD	African Centre for the Constructive Resolution of Disputes
AFRICOM	US Africa Command
AMIB	African Union Mission in Burundi
AMIS	African Union Mission in Sudan
AMISOM	African Union Mission in Somalia
ANC	African National Congress
APRM	Africa Peer Review Mechanism
ASF	African Standby Force
AU	African Union
CAR	Central African Republic
CBOs	Community-based organizations
CCM	Chama Cha Mapinduzi – 'Movement for the Revolution'
CCR	Centre for Conflict Resolution
CEWARN	Conflict Early Warning and Response Mechanism
CEWS	Continental Early Warning System
CFC	Ceasefire Commission
CMF	Commonwealth Monitoring Force
COMESA	Common Market for Eastern and Southern Africa
CPEs	Complex political emergencies
CPI	Corruption Perception Index
CPIA	Country Policy and Institutional Assessment
CUF	Civic United Front
DDR	Demobilization, disarmament and reintegration
DRC	Democratic Republic of Congo
ECOMOG	Economic Community of West African States Ceasefire Monitoring Group
ECOWAS	Economic Community of West African States
EITI	Extractive Industries Transparency Initiative
EU	European Union
FDC	Forum for Democratic Change
FDI	Foreign direct investment
GDI	Gross domestic income
GDP	Gross domestic product
GNP	Gross national product
GROs	Grassroots organizations
HDI	Human Development Index
HIPC	Heavily Indebted Poor Countries Initiative

HIV/AIDS	Human Immunodeficiency Virus/Acquired Immune Deficiency Syndrome
ICISS	International Commission on Intervention and State Sovereignty
ICTR	International Criminal Tribunal for Rwanda
IFIs	International financial institutions
IGAD	Inter-Governmental Authority on Development
IGASOM	Inter-Governmental Authority on Development, Peace Support Mission to Somalia
IMF	International Monetary Fund
IOs	International organizations
ISS	Institute for Security Studies
LDCs	Least-developed countries
LICs	Low-intensity conflicts
LICUS	Low-income countries under stress
LRA	Lord's Resistance Army
LURD	Liberians United for Reconciliation and Democracy
LWF	Lutheran World Federation
MDC	Movement for Democratic Change
MDGs	Millennium Development Goals
MDRI	Multilateral Debt Relief Initiative
MINURSO	United Nations Mission for the Referendum in Western Sahara
MMD	Movement for Multi-party Democracy
MODEL	Movement for Democracy in Liberia
MONUC	United Nations Mission in the Democratic Republic of Congo
MOSOP	Movement for the Survival of the Ogoni People
MSC	Military staff committee
NATO	North Atlantic Treaty Organization
NEPAD	New Partnership for African Development
NEPRU	Namibia Economic Policy Research Unit
NGOs	Non-governmental organizations
NPFL	National Patriotic Front of Liberia
NPI	Nairobi Peace Initiative
NPP	New Patriotic Party
NRGSS	National, regional and global state security
NRLFSA	National Religious Leaders' Forum of South Africa
OAU	Organization of African Unity
ODA	Overseas Development Assistance
OECD	Organisation for Economic Co-operation and Development
ONUB	United Nations Mission in Burundi (acronym in French)
ONUC	United Nations Operation in the Congo
PBC	Peacebuilding Commission
PBF	Peacebuilding Fund

PPRD	People's Party for Reconstruction and Democracy
PSC	Peace and Security Council
PSC	Protracted social conflict
RECs	Regional economic communities
RUF	Revolutionary United Front
SADC	Southern African Development Community
SADC-AAF	Southern African Development Community Allied Armed Forces
SADCC	Southern African Development Coordinating Conference
SAP	Structural adjustment programmes
SDF	Social Democratic Front
SIPRI	Stockholm International Peace Research Institute
SPLM	Sudanese People's Liberation Movement
SPLM/A	Sudanese People's Liberation Movement Army
SWAPO	South West Africa People's Organization
TRC	Truth and Reconciliation Commission
TRIPS	Trade-Related Aspects of Intellectual Property
UK	United Kingdom
UN	United Nations
UNCAC	United Nations Convention Against Corruption
UNCTAD	United Nations Conference on Trade and Development
UNDP	United Nations Development Programme
UNESCO	United Nations Educational, Scientific and Cultural Organization
UNMEE	United Nations Mission in Ethiopia and Eritrea
UNMIL	United Nations Mission in Liberia
UNMIS	United Nations Mission in Sudan
UNOCI	United Nations Operation in Côte d'Ivoire
UNTAG	United Nations Transitional Assistance Group
UNTSO	United Nations Truce Supervision Organization
US	United States of America
USIP	United States Institute for Peace
WANEP	West Africa Network for Peacebuilding
WB	World Bank
WMAP	Liberian Women Mass Action for Peace
WTO	World Trade Organization
ZANU	Zimbabwe African National Union
ZANU-PF	Zimbabwe African National Union Patriotic Front
ZAPU	Zimbabwe African People's Union

ONE | **Understanding concepts and debates**

1 | Introduction: understanding the context of peace and conflict in Africa

DAVID J. FRANCIS

Africa: context of peace and conflict

For most of the post-colonial history of Africa peace has remained elusive. Peace and development have proved far more difficult and complex to achieve than the Afro-optimists envisaged in the immediate post-independence period, owing to a range of domestic and external factors. Two contrasting iconic images have dominated the public, if not the global, perception of Africa. First, the image of the dangerous and mysterious Africa as represented by perennial violent wars and bloody armed conflicts, perpetual political instability, unrelenting economic crises, famine, disease and poverty – all symbolizing the 'hopeless continent' and the African predicament. Second, the wildlife safari and the Hollywood film industry image of Africa. This is represented by the rise of tourism and increase in popularity of the wildlife safari on the continent, and its portrayal by *National Geographic* magazine pictures and Hollywood movies in terms of extremes, i.e. of a romanticized place where lions, elephants and giraffes roam freely in a state of nature – e.g. *The African Queen* (1951), *Out of Africa* (1985) and *The Lion King* (1994) – but at the same time a dangerous, mysterious and exotic continent – e.g. *Dogs of War* (1980), *Black Hawk Down* (2001) and *Blood Diamond* (2006). These contrasting representations of Africa have not only been instrumental in shaping and reinforcing public perceptions about the continent, but have also legitimized the dominant worldview of a 'tragic continent' and a 'basket case'. It is therefore not surprising that the greater part of the media news coverage of Africa reflects the sensational and stereotypical presentations of the continent. According to Robert Stock, 'Africa's success stories have generated little media interest. The Western media's negative stereotyped reporting of African events have been instrumental in convincing the Western public as well as politicians, that Africa is a hopeless case' (Stock 2004: 35).[1] To some extent, therefore, this dominant presentation of the continent by the international media is possible only because Africa is not only the poorest region of the world but also the 'least-known continent' in the twenty-first century (ibid.: 6, 15).

These dominant presentations not only give the impression that Africa is a homogenous continent, but also fundamentally constrain our understanding of the nature, dynamics and complexities of peace and conflict in Africa. There are two common stereotypes used to convey the notion of a homogenous continent. First, 'Africa as a country', which depicts and describes the entire

3

continent as a single country.[2] C. P. Eze's recent book *Don't Africa Me* (2008) rejects the stereotypical presentation and tendency to homogenize the continent as if it were a single country. Second is the perception of Africa as a single region, not only in terms of continental size but more so in subregional terms, whereby there is no differentiation between what is often described as the 'five Africas', i.e. West, southern, East and Central, Horn and Maghreb North. These stereotypes and simplified depictions mask the important fact that Africa is a diverse, heterogeneous and complex continent, and this is reflected in its various peoples, cultures, ecological settings, historical experiences, and political and socio-economic geographies. Hence, one can safely talk about 'not one but many Africas' (Chazan et al. 1999: 14). As a dynamic continent, and since the pre-colonial era, Africa has been marked and transformed by certain dominant trends, patterns and influences, including strong, viable and developed pre-colonial empires and indigenous civilizations, slavery, colonialism, imperialism, decolonization and neocolonialism, cold war politics, post-colonial patrimonial states, and contemporary wars and armed conflicts. But a dominant feature of contemporary Africa is the trajectory of simultaneous advancement and reversal at both continental and regional levels. What is more, Africa in the first decade of the twenty-first century is very different from the Africa of the mid-twentieth century. The pattern of continuity and change remains a dominant feature of the continent.

Therefore, to understand the context of Africa and African politics and how this creates the conditions for wars and armed conflicts, insecurities and under-development, and the possibilities for peace and non-violent conflict transformation, we have to start with the 'dehomogenization' of African politics, i.e. the appreciation that we are not talking about a single, monolithic, homogenous and static sociocultural, political, economic, behavioural and attitudinal pattern of governance (Charlton 1983: 32–48). Despite the diversity and heterogeneity of the continent and African politics, however, there are also commonalities in terms of the dominance of the state and patterns of domestic politics based on neo-patrimonialism, excessive levels of external dependence, the rural–urban divide and the predominance of a rural population, and what Naomi Chazan et al. described as the 'Africanisation and localisation of politics' (1999: 14).

What does this analysis say about the context of contemporary Africa in relation to the problems and challenges of peace and conflict? Africa is a resource-rich continent and one of the most resource-endowed in the world. Of the twenty-one known minerals, the top five in terms of exports are crude oil, other petroleum products, natural gas, diamonds and coal. To illustrate its resource abundance, Africa produces an estimated 10 million barrels of oil per year, and its total share of world crude oil production is about 12 per cent. Nigeria, a leading oil producer, accounts for more than a quarter of Africa's oil production. In addition, Africa accounts for 18 per cent of the world's liquefied natural gas. Africa's abundant mineral and human resources, and the enormous wealth they produce, have not, however, translated into poverty reduction, long-term economic growth, increased livelihood or welfare for the majority of Africans. This paradox of 'poverty amidst plenty', and what some analysts describe as the 'natural resource curse', is largely due to bad management of natural resources by corrupt ruling and governing elites, state weakness and a range of external factors (African Development Bank 2007: xv–xix).[3] With the end of the cold war there has been renewed international interest in Africa's natural resources because of the threats to global energy resources and competition posed by the new emerging economic powers of China and India. According to the president of the African Development Bank, Donald Kaberuka,

> The rekindled interest in Africa's resources is largely driven by global economic growth, especially in Asia, and the related demand for fossil fuels and minerals. This situation raises questions: how the continent can best leverage its resources for its development given the complexities and trade-offs. Indeed, the market demand for Africa's natural resources is strong and growing; but Africa needs these resources too for its own development. (ibid.: iii)

What have been the consequences of bad governance and mismanagement of Africa's abundant resources? According to World Bank socio-economic and development indicators for sub-Saharan Africa, out of a population of 770.3 million (2006), the life expectancy at birth is 47.2 years. This is not surprising because only 44.4 per cent of all births are attended by skilled health staff.[4] In addition, only 54.5 per cent (2000) of the total population have access to improved water sources, while 52.9 per cent (2000) of the urban population have access to improved sanitation facilities. While there has been some modest improvement in the economic growth rate for sub-Saharan Africa at 5.6 per cent (2006) annual GDP, the total military expenditure limits the human security impact of this economic growth rate because it accounts for 1.6 per cent (2005) of total GDP. In addition, though there has been a remarkable increase in foreign direct investment (FDI), with net inflows of US$16.6 billion (2005) and a further US$32.6 billion (2005) in Overseas Development Assistance (ODA) – both buoyed by China's renewed 'romance' with Africa and the 2005 G8 aid commitment – long-term indebtedness is still a serious concern with a total of US$176.7 billion (2005) external debt and a total of 8.8 per cent (2005) of debt service on export of goods, services and income.[5] Furthermore, the UNDP Human Development Index (HDI) ranking gives an interesting indication of the level of underdevelopment and insecurities prevalent in Africa. Between 1990 and 2007, Africa's weak and failing states have dominated the bottom ten rankings of the HDI Low Human Development category. In fact, during the same period, two African countries have constantly been listed in the bottom three and ranked as the 'worst place to live in the world': Niger and Sierra Leone (see Table 1). In addition, global

5

TABLE 1.1 Human Development Index 1990–2007: bottom five countries

1990 country ranking	1995 country ranking	2000 country ranking	2005 country ranking	2007 country ranking
170 – Chad	170 – Afghanistan	170 – Burundi	173 – Chad	173 – Mali
171 – Sierra Leone	171 – Ethiopia	171 – Ethiopia	174 – Mali	174 – Niger
172 – Burkina Faso	172 – Mali	172 – Burkina Faso	175 – Burkina Faso	175 – Guinea Bissau
173 – Mali	173 – Sierra Leone	173 – Niger	176 – Sierra Leone	176 – Burkina Faso
174 – Niger	174 – Niger	174 – Sierra Leone	177 – Niger	177 – Sierra Leone

Sources: UNDP Human Development Reports, 1990, 1995, 2000, 2005 and 2007

environmental problems and, in particular, the negative effect of climate change are set to adversely affect Africa. According to the African Development Bank Report (2007), by 2025 almost 50 per cent of Africans will be living in areas of water scarcity or water stress because of increasing depletion and scarcity of water resources. Though Africa accounts for the lowest greenhouse emissions of any continent, it is likely to bear the most disastrous consequences of climate change because of its 'overdependence on natural resources and rain-fed agriculture, land degradation and the on-going deforestation process – compounded by widespread poverty and weak capacity for planning, monitoring and adaptation to the changes' (ibid.: xviii).

In addition, political stability and governance indicators have been rather depressing. According to the Fund for Peace Failed States Index ranking for 2007, eight out of the top ten most unstable countries in the world are in Africa.[6] The 2007 Transparency International Corruption Perception Index (CPI) lists seven African countries as part of the twenty countries ranked as highly corrupt, with Somalia ranked the second-most corrupt country in the world.[7] Both the CPI and the Failed States Index are problematic, however, for several reasons. In particular, the Failed States Index uses three broad indicators (social, economic and political) to determine the level of instability or judge the 'most critical cause of state failure'. The broad and specific indicators used to measure instability are difficult to quantify. Since this exercise is not 'rocket science', the index gives only an indication of the level of instability or cause of state failure, bearing in mind that these putative indicators are often clouded by political and hegemonic biases. For example, Sudan and the crisis in Darfur cannot be compared with what is globally acknowledged as the 'chaos and mayhem' that prevails in Iraq and Afghanistan. Yet these countries are ranked second (Iraq) and eighth (Afghanistan) in the Failed States Index.

Wars and armed conflicts have dominated the presentation and international media coverage of Africa because of the high incidence of political violence, and the frequency and multiplicity of wars and armed conflicts. According to the Uppsala University conflict database, Africa has had more wars and armed conflicts than any other region in the world. Based on the survey of conflicts by region between 1946 and 2006, Africa had the highest number of conflicts (74) in comparison to Asia (68), the Middle East (32), Europe (32) and the Americas (26).[8] Based on this survey, the period 1990–2002 witnessed the intensification of wars and armed conflicts in Africa. This is not surprising because this period also witnessed the end of the cold war and its negative impact on the continent led to the emergence of what has been described as 'post-Cold War wars' in Africa, driven by the opportunities of neoliberal globalization (Francis 2006a: 80–85; Kaldor 1999; Duffield 2002).

But all these global indicators and indexes on Africa have one thing in common: the tendency to portray the continent as perpetually dangerous, undeveloped and ungovernable. In several ways, this reinforces the dominant international media presentation of Africa. In addition, these indicators and indexes fail to capture the contradictory trajectory of reversal and advancement that has come to define the continent at the dawn of the twenty-first century. Contrary to most of the conflict data on Africa, the reality is that deadly violence, wars and armed conflicts are on the decrease. Between 2000 and 2002, there were eighteen active wars and armed conflicts in Africa. As of February 2008, there were only five active wars and armed conflicts ongoing on the continent: Sudan (Darfur region), Kenya (post-election violence between December 2007 and February 2008), Somalia (excluding Somaliland), DR Congo (eastern region) and Chad. This decrease in wars in Africa is also reflected in the Uppsala University conflict database survey. The sharp decline in wars and armed conflicts indicates the level and intensity of African and international engagement in preventive diplomacy, conflict management and peacekeeping.

Based on the rather depressing socio-economic, development and governance indicators, some sections of the international community have been unanimous in the view that Africa will fail to meet any of the targets for the Millennium Development Goals (MDGs) by 2015. According to the UN World Summit Declaration (2005): 'Africa is the only continent not on track to meet any of the goals of the Millennium Declaration by 2015'.[9] Given the fact that the MDGs have emerged as a development framework for the global governance institutions, international financial institutions (IFIs) and donor agencies in their development cooperation partnerships with Africa, and in particular low-income countries, the persistent presentation of Africa as being off track in meeting any of the targets raises some concerns. William Easterly argues that the 'MDGs are poorly and arbitrarily designed to measure progress against poverty and deprivation, and [...] their design makes Africa look worse than it really is' (Easterly 2007: 2). Easterly agrees that Africa's performance has been poor, but its 'relative performance looks worse because of the particular way in which the MDGs' targets are set'. Some scholars have been critical of the MDGs in relation to Africa and even question the efficacy of measuring or quantifying social and economic progress, the politics of target-setting and benchmarks that may be disadvantageous to certain regions. In addition, they argue that the goals themselves are far too ambitious and do not take into consideration the continent's particular historical circumstances and development trajectory. They also question the link between increased aid and the likely attainment of the MDGs (ibid.: 1–22; Clement and Moss 2005; Charles et al. 2007: 735–51).

Is Africa a lost cause? Far from being a 'tragic continent' and a mere 'basket case', Africa's peace and security challenges have emerged as a global concern and as rekindled international interest in the continent, as manifested by the 'war on terrorism' and the new predatory capitalist scramble (China and the West) for energy resources (oil and gas) in Africa. This unprecedented international focus on and engagement with Africa really took off in 2005 with former prime minister Tony Blair's Commission for Africa as part of the UK's EU and G8 presidency initiative to put the continent at the top of the international agenda. This has been followed by highly commercialized aid initiatives, fund-raising campaigns and high-profile adoption of African children by Hollywood celebrities, to the extent that some media commentators now allude to 'Brand Africa'.[10] To underscore the growing importance of Africa, in February 2007 President George Bush formally announced the establishment of the US Africa Command – AFRICOM – because 'Africa is growing in military, strategic and economic importance in global affairs'. With a budget of US$75.5 million (1 October 2007–30 September 2008 fiscal year), AFRICOM will be responsible for US security in Africa.[11] The renewed international focus on and engagement with Africa have brought to the fore the imperative for peace and conflict resolution on the continent as a prerequisite for democratic consolidation, political stability, social progress, long-term economic growth and sustainable development.

If this is the case, how do we provide a meaningful interpretation of politics and development in contemporary Africa, irrespective of the diversity and heterogeneity of the continent? The dominant interpretations and approaches to the study and understanding of African politics in the 1960s and 1970s have been modernization and dependency theories. These schools of thought have been the subject of many scholarly publications. This introductory chapter will therefore not attempt to recast the usual debates and interpretations.[12] Against the background of the failure of both modernization and dependency theories to explain politics and development in post-colonial Africa, a new political economy interpretation emerged in the 1980s to provide an understanding of politics, underdevelopment, economic crises, wars and armed conflicts in contemporary Africa. This dominant interpretation – variously described as patrimonialism and neo-patrimonialism, patron-clientelism, personalized rule and prebendal politics – primarily focuses on the importance and interactions of the state and state actions, state leaders and the nature of domestic politics, the historical as well as the domestic sociocultural forces, external factors and the international economy.[13] In general, this political economy interpretation looks at the 'inner workings of power politics within Africa', what the power-holders have done to the post-colonial state, 'its uses and abuses', and the subordination of official state and state governing institutions to the vested interests of the small ruling and governing elites. According to Chazan et al., the instrumental utility of politics and governance in contemporary Africa as represented by neo-patrimonial statist analysts is largely responsible for much of the problems in that:

If Africa is undergoing a process of impoverishment, then leaders of the new state bear much of the blame for this state of affairs. The food crisis of the early 1980s, the debt crisis of the mid-1980s, the civil wars of the 1990s, and the ensuing crisis

9

of governability are the outcome of an extractive view of politics that has guided African ruling classes for over a generation. (Chazan et al. 1999: 22)

It will be helpful at this stage to provide a concise and precise definition of some of these terminologies as the reader will encounter them throughout the book.

Patron-clientelism is a patronage network that binds both patron and client together in a system of exchange in which the relationship is mutually beneficial (offering general or specific support and assistance), but at the same time the power, control and authority lie with the patron. As an instrumental political relationship it is replicated at different levels, including local, national and international, and between individuals, groups, communities and states (see Francis 2001). Political clientelism and ethnic clientelism have been used to describe this mode of governance.

Patrimonialism and neo-patrimonialism are extensions of the politics of patron-clientelism and political patronage. Patrimonialism and neo-patrimonialism, as systems of governance, involve the exercise of political authority based on an individual, whereby patrimony (public resources) is used to serve the private and vested interests of the state power-holders, including the ruling and governing elites. In this system, the state governing institutions are appropriated, used, subverted, privatized, informalized and subordinated to the interests of the personalized ruler, the regime in power and its supporters. There is no distinction between the public (*res publica*) and the private realm of governance, and political ascendancy as well as individual preferment is based on loyalty to the power-holder. Within this system, the power-holder emerges not only as a personalized ruler and the prime purveyor of patrimonial resources but also commands monopoly over all formal political activity, whereby the formal state and governmental institutions are subordinated to the leader's vested and strategic interests (Yates 1996: 5; Weber 1958). Patrimonialism and neo-patrimonialism have been generally characterized as prebendal politics to describe personal benefits derived or acquired from patrimony and/or public office. In addition, these concepts have been applied to the context of resource-rich states that receive and depend on external rents through the exploitation of extractive industries and economies such as oil and diamonds. This analysis is referred to as rentierism or the rentier state (Mahdavy 1970; Omeje 2008: 1–25).

Four books have been influential in the international understanding of neo-patrimonialism in contemporary Africa: Jean-François Bayart's *The State in Africa: The politics of the belly* (1993), Bayart et al., *The Criminalization of the State in Africa* (1999), William Reno's *Warlord Politics and African States* (1998) and Berdal and Malone's *Greed and Grievance: Economic agendas in civil wars* (2000). These books have generated much controversy as well as criticism, but their primary contribution is the focus on how the state and its power-holders in Africa have become avenues and channels for organized criminal activity in the form of informalization and privatization of state governing institutions, large-scale fraud and smuggling, the emergence of private militias and the privatization of civil wars, the growth of an economy of plunder, and the 're-traditionalization of society' through the use of witchcraft and occult practice in governance and civil wars; all of these within the broader context of the opportunities and outlets provided by neoliberal globalization (Bayart et al. 1999; Berdal and Malone 2000). A version of this neo-patrimonial interpretation of politics and development in contemporary Africa is the controversial concept of 'political instrumentality of disorder' advanced by Patrick Chabal and Jean-Pascal Daloz (1999). These authors define the political instrumentality of disorder as a 'process by which political actors in Africa seek to maximize their returns on the state of confusion, uncertainty, and sometimes even chaos, which characterises most African polities'. The justification is that 'what all African states share is a generalised system of patrimonialism and an acute degree of apparent disorder' (ibid.: xviii, xix). This is not only a crude generalization that does not reflect the reality in the majority of African countries, but also falls into the very trap that Chabal and Daloz disparage as 'resorting to the so-called mysteries of Africa's "barbarism"' (ibid.: xvii). In addition, this 'political instrumentality of disorder', when applied to much of Africa, neglects the impact of outstanding and exceptional African leaders who have transcended neo-patrimonialism for long-term development commitments, such as Julius Nyerere of Tanzania, Seretse Khama and Quett Masire of Botswana and Nelson Mandela of South Africa.[14]

Neo-patrimonialism and its applications have, however, been problematic because the state in Africa is not a homogenous entity, but rather a product of different and complex state–society relations. In fact, politics in Africa and the issues that cause and instigate wars and conflicts are not simply about leaders or 'personalized rule', but rather about a whole range of complex local and external socio-economic factors, formal and informal contested alliances around identity, resources and the struggle for access to state power and its patrimonial resources. In addition, the neo-patrimonial state and personalized rule do not exist or operate in a vacuum. External factors and international conditions such as the cold war imperatives made it possible to prop up and sustain bloody dictators and autocrats such as President Mobutu of Zaire and the self-styled Emperor Bokassa of the Central African Republic. Therefore, Chazan et al. argue that 'Politics in Africa (as elsewhere), however, cannot be reduced so easily to the activities of actors on the national scene. State institutions interact, with governments depending on changing conditions; and power constellations are not entirely state-centric' (Chazan et al. 1999: 23). Ibrahim Abdullah's edited volume, *Between Democracy and Terror: The Sierra Leone Civil War* (2004), subjects the neo-patrimonial state analysis in relation to peace, conflict and war in contemporary Africa to serious scrutiny. Through a case study of Sierra Leone

– the internationally recognized proxy for simplifying warlord politics and the collapse of the neo-patrimonial state – Abdullah and Yusuf Bangura challenge the application of patrimonial analysis as the only explanatory variable for the civil war. Abdullah argues that 'To privilege an abstract market-centred analysis, to use the now popular binary – greed and grievance – in explaining the Sierra Leone crisis is to neglect the historical process and the multiple actors in the drama of the war and its continuation' (Abdullah 2004: 2). Both Abdullah and Bangura posit that rather than simplify the logic of neo-patrimonialism and how this leads to wars and armed conflict, it is important to interrogate the specific forms of patrimonial accumulation within certain forms of political development and how this may produce violent crisis and war (Bangura 2004: 13–40). Abdullah's seminal book draws attention to the fact that neo-patrimonialism is not only an insufficient explanation of politics in Africa, but also only one plausible interpretation of the undercurrents and drivers of peace and conflict in Africa. In fact, the state–society relationship has emerged as an important lens through which to understand political as well as development dynamics in relation to peace and conflict in contemporary Africa. This politico-development interaction framework looks beyond the state and state institutions as well as political leaders, and instead focuses on the interaction of external actors and forces and domestic sociocultural and economic activities, forces and institutions in Africa. Therefore, if peace has been elusive, in our attempt to understand the problems and challenges of peace and conflict and, in particular, the possibilities and opportunities for peace and conflict resolution, we have to explore a range of domestic and external factors and actors, including political, sociocultural, economic, developmental, military and security issues, as well as state and non-state actors. This is the primary preoccupation of the contributions in this edited volume.

Outline of the book

This book has two primary objectives. First, to present in a single volume a critical understanding of the main concepts, debates and theoretical interpretations of peace and conflict studies in Africa. Second, to critically outline in an advanced and sophisticated overview a distinctive interpretation of peace and conflict, with a particular focus on African indigenous approaches to peace, conflict resolution, security, development and peace-building. But what is new or original about this particular focus, and why does it matter to academics, policy practitioners, and humanitarian and development interveners? There is no single text that specifically addresses the evident gap in the literature on peace and conflict research in Africa. This is not to say that other related and thematically focused books on peace and conflict studies do not exist. A simple glance at the indicative readings outlined for most of the course programmes at undergraduate and postgraduate levels relating to African peace, conflict and development studies, including African politics, delivered at Western universities (in the UK, western Europe and North America, as well as Australia and New Zealand), shows no specifically recommended book on African peace and conflict studies. A few recently published books relating to the theme focus more on generic issues and case studies, with a preoccupation with sociological case studies and mainstream African politics and international relations. This book is therefore an attempt to fill the gap in the literature on African peace and conflict research.

Furthermore, the wars and armed conflicts ongoing in Africa, and the difficulties and challenges to be overcome to resolve, manage and build the peace in these war-torn and post-conflict societies, have led to the emergence of a new 'peace industry' whereby most African universities are offering course programmes in peace and conflict studies. In addition, a range of NGOs and policy research institutes have mushroomed, offering expertise to deliver education and applied skills training programmes on Education for Peace, conflict resolution and peace-building. Based on the curriculum development and programme implementation work of the Africa Centre at the University of Bradford in more than eight transition countries in Africa, we have found that most of the course and training programmes are based on ad hoc improvisation and lack serious academic foundation. The main problem identified, in addition to the lack of trained and qualified experts, is the lack of a distinctive text on African peace and conflict studies that brings together both the African and dominant Western approaches to peace, conflict, security and development. This book has therefore been developed with a view to addressing this critical knowledge gap for a range of university students, policy-makers and practitioners, diplomats, researchers and education specialists, and humanitarian and development practitioners in the field.

Importantly, this edited volume is an attempt to present a radical interpretation of peace and conflict studies in Africa that will complement the understanding of the dominant Western literature and knowledge transfer programmes on Education for Peace in Africa. The 'exportation' of peace and conflict studies in Africa since the 1990s has been largely devoid of serious academic and intellectual knowledge of African approaches to peace-building and conflict resolution. It is as if the continent, believed to be the cradle of humanity, had no such societal, cultural and traditional resources for the prevention, management and resolution of conflicts. This book makes an original contribution by critically outlining the conceptual and theoretical debates and thematic issues in peace and conflict research, from a distinctively Africanist perspective that not only endeavours to deconstruct the dominant discourses and interpretations but also, and most importantly, to bring to the fore the much-neglected African understanding of and approaches to peace and conflict resolution.

The book is organized into eleven chapters in two parts dealing with concepts and theoretical debates and issues in peace and conflict in Africa. Given the broad spectrum of peace and conflict in the context of Africa, the book is eclectic in its coverage of some of the important themes pertinent to the understanding of peace and conflict. As such, some important themes, such as gender, peacekeeping and development, have not been covered for a variety of reasons. These themes are, however, extensively treated as specific chapter contributions in this edited volume.

This introduction, Chapter 1, sets the context for understanding peace and conflict in Africa. The critical focus of the contextual outline is to demonstrate that peace and conflict do not exist or operate in a vacuum or isolation, but essentially interact with and are influenced by specific historical and sociocultural forces, the nature of domestic politics and its international dimensions.

In Chapter 2, Tim Murithi conceptualizes indigenous and endogenous approaches to peace-building, conflict management and resolution in post-colonial Africa. Through the examples of indigenous peace processes practised by the Tiv community in Nigeria, the *guurti* system in Somaliland (northern Somalia), the *Mato Oput* peace-building among the Acholi in northern Uganda, and the *ubuntu* reconciliation tradition in southern Africa, Murithi interrogates the relevance and potential utility of these indigenous practices and resources to the management and resolution of modern conflicts in Africa.

Chapter 3 provides a critical conceptualization and understanding of the meaning and construction of peace in Africa, irrespective of the diversity and heterogeneity of the continent. Isaac Albert utilizes a philosophical framework for the understanding of peace in the context of Africa by drawing from the continent's rich traditional resources, such as proverbs, songs, elders' and traditional chiefs' cultural systems, folklore and religious belief systems.

In Chapter 4 João Gomes Porto presents an analytical interpretation of the conflict analysis perspective and its application to the context of Africa. Porto's primary focus in examining the theories of conflict analysis is to challenge some of the simplistic but dominant interpretations used to explain peace and conflict in Africa, such as the 'greed and grievance' thesis and the 'resource curse' interpretations.

Chapter 5 focuses on the definition and theoretical interpretations of conflict resolution in Africa. Kenneth Omeje critically examines the different conflict management and resolution strategies and interventions used to contain, stabilize, manage and resolve violent and bloody wars and armed conflicts in Africa with the examples of ECOWAS, SADC, IGAD and the African Union.

In Chapter 6, Nana Poku examines the concept and practice of security in the African context within the framework of the African state system and the state problematic in generating insecurity and underdevelopment in the continent. To illustrate the challenges of Africa's security problematic, Poku highlights some of the critical issues, such as poverty, underdevelopment, the difficulties faced by the continent in achieving the targets of the Millennium Development Goals, the HIV/AIDS pandemic, and how all these are further compounded by the debt burden, wars and political instability.

In Chapter 7, Tony Karbo defines and conceptualizes the dominant debates and interpretations of peace-building and examines why and how African indigenous approaches to peace-building have been neglected through the imposition of the liberal peace project in post-war peace-building and reconstruction, what he describes as the 'commercialization' and 'NGO-ization' of peace-building in Africa.

In Chapter 8, Jannie Malan defines and conceptualizes the key debates and theoretical approaches to the understanding of transitional justice in Africa. Through the case studies of the *Gacaca* traditional approach to justice and reconciliation, as well as the International Criminal Court for Rwanda and the Truth and Reconciliation model of South Africa, Malan critically evaluates the implications of these two contradictory models for peace-building, justice and reconciliation in Africa. Malan demonstrates how these models enable an understanding of the link between democracy/democratization and the opportunities as well as the challenges for peace and conflict in Africa.

In Chapter 9 Belachew Gebrewold defines and conceptualizes the notion and construction of democracy and democratization and their application in the context of Africa. A major focus of the chapter is the examination of the problems, 'dangers', challenges and opportunities of democracy and the democratization experiment in post-colonial Africa. Gebrewold argues that though 'democracy' is not alien in the continent, the consolidation of democracy as an 'associational life' is challenged by several factors, including lack of long-term democratic institutions and culture, ethnicity and neo-patrimonial politicization of ethnicity, bad governance and the strategic interests of some sections of the international community.

In Chapter 10, Mohamed Salih examines the different interpretations and theoretical understanding of poverty and human security in the context of Africa. In exploring the poverty–human security nexus, he focuses on the practice and policy-relevant implications of the human security dimensions of NEPAD and the MDGs in Africa. Africa's place in the context of globalization has been the focus of controversial policy and academic debates.

In Chapter 11 Jim Whitman provides a lucid conceptualization and interpretation of globalization and looks at the nature of FDI, China in Africa and the mobile phone revolution and Internet communications/digital divide.

The book concludes with an overview of the key themes and arguments advanced as critical to the understanding and appreciation of the problems, challenges and opportunities for peace and conflict in Africa.

Introduction

15

2 | African indigenous and endogenous approaches to peace and conflict resolution

TIM MURITHI

Externally driven international efforts to resolve conflict in Africa are often faced with the limitation that the local parties are sometimes unwilling, or unable, to relate to such initiatives. Official high-level diplomacy tends to focus on promoting dialogue between the leaders of warring parties based on the assumption that these are the legitimate representatives of the people. This may be an erroneous assumption. Ultimately peace processes must also include local populations in order to be effectively grounded in their realities and so able to address their grievances. Indigenous and endogenous approaches to peace and conflict resolution in Africa provide us with insights into how more inclusive and community-based processes can be utilized. Indigenous and endogenous peace processes are endowed with valuable insights that can inform the rebuilding of social trust and restoration of the conditions for communal coexistence. This chapter will argue that there are important insights to be gained from such approaches which researchers, policy-makers and peacemakers in the international community can benefit from.

International initiatives in Africa to promote preventive diplomacy, prevent, manage and resolve conflict and promote development have traditionally neglected indigenous resources and capacities for peace-building and reconstruction. This chapter explores 'why' and 'how' this neglect has come about. It will also discuss four case studies to illustrate the potential utility of indigenous resources to modern conflict resolution in Africa. Specifically, it will discuss examples of indigenous peace processes from the Tiv community in Nigeria, the *guurti* system utilized to promote stability in Somaliland (northern Somalia), the *Mato Oput* peacemaking process found among the Acholi of northern Uganda and the application of *ubuntu*[1] to reconciliation based on experiences drawn from South Africa. Overall what can be gleaned from these approaches is their emphasis and the value that they place on achieving peace through forgiveness, healing, reconciliation and restorative justice.

The chapter will avoid the tendency to over-romanticize indigenous approaches to peacemaking and will also discuss some of the limitations inherent in these processes. Specifically, it will highlight the fact that even though indigenous processes are more inclusive they tend to be slow in bringing about agreement because they proceed on the basis of consensus-building. In addition, some of these traditions have been drawn from patriarchal societies, so there is a need to temper the progressive values that can be learned from these processes with the positive advances that have been made in promoting gender equality in peacemaking processes in Africa. Ultimately, this chapter will draw out some of the valuable insights that can contribute to the ongoing policy and theoretical debates about the importance of utilizing indigenous and endogenous processes in current efforts to make peace in Africa.

Contextualizing the indigenous and the endogenous

The types of intra-state conflicts that we are witnessing today in Africa divide the population of a state by undermining interpersonal and social trust, and consequently they destroy the social norms, values and institutions that have regulated and coordinated cooperation and collective action for the well-being of the community. This makes it very difficult for both the social groups and the state itself to recover their cohesion after hostilities cease in the post-conflict situation. It is therefore useful to examine whether there are indigenous and endogenous approaches to peace and conflict resolution that emphasize the re-building of social trust through reconciliation. It is particularly of interest to look at these issues through the prism of the rebuilding of social trust, because if our emphasis during the peacemaking process is on the renewal and reconstruction of society then the mechanisms and institutions that are put in place to oversee this process need to place an emphasis on the healing of social divisions, the redressing of the exclusion and inequality that may exist in a given community. This in turn means focusing on the restoration of broken relationships, through the involvement and participation of the family, community and even the nation as a whole. It means highlighting their strengths in supporting local governance, constructing consensus and initiating processes of reconciliation. It also means pointing out that a reliance on indigenous approaches can limit the flexibility of a process owing to the adherence of cultural norms, some of which may not be gender sensitive. Nonetheless, incorporating the insights and best practices of indigenous processes into official peace, to create a hybrid peace process, can improve the efficacy of peacemaking.

The term indigenous refers to that which is inherent to a given society but also that which is innate and instinctive. The term endogenous refers to that which emerges from a society. Both definitions are instructive because when we allude to indigenous and endogenous approaches to peace and conflict resolution, we are simultaneously referring to processes that are inherent in a given society following years of tradition, but also to those that are generated and systematically reproduced by such a society. The fact that there are peace processes that are innate or instinctive to a particular society should at once highlight the value of such processes in promoting order and stability. Indigenous and endogenous processes have been internalized by years of tradition and therefore the values and practices that they propose do not seem to be strange

17

to their referent community. Combining the notion of indigeneity with that of endogeneity may seem unnecessary on the surface, since both terms have virtually similar meanings. The distinction is, however, a subtle but important one. Indigenous processes may have been formulated over centuries and can thus be considered inherent, innate and instinctive to a society. Endogenous processes emphasize the fact that there is a temporal process of continuously reformulating and crafting additional ways of doing things. Thus endogenous processes have organically emerged from a society and indigenous processes are considered virtually innate to a given society. The notion of endogeneity also permits the possibility of combining indigenous approaches to peacemaking with so-called 'modern' or official processes of conflict resolution. In effect, both concepts are inextricably linked and mutually reinforcing, and in some cases they are the glue for sociocultural and political cohesion. By defining how social relations are maintained and rebuilt these approaches create a framework within which members of a community may interact and coexist. Ultimately, it is clear that the link between indigenous and endogenous approaches illustrates that societies, customs and traditions are not static but dynamic and change over time. This means that even as far as peacemaking processes are concerned there is continuity and change.

The global preponderance of indigenous and endogenous approaches

Virtually all societies around the world have both indigenous and endogenous values, resources and institutions. Therefore, even though this chapter will focus on Africa, it is evident that the continent is not an exception to the rule. Peacemaking and peace-building in Africa are, however, still predominantly being taught and practised through models developed from Eurocentric traditions. The mainstream and dominant literature in peace studies works on the premise that the values, resources and institutions that have been developed by Eurocentric Western tradition, broadly defined as the Judaeo-Christian heritage, have a universality and can easily be transposed on to other societies. The Judaeo-Christian Western traditions have developed their own notions of peacemaking and reconciliation. The greater part of academic research on peacemaking has a distinctively Western and Eurocentric bias. It is therefore necessary to rectify this asymmetrical growth of knowledge as far as peacemaking is concerned.

Selected indigenous and endogenous conflict resolution processes in Africa

The jir *mediation forum of the Tiv of Nigeria* Even though disputes within and between communities have been a feature of the African experience, it is also evident that early mechanisms of indigenous conflict resolution in pre-colonial Africa had a significant degree of success in maintaining order and ensuring the peaceful coexistence of groups (Yakubu 1995). This recurrent nature of wars and instability has concomitantly meant that indigenous resources have been equally important in ensuring that peacebuilding and conflict resolution prevail in these communities. Derry Yakubu observes that in most African societies 'the resolution of conflict was guided by the principle of consensus, collective responsibility and communal solidarity. This meant that communities were collectively responsible for the harmony and discord caused by their members.'[2] For the Tiv people of Nigeria, the discursive assembly was made possible by the convening of the *jir* or the 'dispute mediation session' in the communal square. The leaders of the communities in dispute sat in a semicircle facing the audience, which also sat in a semicircle to complete a full circle, with the disputants located within the circle. Rather than legal or political codes or laws, the Tiv relied on cultural norms, values and the communal moral conscience to inform the resolution of conflict.

The Tiv approach to conflict resolution had five key elements including: i) a commitment to maintaining order and ensuring the peaceful coexistence of groups; ii) a desire to ensure that the community remained a cohesive unit; iii) the fact that the leadership was not there to decide a particular issue, but to encourage the disputing parties to reconcile between themselves; iv) the fact that the whole process was consensual and every member of the community was free to participate and contribute to the settlement process; and finally v) the emphasis that was placed on all sides gaining from the process based on the belief that a settlement or resolution could not follow unless the dispute mediation session (*jir*) had been satisfactorily concluded.

CONTEMPORARY APPLICATIONS OF THE JIR APPROACH In 1994, Martin Dent, an academic and peace practitioner, was involved in overseeing a consensual mediation process among the segmented Tiv peoples of south-eastern Nigeria. Dent was a former colonial district officer in Tivland, Nigeria, in the 1950s, who befriended the Tiv peoples. This relationship contributed to his dismissal by the British head of the civil service in northern Nigeria for what was considered a lack of 'loyalty' to the British Empire when responding to a series of riots in the area.[3]

In 1994, protracted communal clashes had been taking place between the Kusuv community and the Ikurav-Tiev community over their boundaries along the Kungwa Jov river. Both sides had been systematically sending raiding parties to carry out killings and to destroy property and houses across the river.

Dent was familiar with the Tiv mediation process and was invited in 1994 by the communities to mediate in this dispute. He met the leaders of both communities and realized that the sentiments on both sides were in favour of attempting to find a resolution. The central authorities had been relatively inactive in dealing with the dispute. By invoking and referring to indigenous Tiv traditions, Dent brought together fifty community members from both sides in the traditional council chamber in what was effectively the *jir* (dispute mediation session). During the process, he encouraged the discussion to focus on the 'causes' of the conflict. As the session progressed, Dent proposed a solution that would recognize the Kungwa Jov river as a boundary, but at the same time it would have to provide the Ikurav-Tiev with some land beyond the river.

Initially both communities had entrenched positions and at one point no progress was being made, culminating in an impasse. Dent persisted and urged both groups to forget about the past and focus on a new future for their mutual benefit. Since the parties were predisposed towards finding a solution, the inclusive nature of his arguments to all the parties contributed to finding an agreement. The impasse was broken as 'more and more speakers asked for a declaration of peace to end the ruinous quarrel that had caused so much bloodshed' (Dent 1994: 6). The leaders of the two groups agreed to end hostilities and signed a peace treaty. The momentum for peace was under way at this stage and Dent, anxious to make sure that they consolidated the peacemaking process, sought the backing of the governmental authorities (the state commission of inquiry and boundary settlements) so as to work towards a final settlement.[4]

Indigenous conflict resolution in Somaliland In northern Somalia, also known as Somaliland, people rely upon their traditional clan elders as 'the repositories of moral authority and catalysts for societal harmony with regards to dispute resolution and the socio-economic distribution of resources' (see Murithi 2000). Rules of self-governance within units are adapted and based upon the principles of inclusion, consensus and kinship among the elders and society. According to Haron Yusuf and Robin Le Mare, 'two key elements of the kinship are blood ties and a concept known as *Xeer* (pronounced "hair"), which is, essentially, an unwritten but loosely accepted code of conduct' (Yusuf and Le Mare 2005: 459). The *Xeer* governs relations among members of different clan units regarding the sharing of common pool resources, such as grazing land and water resources. *Xeer* emphasizes 'the values of *interdependence and inclusiveness* and forms the basis for social contracts or covenants between lineage groups'.[5] This concept also defines obligations, rights and collective responsibilities (including sanctions) of the group. Within this contract members are pledged to support each other. *Xeer* does not eliminate strife but provides accepted and workable ways of dealing with disputes and conflicts.

According to Yusuf and Le Mare, 'when disputes arise over matters such as grazing rights, water, or other resources, or political influence, they are arbitrated by what is known as a *shir* – council of elders'. The *shir* 'deals with relations between groups, in war and peacetime, and lays down the laws and principles by which members act'. When the *shir* of different clans meet, they form an inter-clan mediating council known as the *guurti*. The *shir* and *guurti* act as mediators and operate in open assembly, not secretly. The *guurti* can mediate between Somalis and sanction, monitor and reinforce the adherence to the *Xeer*.

In this regard, this indigenous institution maintains clan coexistence and social order by managing disputes when they arise.

CONTEMPORARY APPLICATIONS OF THE INDIGENOUS SOMALI CONFLICT RESOLUTION SYSTEM Following the collapse of the Somali state in 1991, the breakaway territory of northern Somalia or Somaliland, with its capital in Hergesia, utilized indigenous mechanisms to make peace. In contrast, south Somalia, with its capital in Mogadishu, was, and remains, reft by violent conflict. In 1991, Somaliland's elders organized inter-clan reconciliation conferences, which were followed by meetings at the district and regional levels. In January 1993, a conference held in a town called Erigavo produced a peace charter which brought hostilities to an end in several parts of Somaliland and recognized individuals' rights to move, trade and pursue their aspirations within the clans' boundaries. This was effectively a peace agreement that 'stipulated the return of property, land, and other resources occupied, stolen, or looted during the war. Conflict resolution committees were set up to keep the peace and interpret the charter.' In effect, this operationalized a monitoring system that maintained the peace in the region, despite the tension in the less stable neighbouring regions.

The Erigavo conference led to the Borama peace conference, which was held between January and May 1993 and 'brought together more than 150 *guurti* members from all of Somaliland's clans, plus hundreds of delegates and observers from inside and outside the country'. As a result of the mediation by the *guurti*, Somaliland managed to achieve:

- The peaceful transfer of power from the armed factions to a president, Mohamed Egal, who was elected by the council of elders and assembly in May 1993;
- A Peace Charter that established a national security framework;
- A National Charter that established a bicameral legislature, creating for the first time an Assembly of Elders – or national *guurti* – as a non-elected upper house;
- An elected lower house.

In the intervening years, despite difficulties in implementing the provisions in the Peace Charter, using indigenous mechanisms Somaliland managed to maintain a relatively high degree of peace. Today, a relatively peaceful Somaliland has applied for membership of the African Union and has requested the UN to grant it special status as it had previously done for Kosovo and Timor Leste (Jama 2003).

Endogenous reconciliation in northern Uganda In northern Uganda the government is in conflict with a resistance movement calling itself the Lord's Resistance Army (LRA), which continues to make incursions from the neighbouring country of Sudan. In Uganda the rebel movement has been known to carry out abductions of innocent civilians including children. The Sudanese government is itself embroiled in a conflict situation with a rebel movement in the south of the Sudan being conducted by the Sudanese People's Liberation Movement (SPLM), which has bases in Uganda. Both of these conflicts form part of the same conflict system. In both the social provisions, which normally would have been provided for by the state (Govier 1998), are also lacking. The majority of people from these region are from the Acholi ethnic group. Many Acholi have found themselves divided by their different loyalties: many support the rebellion owing to grievances that they hold against regimes that have ruled over them, while others remain neutral and others support the government owing to the rebel incursions and their practice of abducting children to join the ranks of its soldiers. Social cohesion is fragmented and the persistence of violence and abductions has thoroughly undermined the levels of social trust. From this complex matrix of factors brought about by violent conflict there has developed an urgent need to identify mechanisms and institutions for conflict resolution which can achieve the medium-to-long-term goal of rebuilding social trust and reconciliation.

Reconciliation remains essentially contested in terms of what it is and how it can be brought about. There is much debate as to whether institutions can play a significant role in fostering reconciliation. Part of the problem lies in the fact that most of the institutions that exist in the realm of international and domestic politics were not designed with a view to fostering reconciliation or rebuilding social trust. Many of these institutions, such as international and subregional organizations and courts, play more of a conflict regulation and conflict management role. Whether we can restructure international and domestic political and legal institutions to promote reconciliation raises the much larger issue – which is beyond the scope of this section – of how it is possible to promote closer ties and even an interpenetration between law, politics and morality.

To help us shed more light on this challenge some of the features of the reconciliation mechanism found among the Acholi may be informative. The Acholi have maintained their conflict resolution and reconciliation mechanism, called the *Mato Oput*, which also served as an institution for maintaining law and order within the society (Conciliation Resources 2002). This mechanism pre-dated the colonial period and is still functioning in some areas. The Acholi place a high value on communal life. Maintaining positive relations within society is a collective task in which everyone is involved. A dispute between fellow members of the community is not merely perceived as a matter of curiosity regarding the affairs of one's neighbours, but in a very real sense an emerging conflict belongs to the community itself. Each member of the Acholi community is viewed as being to varying degrees related to each of the disputants. To the extent that somebody is willing to acknowledge this fundamental unity, then people can feel either some sense of having been wronged or some sense of responsibility for the wrong that has been done. Owing to this linkage, a lawbreaking individual thus transforms his or her group into a lawbreaking group. In the same way a disputing individual transforms his or her group into a disputing group. It therefore follows that if an individual is wronged he or she may depend upon his or her group when seeking a remedy to what has transpired, for in a sense they too have been wronged. On this basis, therefore, the Acholi society developed the *Mato Oput* process for resolving disputes and promoting reconciliation based on the principle of consensus-building (Kacoke Madit 2000). Consensus-building is embraced by the Acholi as an endogenous cultural pillar of their efforts to regulate relationships between members of a community.

The Acholi leadership structures are based on models designed to build consensus. There are Councils of Elders or community leadership councils made up of both men and women. All members of the society have a say in matters affecting the community. With the passage of time, however, colonialism and the onset of post-colonial regimes have undermined the adherence to this value system among most of the population. Today there are ongoing efforts to revive this way of thinking as a means of promoting more sustainable peace by using consensus to determine wrongdoing as well as to suggest remedial action.

The peace process in the Acholi context involves a high degree of public partici-pation. As noted earlier, under the timeless Acholi world-view a conflict between two members of a community is regarded as a problem that afflicts the entire community. In order to restore harmony and rebuild social trust there must be a general satisfaction among the public, in particular the disputants, with both the procedure and the outcome of the dispute resolution effort. The *Mato Oput* process therefore allows members of the public to share their views and to make their opinions known. Through a public assembly known as the *Kacoke Madit* those supervising the reconciliation process, normally comprised of the Council of Elders (who have an advisory function with respect to the chiefs), listen to the views of the members of the society, who have a right to put questions to the victims, perpetrators and witnesses, as well as make suggestions to the council.

Owing to the emphasis placed on inclusion and participation in the peace process, it can at times be a lengthy affair. The victims, perpetrators or disputants have to undertake certain commitments. The process generally proceeds through the following five stages:

1 Perpetrators are encouraged to acknowledge responsibility or guilt for the wrongs done following the presentation of evidence by witnesses and the public and investigation by the Council of Elders.
2 Perpetrators are encouraged to repent and demonstrate genuine remorse.
3 Perpetrators are encouraged to ask for forgiveness from the victims and victims are encouraged to show mercy and grant forgiveness to the perpetrators.

4 If the previous stage is carried out satisfactorily, perpetrators, where possible, and at the suggestion of the Council of Elders, pay compensation to the victims (this in many instances is a symbolic gesture that seeks to reinforce the genuine remorse of the perpetrator).

5 The process concludes with an act of reconciliation between the representatives of the victims and the representatives of the perpetrators. This act of reconciliation is conducted through the ceremony of *Mato Oput*, which is the drinking of a bitter-tasting herb derived from the *Oput* tree. The bitter drink *Oput* symbolizes the psychological bitterness that prevailed in the minds of the parties during the conflict situation. The act of drinking it is an indication that an effort will be made to transcend this bitterness in order to restore harmony and rebuild trust.

In Acholi society the *Mato Oput* process covers offences across the board from minor injustices like theft to more serious issues involving violence between members of a society, the taking of the life of a person, even accidentally, and conflict situations. The Acholis avoid resorting to retributive justice and in particular the death penalty because of the way the society views itself and the value that it attaches to each of its members. Even though the demand for vengeance may be great among some of the victims, the death penalty for murder would serve only to multiply the effects of suffering in other parts of the society and ultimately undermine any possibility of re-establishing harmonious coexistence at a future stage.

Depending on the level of the offence the *Mato Oput* reconciliation act is followed by two other ceremonies. In all dispute situations the community leaders or Council of Elders of both genders – the male leaders are referred to as *Rwodi Moo* and the female leaders are known as the *Rwodi Mon* – give a final verbal blessing to mark the end of the conflict. In the case of a murder, or a warring situation, there is the 'bending of the spears' ceremony undertaken by the two parties to symbolize the end to the conflict and the disposal of the instruments of its execution (Pain 1997).

It is evident, then, that the guiding principle and values are based on the notion that the parties must be reconciled in order to rebuild social trust and maintain social cohesion, and thus to prevent a culture of vendetta or feud from developing and escalating between individuals, families and other parts of the society. This is one reason why the *Mato Oput* act of reconciliation always includes the disputants, victims, perpetrators and their representatives. Public consensus also plays a significant role in the post-conflict situation, particularly when social pressure is utilized to monitor and encourage the various parties to implement peace agreements. Any breach of the act of reconciliation by either side would represent a far worse offence than the original offence because it would set a precedent that could eventually lead to the fragmentation of communal life.

In sum, the Acholi endogenous method for resolving disputes provides us with some practical insights as to how we can refer to culture in our efforts to establish mechanisms for promoting reconciliation and rebuilding social trust, across Africa as well as in other parts of the world. Civil society groups, religious leaders and parliamentarians in the Acholi community of northern Uganda, together with Acholis in the diaspora, have been advocating the revitalization and integration of the *Mato Oput* into current peace initiatives. The process is being utilized in various local efforts within the region with significant results in terms of the termination of violent conflict and the healing of communities. Many believe that drawing upon certain elements of the *Mato Oput* mechanism can also contribute towards healing tensions between the Lord's Resistance Army and the government of Uganda. There have been efforts to establish a Government Amnesty Bill to bring aspects of the *Mato Oput* mechanism and pardon initiatives into the reconciliation to reintegrate perpetrators, some of whom are still children, back into society. The current government of Uganda, under the leadership of President Yoweri Museveni, has tacitly validated the use of *Mato Oput* in the peace-building processes with the LRA. Specifically, the commander of the army, General Aronda, and the chief peace negotiator, Dr Rugunda, participated in a series of *Mato Oput* ceremonies that were convened across Acholiland. As with any political process there are of course still obstacles with regards to policy implementation, which undermine the use of these mechanisms in current peace efforts. Continued leadership and vision on all sides will be required to see some of these initiatives through.

In terms of the institutionalization of the reconciliation into mechanisms for restoring peace with justice there are also some limitations. The element of volunteerism as far as the acknowledgement of guilt by the perpetrators is concerned would obviously impact on the efficacy of such a system. When it comes to talking about 'truth' there are also no guarantees that the victims will be willing to accept the version of truth espoused by the perpetrators or forgive them for the wrongs that they have done. Perpetrators themselves may in many instances be reluctant to acknowledge their wrongdoing owing to a natural fear of persecution. The modest inroads made by the Acholi system of reconciliation in terms of its impact on government policy suggest that there is an opportunity for promoting the legal acceptance of endogenous approaches within national constitutions as alternative forms of restorative justice. The interpenetration or cross-fertilization between law, politics, morality and social values is indeed possible, but beyond that it is necessary and desirable in the interests of building sustainable peace and democratization through reconciliation. One key inference that we can draw from the Acholi endogenous system of reconciliation and the cultural wisdom handed down through generations of these people is that punitive action within the context of retributive justice may effectively decrease social trust and undermine reconciliation in the medium to long term, and therefore such action is ineffective as a strategy for promoting social cohesion.

Ubuntu and culturally inspired reconciliation

Given the diversity of Africa, with over five thousand different ethnic groups in fifty-three countries, understanding different belief systems and value judgements is essential. The concept of *ubuntu* is one such system of belief which underpins several African societies, including the Xhosa, Zulu, Swazi and Ndebele, which have and continue to conduct and manage their political affairs in a communal setting or 'under the acacia', to borrow a metaphor. It is not possible to give a definite statistical account of the number of the communities or countries that practise *ubuntu*. It is sufficient to note that the *ubuntu* approach is utilized in a number of societies and communities that are spread out across southern, Central and East Africa.

Ubuntu acknowledges the interconnectedness of humanity at all times. In Xhosa, *Ubuntu ungamntu ngabanye abantu*, 'a person is a person through other people', or in Zulu, *Umuntu ngumuntu ngabanye*, 'I am human because I belong, I participate, I share'. This has a profound effect upon perceptions of how conflict should be resolved through conflict resolution. Through an inclusive community-wide conflict resolution and reconciliation forum known as a *lekgotla*, a Council of Elders or the king himself mediates using this notion of *ubuntu* to highlight the importance of peacemaking through the principles of reciprocity, inclusivity and a sense of shared destiny between peoples. In *ubuntu* societies the entire society is typically involved at various levels in trying to find a solution to a problem, which is viewed as threatening the social cohesion of the community. Any member of the society has the right to question victims, perpetrators and witnesses as well as to put suggestions to the Council of Elders on possible ways forward. The Council of Elders in its capacity as an intermediary has an investigative function and it also plays an advisory role to the king. By listening to the views of the members of the society, the Council of Elders advises on solutions that may promote peace and reconciliation between the aggrieved parties and thus maintain the overall objective of sustaining the unity and cohesion of the community.[6]

Contemporary applications of ubuntu Further research needs to be undertaken to document the application of *ubuntu* to conflict resolution, particularly in the rural communities in southern Africa. There is a rich oral history of this tradition, but a dearth of documentary records. According to Nomonde Masina, the Xhosa community in South Africa, particularly in the rural areas, has maintained a strong bond with its traditions and peacemaking predicated on the principle of *ubuntu* continues to be practised, particularly with reference to family and marriage disputes, theft, damage to property, murder and conflict (Masina 2000).

Ubuntu approaches emphasize a link between conflict resolution and reconciliation, rather than viewing them as separate phases.

Speaking from his own experience, and based on his own opinion, Archbishop Desmond Tutu, as chairman of the South African Truth and Reconciliation Commission, reflects in his book *No Future without Forgiveness* that he drew upon both his Christian and his cultural values to guide him in his functions. In particular, he highlights the fact that he constantly referred to the notion of *ubuntu* when he was guiding and advising witnesses, victims and perpetrators during the commission hearings (Tutu 1999: 34). The guiding principle of *ubuntu* was based on the notion that parties need to be reconciled in order to rebuild and maintain social trust and social cohesion, with a view to preventing a culture of vendetta or retribution from developing and escalating between individuals, families and the society as a whole. We continue to observe how individuals and sections of society in the Republic of South Africa, epitomized by Nelson Mandela and Desmond Tutu as well as thousands of other citizens, have drawn upon these aspects of their cultural values and attitudes to enable the country to move beyond its violent past. The South African Truth and Reconciliation Commission, which has as many critics as it has supporters, also relied on the willingness of victims to recognize the humanity of the perpetrators, and there are documented cases of victims forgiving particular perpetrators (Villa-Vicencio and Verwoerd 2000). Archbishop Tutu himself would always advise victims, if they felt themselves able to do so, to forgive. His guiding principle was that without forgiveness predicated on the notion of *ubuntu*, which he always took the opportunity to explain, there could be no future for the new republic. South Africa is a model of unity in diversity, and has been referred to as the 'rainbow nation'. It is clear that different groups and individual members of the society would have drawn from aspects of their own cultures when dealing with the process of transition. Many drew upon their own family values and their religious background. An analysis of all the different cultural backgrounds and belief systems, and the way in which they informed the peace process, is beyond the scope of this paper. We cannot, however, discount the fact that *ubuntu*, an African way of viewing the world, informed the attitudes of a significant number of ethnic groups and individuals, some of whom were involved in reconciling groups and guiding the nation through its troubled phase.

The strengths of indigenous processes

Based on the discussions above we can identify key strengths of indigenous and endogenous conflict resolution processes. First, they are familiar to the communities where they are being utilized and appeal to the local cultural norms and leadership structures. Therefore, the outcomes they produce are more likely to be internalized by the parties. Second, the cases illustrated in this chapter demonstrate that indigenous processes are inclusive, promote public participation and seek consensus in addressing the root causes of conflict.[7] Third, there is a value-added element in terms of sustaining peace when these processes draw upon local cultural assumptions, norms and values as well as traditional and grassroots notions of justice and community-based political dialogue. In this regard, they ensure the local ownership of peace processes. Fourth, indigenous processes are cost effective in the sense that they rely on a community's own internal resources rather than the infusion of funds from external actors. The Somaliland experience was instructive in this regard. Ultimately, such a degree of self-sufficiency and self-sustainability can also protect a peace process from external pressures of resource mobilization. Fifth, indigenous approaches emphasize and place a higher value on the nexus between mediation and reconciliation rather than viewing them as separate and distinct processes. Finally, indigenous approaches emphasize the importance of a sustained and continuous peace effort. For example, the Borama conference peace-building took place over five months. This is in contrast to other 'modern' or official processes, which are intermittent and episodic, thanks often to the high costs involved of maintaining parties at a particular venue.

The limitations of indigenous and endogenous peace processes

We should avoid the tendency to over-romanticize indigenous approaches to peacemaking and also discuss some of the limitations inherent in these processes. Paradoxically, the duration of indigenous peacemaking can be viewed as a weakness, because, depending on the willingness of parties to achieve consensus, such processes can become indefinite. While indigenous processes are inclusive and consensual, for a variety of reasons, often they do not necessarily proceed on the basis of socio-political expediency. An inclusive process is, however, more likely to have widespread legitimacy and acceptance. Ideally, a peace process with a small number of interlocutors is more likely to lead to an agreed outcome and to facilitate relationships of trust, which are critical to agreement. Such a narrow process can, however, also bring the legitimacy of the process itself into question, if powerful actors are left out. There is a trade-off to be considered when addressing the issue of inclusion or exclusion in peace processes.

Gender exclusion and the paternalism inherent in human societies While indigenous processes contain a range of progressive values, some of their practices are patriarchal and therefore not gender sensitive. This interestingly enough is not a phenomenon that is restricted to the African experience. Western and Eurocentric traditions and cultural practices have historically excluded women from the political decision-making and problem-solving roles. This has had the effect of undermining the role of women in peace and peacemaking processes. More often than not, even 'modern' or official peace processes consider women's concerns only 'as an afterthought' (International Crisis Group 2006). There have been recent events to mainstream gender equality in the knowledge and practice of peacemaking. Indigenous approaches to peace have not been an exception to the rule. In the practice of solving social and political problems traditional cultural practices also tended to relegate the role of women. There is therefore a need to temper the progressive values that can be learned from these indigenous processes with the positive advances that have been made in promoting gender equality in peacemaking processes in Africa.

Reintegrating child soldiers in the aftermath of conflict There are situations in which even indigenous approaches face limitations in their ability to provide the necessary resources to heal families and societies. The impact of protracted wars and gratuitous violence means that in some instances child soldiers have been forced to kill parents, elders and chiefs. This was the experience in Sierra Leone following the recruitment of child soldiers by the Revolutionary United Front (RUF). In some instances the children were subsequently forced to commit atrocities against their own family members. In these circumstances, in terms of healing the individual, where family in some instances is non-existent, clearly indigenous resources and institutions face a substantial challenge. Ultimately, this calls into question the universal relevance and utility of traditional cultural resources in the aftermath of war.

Complementing official state and international peace processes

The discussion of indigenous and endogenous processes points to a number of strengths and limitations in terms of their effectiveness. Indigenous and endogenous peace and conflict resolution approaches are generally not recognized by the governments as viable alternatives to promoting peace at a grassroots level. This means, therefore, that there is a lack of interface with official national and international peacemaking efforts. Furthermore, in the aftermath of conflict, indigenous and endogenous principles are rarely consulted in terms of the development of constitutional and legal frameworks to oversee the vital transition to democratic governance.

Recent research has suggested that it may be worthwhile to think in terms of a 'hybrid approach' that might take best practices from indigenous and so-called 'modern' or official approaches to peace and conflict resolution. A hybrid approach would rely upon a combination of official and indigenous values, principles and norms. Such an approach would encourage parallel forums and interactive problem-solving workshops, utilizing indigenous and official approaches, to bring together key opinion leaders and civil society at the regional, national or local levels. Ultimately, a hybrid approach would strive to facilitate national peace talks, which can be sequenced to complement an official mediation process and can also bring community leaders and civil society into the process.

Conclusion

A review of indigenous and endogenous processes demonstrates their strengths in capitalizing upon local and regional cultural norms, integrating community leaders, constructing consensus and emphasizing the link between mediation and reconciliation. If strengthened at the local level, and nationally and internationally recognized, such processes may play a greater role in preventive diplomacy, peacemaking and peace-building.

Ultimately, based on the discussions in this chapter, we should acknowledge that indigenous processes are able to construct consensus, facilitate inclusion and integrate judicial norms recognized and respected by the community. Since indigenous approaches rely on traditional norms that have been developed over centuries the values and principles that they espouse can be more easily referenced and internalized by the communities in which they function. While there are limitations to the implementation of indigenous strategies for building peace, notably the inherent predisposition towards gender exclusion, there are nevertheless progressive values that can be gleaned to inform conflict resolution processes. These progressive values and principles should therefore be documented further and utilized in ongoing and future conflict situations.

In terms of the way forward, it is clear from this discussion that there is much that we can learn from different cultures around the world. In the case of peacemaking and peace-building in Africa it is therefore vital to promote the incorporation of mechanisms and institutions of restorative justice within the constitutions of states and societies in transition so that they are more accessible and more widely utilized as acceptable and legitimate forms of the rule of law. It is evident that additional research and analysis are required with a view to gaining more insights into practical strategies for utilizing indigenous and endogenous approaches to peace and conflict resolution in Africa.

3 | Understanding peace in Africa

ISAAC O. ALBERT

Conflicts constitute a major threat to African development in terms of loss of human life, destruction of property, displacement of people, sometimes across international borders, and diversion of resources meant for promoting sustainable development into arms purchase and funding of expensive peacekeeping support operations. A lot has been published on these conflicts and efforts at transforming them. A large number of these publications adopt the top-down (state-centric and 'globalizing') approach to the discourse. They were produced in the context of 'international peace, security and cooperation' at the end of the cold war and therefore focus exclusively on how members of the international community come to make, create and keep peace (Sorbo and Vale 1997) on the continent. Atomized in these publications are issues relating to traditional conflict management mechanisms. Academic researchers are not the only ones to blame in this respect. The local and international non-governmental organizations (NGOs), global governance institutions, the international community and international cooperation development agencies working on the continent are equally guilty. The Western-oriented conflict management systems they force on the African people are often framed in the context of the 'liberal peace project' (see Fischer 2000; Rosato 2003; Barbieri 2005). The objective of the latter, which promotes retributive/punitive justice, is the protection of the hegemonic and economic interests of the Western world in Africa. This top-down approach not only hides the contributions that traditional conflict management systems in Africa can make towards ensuring peace but sometimes perpetuates conflict situations.

The present chapter adopts a 'bottom-up' approach which places emphasis on how Africans provide peace for themselves. At the end of the chapter, a suggestion is made regarding the integration of the traditional and Western models of conflict management in engaging with the contemporary conflicts on the African continent. The central message of the chapter is aptly captured by a Chinese poem which says: 'Go to the people ... start with what they know; build on what they have ... and in the end, the people will remark we have done it ourselves' (www.crcvt.org). The position of Vraalson on conflict management in Africa is equally instructive. He observed that:

> ... any successful attempt to resolve conflicts and make peace in Africa must be a genuine recognition of, and respect for, the identity of the peoples of the

continent, their traditions and their proud cultural heritage. To this should be added an intimate knowledge of the historical facts as well as an understanding of the prevailing social and economic conditions on the continent as fashioned by centuries of colonial domination and oppression. (Vraalsen 1997: 22)

What are the reasons for the bottom-up approach adopted in this chapter? The first is implied in the foregoing: it is that hitherto the emphasis of academic and policy analysts regarding peace in Africa has been on what others are doing or can do for Africa rather than what the people can do for themselves. The second is that the formal conflict resolution mechanisms (e.g. court systems) in Africa today lack credibility, and this strengthens recourse to traditional mechanisms of settling conflicts. The background to this problem is that the state, which is needed for anchoring the formal justice system in any society, hardly exists in many parts of contemporary Africa in the Western-style Weberian/Westphalian sense of the term. Many of the states are weak and have been 'replaced' by criminal and political 'godfathers', 'warlords', militia leaders and fundamentalist religious movements, which, as in other Third World countries, are linked with pre-state traditional social and political institutions. The conflicts generated by these alternative state systems 'characteristically combine modern and pre-modern or traditional causes, motives and forms of conflict. It is not only that under the umbrella of current internal wars traditional conflicts between different clans or "tribes" or other traditional societal groups are fought out violently, but those wars themselves become permeated by traditional causes and forms of violence' (Boege 2006: 2). The paradox is that issues of culture and tradition are usually atomized in the peace processes put in place for engaging these social systems and the conflicts they generate.

The judicial system in these fragile African states faces one other key problem that strengthens recourse to the indigenous conflict management systems. In the sense that it is litigious and based on Western value systems, many Africans perceive it to be more framed towards breaking relationships than strengthening them at the end of a conflict (Albert et al. 1995). Hence, a popular Yoruba adage says '*A kiti kotu bo ka sore*' (you do not return from a court of law and remain friends).

The legal fees that litigants are expected to pay are often prohibitive for the ordinary citizen. Within this framework, formal justice is considered to be exclusively meant for the rich. The paradox is that the continent is dominated by the poor (ibid.; Cappelleti 1978; Goldberg et al. 1985; Uwazie 2000: 15–30). What makes the formal justice system so expensive is not just the cost of hiring an attorney but also what is required for 'bribing the police or court registrar before one's case is filed' (Uwazie 2000: 28). Uwazie provided one other reason why more people are drifting from the formal to the informal conflict resolution systems: 'The rules and legal jargon of the English-based legal system are often too confusing. The distance of the police station or courthouse from the disputants further inhibits access' (ibid.).

The need to adopt a bottom-up approach in this chapter is further strengthened by the fact that, since the 1990s, the United Nations peacekeeping operations in Africa require that the 'peacekeepers' engage the people more directly. The peace operations encompass a wide range of elements: supervision of ceasefire agreements; regrouping and demobilization of armed forces; destruction of weapons surrendered in disarmament exercises; reintegration of former combatants into civilian life; design and implementation of mine clearance programmes; facilitating the return of refugees and displaced persons; provision of humanitarian assistance; training of new police forces; monitoring respect for human rights; support for implementation of constitutional, judicial and electoral reforms; and support for economic rehabilitation and reconstruction. It is difficult for peacekeepers, whether military or civilian, to accomplish all these without working with local partners using indigenous knowledge systems. The most daunting of the tasks has to do with conflict management and resolution.

Understanding peace 'globally'

The subject matter of peace in Africa is better appreciated if linked up with extant global debates. The first point to be made here is that peace is a universal concept. Every society desires it; none can exist without it. The term features prominently in the two leading religions in the world – Christianity and Islam. For example, the salutation '*Shalom*' is as popular among the Christians and Jews as '*Asalaam aleikum*' is among the Muslims. Both terms mean 'Peace be unto you'. The troubling paradox, however, is that there is no consensus in the world today, even among the adherents of the leading religions, on what constitutes peace. More contentious is the debate on how peace can be attained. We are therefore not too surprised that one of the most destructive nuclear bombs ever invented by man was nicknamed 'The Peacemaker' in the 1980s (Assefa 1993: 1). One of the clichés in international relations is 'If you need peace, prepare for war'. What we have now is a situation where everybody does his own thing and hangs the label of 'peace' on it.

The most simplistic but popular understanding of peace is that it is the opposite of conflict or violence. A major shortcoming of this understanding of the concept is that it lays exclusive emphasis on overt violence; it is silent on how to contend with psychological and structural violence, which Assefa defined as the 'social and personal violence arising from unjust, repressive, and oppressive national or international political and social structures' (ibid.: 3). This kind of peace is technically referred to as 'negative peace'. This concept was introduced by Galtung in the editorial to the first edition of the *Journal of Peace Research*. He defined negative peace as 'the absence of violence, absence of war', and positive peace as 'the integration of human society' (1964b: 2).

'Positive peace' considers the prevention of violence (or warlessness) as a limited goal on the ground that it does not address the structural violence that bedevils the world or which underpins a violent situation. It is argued, for example, that there are several societies that are not at war today but which are ruled by despots, exploited by corrupt elites or bedevilled by crime and self-destruction. Such a society cannot be said to be at peace, and its problems cannot be understood in the context of negative peace. The position of the advocates of 'positive peace' is thus that sustainable peace requires egalitarian distribution of resources and fighting against anything that compromises basic human existence and survival.

The concept of positive peace has its own problems. One is that it tends to define peace from the perspective of the values of certain societies rather than 'global society' (Fogarty 2000: 26). To the Catholics, for example, peace is a logical outcome of truth, justice, freedom and love. The Muslims, Hindus and people of other faiths are bound to define peace differently based on the dominant values in their religions. This is because what ensures and assures basic human survival differs from one society to the other. Commenting on this, Fogarty (ibid.: 27) observed:

> ... it is clear that ideals of justice vary widely from one culture to the next. In contemporary American society, for example, one basic tenet of justice is that all people should have equal opportunities for success or failure; but that neither success nor failure should be guaranteed (the extent to which this ideal is practiced is another matter). But there have been, and still are, many cultures in which this definition would be considered a grave injustice, or a nonsensical ideal. In some cultures tradition may specify that birthright or religious status, or age, or gender justly ascribes status and confers privilege on some, subservience on others.

Students of positive peace in Western society define peace as an outcome of democracy, social equality and 'justice'.

Taking the above into consideration, Ishida (1969) has, within the context of cold war politics, suggested an East–West dichotomy in the conceptualization of peace. In the East, as in the continent of Africa, peace is considered to be a product of the individual's conformity to societal customs and norms. In the Western world, on the other hand, peace is a social system aimed at assuring prosperity. Agreeing with this position, Galtung (1981) presents the difference between the Eastern and Western perception of the concept of peace as one of 'social cosmology'.

Concerned about the need to craft a 'global' definition of peace, Fogarty (2000: 28–9) has identified four major characteristics that a definition of the concept must possess. The first is that the definition should be universally applicable and not culture specific. He argued, for example, that 'the peaceability of a society should be judged independent of whether it incorporates a democratic political system, a monarchy, or a tribal council. Certainly it should be independent of the precepts of any particular kind of religion.' In other words, the definition should be applicable to peoples of different parts of the world. The second characteristic of a good definition of peace is that it should avoid reductionism. In other words, peace ought to be conceived not as a characteristic of an individual but of groups and societies.

The third major issue is that the definition must go beyond the conception of peace as merely the absence of war. The definition must capture a broad spectrum of what is needed for maintaining decent living – absence of human suffering in its physical, psychological and structural dimensions. The definition should include safety from diseases and the like. In other words, the definition must reflect the reality of both the negative and the positive peace. The fourth and last issue is that the definition needs to be consistent with major ideas in sociological theory, most especially liberty and freedom.

The way the world is structured today makes it impossible to have the kind of all-embracing definition of peace that Fogarty was calling for. It is thus more convenient to focus our discussion on how to achieve global peace than on how to reach consensus on a global definition of peace.

The challenge of globalization has brought into the limelight three important values within which peace objectives are now pursued around the world: respect for life and human dignity (Harris 1990), universal responsibility (Reardon 1988; Brenes 1990) and global cooperation (Fischer 1996). These objectives allow us to be persuaded by Johnson's (1976) position on the concept of peace. He identified three concepts of peace as part of his own mission of adding to the intellectual depth of the field of peace studies: (i) peace as a world without war; (ii) peace as world justice; and (iii) peace as world order. It is argued in this chapter that before we can realize the three dimensions of peace alluded to by Johnson, the world-view of different peoples of the world must be taken into consideration. Our argument is that Africa is an important jurisdiction in the world. The people's conception of peace, justice and order must be factored into the global peace agenda.

A philosophical framework of peace in Africa

The meaning of peace in the Western world and Africa is rooted in the philosophical and political thoughts of the peoples as evident in their 'traditional religions'. While the African understanding of the concept of peace is rooted in the culture and traditions of the people as expressed in their now demonized traditional religions, the Western conception of peace has its origin in (i) the Ancient Judaic concept of *shalom*, which emphasizes the will of God, justice and prosperity; (ii) the Greek concept of *eirene* focusing on prosperity and order; and (iii) the Roman concept of *pax*, focusing on order and mental tranquillity. The

35

thread that runs through the three Western concepts is *prosperity* and *order*. The latter refers essentially to rule of law (Rinehart 2005: 2). The argument here is that war, conflict or violence reduces prosperity and the only way to promote prosperity is to step up the enforcement of the rule of law. Peace, looked at from this perspective, refers to the maintenance of law and order, the pursuit of stability and a relatively safe social and political order.

As in the Western conception of the term, Africans believe that peace has relationships with prosperity. For example, a Basotho proverb says 'peace is prosperity' (*Khotso ken ala*) (Mokitimi 1997). A popular Hausa proverb also says '*salama maganin zama duniya*' (peace is the forerunner of healthy human existence). The understanding here is that it is only when there is peace in a society that it can experience prosperity in terms of having the freedom to plant and harvest crops. This peaceful atmosphere would also enable members of the society to sell their products and use the resources to improve their living standards.

The point of departure between the Western and African perceptions of peace, however, is that whereas the former places heavy emphasis on the need to preserve material prosperity, the emphasis of the latter is on morality in human interaction. In other words, whereas the Western conception of peace is based on prosperity and order, that of Africans is based on morality and order. In both milieux order is constant, but in the African setting morality is the most important factor for consideration. Hence a popular Yoruba adage says:

> Bi a ba nwowo lọ
> Ta pade iyi lọna
> Nse lo yẹ ka pada sile
> Nitori kini
> Taba lowo iyi lo ye ka fira
> If we set out on a journey for wealth
> And we come across honour
> It is necessary to return home
> Why
> The best money can buy is honour

To Africans, peace emanates from both God and man. There are things that only God can provide; there are things man has to do. To this end, peace is a spiritual and moral value located in the religious belief systems of the people as handed down from one generation to another. Though predominantly adherents of the religions of Christianity and Islam, contemporary Africans often try to explain the circumstances around them from the context of traditional religions. This is because the traditional African religion is not only a matter of *belief*, but also *worship* and, more importantly, *human conduct*. While 'modernity' has taken the belief and worship aspects of African religion away from the people, many still hold tenaciously to the human conduct aspect because it promotes community-centred morality and provides the indicators by which individuals can describe themselves as good citizens. It strengthens community bonds, most especially through sharing and promotion of justice. Rather than being 'killed' by Western and oriental influences, the moral conduct aspects of traditional African religion are in fact strengthened in some cases, most especially in the upbringing of the young. The latter consists of the transmission of knowledge on traditional etiquettes and observance of essential taboos needed for maintaining a state of tranquillity in the society. The opinion of Onah (www.afrikaworld.net/afrel/goddionah.htm) on this is enriching:

> Belief in God and in the other spiritual beings implies a certain type of conduct, conduct that respects the order established by God and watched over by the divinities and the ancestors. At the centre of the traditional African morality is human life. Africans have a sacred reverence for life, for it is believed to be the greatest of God's gifts to humans. To protect and nurture their lives, all human beings are inserted within a given community and it is within this community that one works out one's destiny and every aspect of individual life. The promotion of life is therefore the determinant principle of African traditional morality and this promotion is guaranteed only in the community. Living harmoniously within a community is therefore a moral obligation ordained by God for the promotion of life. Religion provides the basic infra-structure on which this life-centred, community-oriented morality is based ... The implication is that one has an obligation to maintain harmonious relationships with all the members of the community and to do what is necessary to repair every breach of harmony and to strengthen the community bonds, especially through justice and sharing.

While the human conduct aspects focus on moderating human interactions in a way that could prevent disagreements from escalating into violence or violence from spiralling out of control, the belief and worship aspects pertain more to prayers and incantations targeted at placating the gods or evoking peace for adherents. The following Kikuyu (Kenya) litany of peace addressed to Ngai, the Supreme Being, is an example (see Shorter 1975: 125–6; Mbiti 1975: 162–3):

Praise ye Ngai ... – Peace be with us
(Say that the elders may have wisdom and speak with one voice.
Praise ye, Ngai. Peace be with us)
Say that the country may have tranquillity
Peace be with us.
And the people may continue to increase
Peace be with us.
Say that the people and the flock and the herds
May prosper and be free from illness – Peace be with us.
(Say ... [that] the fields may bear much fruit

And the land may continue to be fertile.
Praise ye, Ngai. Peace be with us)
May peace reign over earth,
May the gourd cup agree with vessel – Peace be with us.
May their heads agree and every ill word be driven out into the wilderness,
into the virgin forest.
Praise ye Ngai ... – Peace be with us.

This type of prayer, which is common to many parts of Africa, testifies to the fact that Africans recognize God as the author of peace. It also underscores the people's belief that peace is not only a matter of human interaction but also includes issues like food security, health, a state of harmony between man and his environment and 'elders' readiness to "speak with one voice"'.

The contents of the following prayer also suggest that Africans perceive peace to include issues of inter-ethnic and racial harmony:

May God grant us peace and health of the body,
Let the black and red people live on earth in peace
And live in the world to come in joyful heart
May our life be long and deep
And a white hen guide our way towards heaven (the sky).

The aspect of this prayer dealing with 'our life' being 'long and deep' is also significant. It suggests that Africans not only see the end product of peace as giving the opportunity to live long on the surface of earth but more importantly to live a quality life. What matters is not just the length of life but the 'depth' of it.

Peace-building is often built into role expectations in many African societies. There are things that the young must do, there are things that women must do, and there are things that the elderly in the society must do. For example, the first prayer cited above enjoins elders to speak with one voice. The prayer asks for there to be agreement between the gourd cup and the vessel as well as the banishment of every ill word. When an elderly person fails to conduct himself properly in the Yoruba culture, he is referred to as an *Agba iya* (a worthless elder). Such an elder stands the chance of being ridiculed in the society, as testified to in a Yoruba proverb that says: '*Agbalagba to wewu aseju ete ni yoo fii ri*' (an elder that exceeds his bounds is bound to be disgraced; Adewoye 1987: 8). Therefore everybody tries as much as possible to conform to the norms of the society.

As the elders try to conduct themselves in a manner that will ensure harmony in the society, they also ensure that the young are trained into responsible adulthood. Women are predominantly charged with the responsibility of shaping the character of children. This issue was clearly underscored in a recent UNESCO (2003) publication. The different case studies in the publication, from six African countries – Burundi, Cameroon, Central African Republic, Namibia, Somali and Tanzania – all showed that women contribute significantly to peace in Africa by serving as the first peace educators to their children, most especially in the areas of (i) responsibility through reciprocity; (ii) honesty and loyalty through mutuality and deference; (iii) faith and compassion through inner strength and self-control. The children are taught stories and songs that extol high morality and respect for societal norms. They are also exposed to myths that portray the dire consequences of engaging in unbecoming behaviours or activities in the society. Commenting on the role of mothers in moulding the behaviour of children, Ntahobari and Ndayiziga (2003: 18) noted in their chapter on Burundi:

> It was primarily the mother that had responsibility for the upbringing of the children. Children, especially when very young, remained with their mother, who would look after both boys and girls until they reached a given age (for boys, until the time when their father took over the responsibility). There were strict rules to be complied with on how to dress, speak, eat and even walk and sit (especially for girls).

A respondent in the Burundian study further sheds light on the role of women in shaping the young for peace in a typical African society:

> Children live in the home of their birth, observing what is done, watching their parents and elders and following their example. This period of extended observation is supervised by the mother, who has her young children constantly at her side, giving them punishments scaled to their years, so that from an early age, children come to acquire an appetite for those human qualities, immensely valuable to the society, that denote a good upbringing. The education of a daughter who had reached the age of puberty was a matter of ongoing concern for her mother, who had to prepare her properly for marriage, so that, once a wife herself, she too would become a factor for stability and peace in her husband's family.

As women engage in preventive diplomacy by building the character of the young in the society in a manner that will support orderliness, the head of the home (the woman's husband) provides the first line of conflict management in the family. Bascom (1984: 44) tried to describe this in one of his works. According to him, the *Bale* (head of a Yoruba community) is responsible for the management of the conflicts within the community: The *Bale* serves as the principal judge of the compound, presiding when disputes are brought before him, but cases are heard by all the elders and by any other members of the community who may be present. If a titled chief lives in the compound, he is also responsible for settling disputes. A husband is responsible for settling quarrels within his own family; but if he is unsuccessful or if an argument involves members of two different families within the compound, it is referred to the *Bale*.

We can make some generalizations about peace in African cosmology from the foregoing. The first is that peace among the people is not an abstract poetic, but a practical concept. It refers to the totality of well-being; not only of the fullness of life when man is on the surface of earth but also hereafter. The Yoruba refer to peace as '*alafia*' – 'the sum total of all that man may desire: an undisturbed harmonious life'. *Alafia*, the Yoruba word for peace, is not only referring to order but also the physical well-being of the individual and his larger community.

The foregoing also suggests that the philosophical and religious underpinnings of peace among the African peoples can be located in two types of knowledge systems: commitment to the cultural values, beliefs and norms of the people on the one hand and role expectations on the other. The latter have to do with the consensus on the beliefs, values and norms of the society physically and, importantly, spiritually defined. In order to have a 'consensus', the people must possess the same idea (*agree*) about a belief, value and norm, they must be *aware* that once in their existence they had such an agreement (i.e. have the agreement as part of their belief systems), and also *understand* the contents and contexts of the agreement and be willing to abide by it (Scheff 1967). This is because the recalcitrance of one member can create problems for other members of the community. Every decent member of the society is thus expected to locate himself in the context of Mbiti's famous phrase: 'I am because we are; and since we are, therefore I am'. South Africans refer to this as *Ubuntu*.

The practice of peace in Africa

Elders and chiefs play decisive roles in traditional conflict management systems in Africa. They are highly respected in the societies. Their 'judicial decisions' are legitimized by their 'knowledge of the traditional ways of life, circumspections, and adherence to the truth' (Ayittey 1991: 48). Pkalya et al. (2004) identified a few other reasons for the respect elders and chiefs enjoy in many African societies:

> The elders have three sources of authority that make them effective in maintain-
> ing peaceful relationships and community way of life. They control access to
> resources and material rights; they have access to networks that go beyond the
> clan boundaries, either identity or generations; and possess supernatural powers
> reinforced by superstitions and witchcraft.

They observed further that:

> The elders function as a court with broad and flexible powers to interpret
> evidence, impose judgments, and manage the process of reconciliation. The
> mediator leads and channels discussions of the problem. Parties typically do
> not address each other, eliminating direct confrontation. Interjections are not
> allowed while parties state their case.

Different forms of adjudicatory systems are woven around the elders and chiefs. The Acholi's *Mato Oput* in northern Uganda is popular in many other parts of the African continent. It involves the appearance of disputants before a council of elders (*Lotido-Apoka*). After a lengthy process involving taking of evidence, cross-examination (Olaoba 2000) and counter-arguments, the root cause of the problem is established, guilt is established and voluntarily admitted, and settlement terms that finally lead to reconciliation between the parties are adopted. Where arms were involved in the conflict, a ceremony known as 'bending of spears' has to be performed, in which the disputants exchange spears and the tips of the spears are bent. This is followed by an oath not to harm each other any longer.

Another significant peacemaking tradition in Africa involving elders can be drawn from the Banyarwanda community in Rwanda. It is popularly known as *Gacaca*. This intricate tradition, which started at community level but soon attained national importance in Rwanda, derived its name from a grass known as *Urucaca*, which grows in homesteads in the country. The conflict management approach places emphasis on three things: dialogue, reconciliation and reparation. Like the Acholi's *Mato Oput*, the process involves elders gathering in front of the *Urucaca* in the homestead to resolve conflicts. Proceedings in a *Gacaca* court involve plaintiffs, defendants and witnesses. Each party is asked to present his/her case. The defendants do not have lawyers but any member of the community can participate and intervene in the proceedings, either against or in favour of the defendant. As usual there is cross-examination of the parties, and the elders, rather than pass judgment per se, try to reconstruct the broken relationship. So productive is this African approach to conflict management that it was incorporated in the official legal system in Rwanda. In 2001, about 260,000 men of integrity, honesty and good conduct were selected from local communities to establish more than ten thousand *Gacaca* tribunals in different parts of Rwanda to find out the truth about the 1994 genocide in the country (Lutheran World Federation 2002: 2).

In Botswana, as in Nigeria, traditional courts are a critical element of the justice system. This traditional conflict resolution system is hierarchical in nature. It starts with the family head, who is considered to be the chief conflict manager within his immediate family. Only the cases that cannot be successfully handled by the family heads get referred to the ward *Kgotla*, namely the war or neighbourhood court. Cases that cannot be successfully settled at *Kgotla* are taken to the main *Kgotla*, presided over by the chief. This pattern of conflict settlement is equally popular among the Mbeere of Kenya:

> Private disputes arising within the family were settled by its head. If the case was unresolvable or if the aggrieved party failed to obtain satisfactory resolution, the case could be appealed to the lineage head, called *mutongoria wa kithaka*. The

lineage head would assess the substance of the case and, if it merited further deliberation, would empanel a group of elders as a family court to adjudicate. Such family courts usually deliberated on disputes involving a father and his son or between and man and his wife. (Ayittey 1991: 40)

Writing on how the above kind of conflict intervention operates among the Igbo-speaking people of Nigeria, Uwazie (2000: 28) observed:

A disputant simply orally complains to the family head or village chief/chairperson. In cases where both disputants are women, the aggrieved party complains by loud shouts of 'egbe-ee' during the particular incident, to be echoed by other women as they rush to the scene. A case may be resolved immediately upon such a complaint, or a date is set for a public hearing at the village square or at another neutral site.

Discussing how this kind of conflict situation is settled in traditional Ashanti society in Ghana, Busia (1967: 51) noted that:

The matter was, in effect, settled by arbitration. A pacification or conciliation (*mpata*) was claimed from the offender for the injured man, who was expected to accept it. Not only as proof that the injury has been annulled but also as a sign that friendly relations had been restored between the parties. The pacification was small: a fowl or a few eggs for the injured man to 'wash his soul' (*adware ne kra*) so that his feelings might be assuaged. In more serious offenses gold-dust to the value of 7 shillings or at most 10 shillings was paid as pacification.

The settlement becomes more challenging when the disputants do not belong to the same lineage or ethnic group. In the latter case, the aggrieved person submits the matter to a respected member of the community for arbitration. The latter would involve an elder from the offender's lineage or group participating in the arbitration process. Other elders might be invited to join the arbitration panel. The elders would determine who was wrong or right and arrive at terms for compensating the injured person. The matter could also be referred to the community leader for arbitration if it could not be settled at that lower level.

The 'house of palaver' (*a berei mu meni saa*) or moot system of the Kpelle of Liberia is another interesting conflict management strategy involving the elders in the society. This informal dispute-settlement forum often consists of an ad hoc group of kinsmen and neighbours gathered by two complainants to settle a dispute involving both of them. In this case, the matter is openly considered by everybody, and the person found to be at fault is made to apologize to the aggrieved party and present a small gift to him/her. At the end of the process, both disputants share a drink and symbolically end the dispute. This kind of dispute-settlement system is also common among the Somali and the Kalahari (Ayittey 1991: 42).

The foregoing does not suggest, however, that the roles of chiefs in conflict resolution and peace-building are infallible. There are many instances in which the chiefs themselves are the major source of violent conflicts. A recent study (Albert 2008) shows how several hundred lives as well as property are lost to chieftaincy disputes in Ghana and Nigeria. Long years of colonial rule, military misadventures, prebendal civil rule, protracted wars and gratuitous violence have given people great respect for the judicial decisions and pronouncements of traditional rulers who embody cultural values and etiquette.

Towards integrating the African and the global

The point made above is that the traditional systems are still vibrant and relevant for making, building and keeping peace in Africa. The continent would become a better place if these local approaches could be integrated with modern approaches for managing conflicts on the continent. This issue was the subject matter of an inter-faith summit organized by the Lutheran World Federation (LWF) and hosted by the National Religious Leaders' Forum of South Africa (NRLFSA) in Johannesburg on 23 October 2002. The meeting concluded, among many other things, that the traditional methods of conflict resolution do in fact work but have not been formally incorporated into the official methods of conflict management in many parts of the continent. It called for a rethink of this paradoxical situation.

Some studies sponsored by the United States Institute for Peace (USIP) on countries of the Horn of Africa (particularly Sudan, Somalia and Ethiopia) in the 1990s came to the same conclusion. They have shown that the failure of more traditional methods, most especially erosion of the authority of traditional rulers and politicians, is partly responsible for many ongoing conflicts in Africa. The problem consists in the fact that the modern elite who have successfully wrested powers from the traditional political elite use such powers to advance personal and narrow group interests and in the process have generated several conflicts for the people of the continent.

The USIP studies also observed that African civil wars are more easily managed when the traditional methods of conflict management on the continent are adapted to modern realities and that traditional authorities (elders and chiefs), women's organizations, local institutions and professional associations have important roles to play in this goal of promoting grassroots peace-building, peacemaking and preventive diplomacy (Smock 1997).

One of the USIP-funded projects, carried out by Wal Duany of the University of Indiana in southern Sudan, came up with nine important lessons on how indigenous knowledge systems can help to establish and consolidate the basis and framework for peace in Africa. Seven of them are related to the objectives of this chapter. First and foremost, the study advised that external actors doing peace work in Africa should take into serious account the cosmologies and theologies of the people. The question to ask in this context must capture the whole essence of the philosophical and religious ideas that lie behind the disputants' understanding of the world. What is their idea of justice and how can this be provided?

The second observation is that the conflict resolution approaches to be adopted in dealing with a particular problem should be drawn from or take into consideration the traditional culture of the people with the guidance of traditional leaders. This is important for refining the peacemaking process. The things to be taken into consideration here include 'communication styles, leadership choices, methods of negotiation, participation of parties to the conflict and the third-party, decision-making structures, the system of recompense for wrongdoing, determination of wrongdoing and appropriate punishment, processes for remorse, confession, forgiveness, and reconciliation, and rituals for marking closure and new beginnings' (ibid.: 5).

The third point is that the peace worker should understand the structure of social institutions and principles guiding interaction of the people. How do the people see themselves and others? How do they culturally relate internally and externally? This aspect of the findings is important in the context of property rights, kinship ties and women as resources for managing disputes.

The fourth point is that the peace process should make provisions for local institutional arrangements for implementing the peace agreements. Achieving this objective could entail efforts at revitalizing traditional systems of order, justice and welfare. Closely related to this is the need to understand the traditional governance and leadership systems in the communities. What are the roles of the elders, custodians of the people's traditions, age-grades, women leaders, indigenous militia and traditional religious leaders? This is with a view to identifying who should do what in the peace process.

The sixth issue is to understand the traditional conflict management processes of the people, and last but not least to frame the peace process as a long-term process of cultural and human interaction rather than a quick-fix system meant for dealing with one particular problem (ibid.: 6).

Conclusion

The main argument of this chapter is that durable peace cannot be attained in Africa until those working for peace on the continent start to factor local approaches into their conflict management strategies. For now, most of the peace activities on the continent are framed in the context of the liberal peace project, which has as its focus Western ideas geared towards protecting the narrowly defined hegemonic and economic interests of the developed world. Though Africans do not have a monopoly of wisdom over how to manage their conflicts, it is also not true that the people lack the traditional values that can be tapped into for strengthening peace processes on the continent. Those who manage conflicts on the continent need to immerse themselves in the sociocultural contexts of the problems they are solving. They need to incorporate the wisdom of elders and chiefs in the African communities into their conflict management traditions. This chapter clearly identifies a number of African traditions and societies from which some best practices can be drawn.

What this chapter is calling for is neither a wholesale importation of the traditional conflict resolution mechanisms in Africa nor a total repudiation of the Western models and values, but rather a revitalization and subsequent inclusion of the African traditional conflict resolution mechanisms in the management of the 'modern conflicts' on the continent. The present situation of marginalizing the traditional approaches in managing contemporary African conflicts is comparable to attempting to fly an aeroplane with one wing. We are therefore not surprised that most of the peace agreements on the continent fail to hold any water.

4 | The mainstreaming of conflict analysis in Africa: contributions from theory[1]

JOÃO GOMES PORTO

In the last decade, conflict analysis has assumed increased importance in the basket of tools used in development assistance, humanitarian relief and peace support operations. The mainstreaming of conflict analysis in the day-to-day practices of a large number of organizations operating in pre-conflict, conflict and post-conflict environments is a remarkable achievement with potentially significant consequences as regards the prevention, management and resolution of violent conflict, as well as the efficacy of assistance. The development and adoption of conflict analysis frameworks demonstrate the practical benefits accrued through the combined efforts of practitioners and academics in the operationalization of years of multidisciplinary research. With the aim of reflecting on some of the challenges as well as the opportunities posed by the application of these analytical tools to African contexts, this chapter reviews some of the defining contributions and debates that, although at the basis of the development of conflict analysis methodologies, are often forgotten given the day-to-day pressures faced by organizations and individuals involved in their application.

A focus on conflict analysis theory – and its potential as part of conflict prevention, management and resolution in African contexts – remains both necessary and urgent. It is urgent because of the inordinate severity of the way conflict affects the lives and livelihoods of millions of Africans. Africa has been the stage for ten high-intensity conflicts in the past twenty-five years, with casualties ranging between 4 and 6 million people, and with an astounding 155 million people directly or indirectly affected by war. Although perhaps a latecomer, Africa's place as an active contributor to what Eric Hobsbawm has termed the 'age of catastrophe' – a twentieth century marked by bloodshed and violence – is, unfortunately, assured.[2] Not only have civil, regional and internationalized wars ravaged large parts of the continent since independence, but the instances where regimes are the chief perpetrators of violence against their own citizens through genocide and mass murder (adequately encapsulated by Rudolph Rummel's expression 'democide') have been pervasive.[3] In this first decade of the twentieth-first century alone, the civil wars in Côte d'Ivoire, Democratic Republic of Congo (DRC), Burundi, Sudan (Darfur as well as Western Upper Nile), Somalia and Guinea Bissau, or the medium-intensity conflicts in the Central African Republic, Nigeria (Niger Delta) and now Chad, have been stark reminders of the severity of violent conflict on Africa's socio-economic development (see Poku et al. 2007). Moreover, the fragility of war-to-peace transitions in countries such as Sierra Leone, Liberia, the DRC and Angola (to name but a few) requires constant attention from all actors involved. The pace at which violence destroys the socio-economic fabric of countries not too long ago regarded as the 'good boys' (Zimbabwe and the very recent case of Kenya come to mind) should remind us of the absolute imperative of conflict prevention, of dealing with situations before they escalate, of benign intervention through peacemaking. For in addition to the human and material costs of war (often in contexts where civilians and civilian infrastructure are directly targeted), violence introduces variables of a psycho-social nature (spirals of retribution and revenge, for example), which require extensive and long-term peace-building and reconciliation in the societies in question long after the guns have fallen silent.

Revisiting conflict analysis theory and practice is also necessary at a time when a large number of organizations involved in conflict prevention, management and resolution (ranging from the African Union to the Regional Economic Communities; from donor agencies to local NGOs; from policy research think tanks to university departments) employ one version or another of so-called conflict assessment tools in their efforts to understand, explain and develop responses to situations of instability on the continent. This is particularly the case with the current operationalization of a number of conflict early warning systems in Africa – including the Continental Early Warning System (CEWS) at the African Union or CEWARN at the Intergovernmental Authority on Development (IGAD) and ECOWARN at the Economic Community of West African States (ECOWAS), to name just a few.

This chapter aims to provide a critical review of the mainstreaming of conflict analysis and assessment frameworks, as well as a preliminary reflection on some of the challenges that the application of these frameworks pose in African contexts. Wherever possible and necessary, it will bridge theory and practice by using findings of a theoretical nature from conflict research, peace studies and international relations. At a very basic level, in its attempt to navigate a treacherous perceptual terrain still littered with single-cause explanations (or at worst propositions of inevitability) of the pervasiveness of conflict on the continent, this chapter should stimulate our thinking on how to approach – and not shy away from – the complexity that characterizes the occurrence of violence. As for the *inevitability of conflict in Africa* proposition, the words of award-winning journalist and author Charlayne Hunter-Gault come to mind: 'If all you hear about year after year is hunger, drought, disease and conflict, *people conclude that Africa's problems are intractable and that nothing in Africa ever changes* [emphasis added]'.[4]

Hunter-Gault's volume *New News Out of Africa: Uncovering the African Renaissance* represents a potent reaction to prevailing orthodoxy on public perceptions of everything *African*, an attempt at offsetting the *'four d's'* that inevitably permeate much of our discourse on Africa: death, disease, disaster and despair (Hunter-Gault 2006). For the author of these pages, this partly requires negotiating the two broad strands that, as noted by Patrick Chabal, have marked reflections on the pervasiveness of violence on the continent. A first argument links 'violence with the social and political pangs of development' in that 'the consolidation of the state and the transformation of society cannot be achieved without force' (Chabal 2005: 1). A second strand of arguments purports to explain the pervasiveness of conflict in Africa by relating its occurrence to the 'features of the modernisation of the African Continent that make it prone to a greater degree (and range) of violence than might otherwise be expected' (ibid.: 1). Often reliant on comparisons with other parts of the world, the first strand tends to explain conflict in Africa as the inevitable result of historical processes of state- and nation-building, in its case made particularly challenging by the legacies of centuries of colonial rule. Paradigmatic of this view, Mohammed Ayoob's *The Third World Security Predicament* closely links efforts at state-building in post-colonial and other states of the South with the inevitability of conflict. In his view, these states experience a *security predicament* that is a consequence of the twin pressures of state-making and the Third World's late entry into the system of states.[5] What happens in Africa as far as political violence is concerned is therefore not necessarily specific, being observed in many parts of the post-colonial world. In the second strand, it is precisely the specificity of Africa's colonial and post-colonial experience (in its political, economic, developmental, social, security dimensions) which is at the root of the occurrence of violence – the intricate and situation-specific ways it affects individual countries woven into a broader set of arguments around the nature of political power and neo-patrimonialism, governance, identity and ethno-linguistic fractionalization, resource scarcity and inequality, among other factors.

Practice and method: the mainstreaming of conflict analysis

Introduction For an increasingly large number and variety of organizations and individuals operating across Africa, undertaking conflict analysis has become synonymous with the use of a very specific instrument and method, minor variations according to the mission and purpose of the agencies concerned notwithstanding. If one recalls that only a decade ago it was *en vogue* within both academic and policy circles to caution against the continued gap between theory and practice, the mainstreaming of conflict analysis – even considering some of the associated and inevitable pitfalls to be discussed below – is nothing but remarkable. It is worth recapping some of the background to these developments. When in the years leading to the end of the cold war an increasing number of social scientists turned their attention to understanding and explaining the wars that then finally began to matter (i.e. internal, civil, societal wars) – turning the page on a somewhat obsessive focus on systemic and other interstate wars – the walls that separated different strands of academia as well as the gap that characterized the interactions between academia and communities of practice finally began to show irreparable cracks. One should recall that within academia, the study of war and armed conflict had for decades remained fragmented between disciplinary boundaries (international relations, strategic studies, sociology, history, peace studies and conflict research), a division that inevitably resulted in conflicting and often mutually exclusive theories and research agendas and, perhaps more importantly, a conspicuous lack of knowledge integration through multidisciplinary approaches. The situation as regards the links between academia and communities of practice operating in countries and regions ravaged by war was even more tenuous (notable exceptions here being development studies and at the time the nascent applied conflict resolution field).

It is therefore not surprising that the initial impetus for some kind of integration (for our purposes here, the focus is on conflict analysis frameworks) came from practitioners from a variety of different organizations and backgrounds. Whether operating in Europe's post-cold-war battlefields of Bosnia-Hercegovina, Nagorno-Karabakh and Georgia or in Africa's wars in Angola, Sudan, Uganda, Zaire/DRC, practitioners required a set of analytical tools that would enable them to better understand – and by consequence prepare and plan for – these situations. As the curtains closed on the final act of the cold war – the dissolution of the USSR in 1991 – classic interstate wars had already become the exception rather than the rule. And yet, as far as mainstream international relations and strategic studies were concerned, the study of war was, by and large, focused on *Big Wars*[6] with system-altering consequences – all other conflicts seen as 'proxy wars', 'small wars' or 'low intensity conflicts' (Siverson and Midlarski 1990: 219). Under the dominance of realist and neo-realist thought, the overwhelming focus was placed on strategic studies' issues, such as national and international security, nuclear deterrence and balances of power, alliances and arms races, as well as the incidence, frequency and duration of interstate wars.[7] An important exception to this, as will be further discussed below, was provided in the guise of the truly revolutionary contributions of the increasingly visible field of peace studies and conflict research through the now classic works of John Burton, Johan Galtung, Edward Azar, Herbert Kelman, Ted Gurr, Louis Kriesberg or pioneers such as Georg Simmel or Quincy Wright, among many others.

Between 1989 and 2006, as recently noted by Harbom and Wallensteen, out of a total of 122 conflicts worldwide, only seven were interstate conflicts, eighty-nine were intra-state conflicts and twenty-six were considered as internationalized intra-state conflicts (when the government, the opposition or both receive military support from other governments) (Arbom and Wallensteen 2007: 623). In Africa, the resumption of large-scale civil war in Angola following the 1992 elections, the 1993 American debacle in Somalia and the international community's failure

49

to act on the genocide in Rwanda in 1994 exposed violence to wider and wider audiences. Ironically, it wasn't that these now-termed 'new wars' or 'wars of the third kind' – to use Kaldor's and Holsti's terminology – had suddenly materialized (Kaldor 1999; Holsti 1996). The trend, of course, had been there for several decades and yet the world was firmly focused on the *strategic level*, paying little attention to the 'subterranean ravages' wrought during the period.[8] 'Internal', 'civil', 'ethnic', 'societal' conflicts, 'new wars' and 'complex humanitarian emergencies' imposed themselves on an international arena no longer able to dismiss them as irrelevant to the strategic equation. It had become increasingly clear that in the new, turbulent and gradually unstable post-cold-war world, Bueno de Mesquita's warning on the dangers of limiting one's attention to global, systemic wars was indeed good advice.[9] And nowhere was this truer than in the African continent, where by the end of the 1990s no subregion was spared the ravages of war (in West Africa, Liberia, Sierra Leone and Guinea Bissau; in the Horn, Ethiopia/Eritrea and Somalia; in the Great Lakes, Uganda, the DRC and Burundi; and in southern Africa, Angola). This caused a fundamental and urgent shift in the analysis of war and armed conflict. These became the conflicts that mattered, for not only could they threaten global and regional peace and stability in their tendency to metastize to neighbouring countries, but they caused unprecedented levels of human and material destruction. Largely focused on a 'Clausewitzian universe' of interstate wars, academia and policy-making circles were largely unprepared for the task of explaining such 'societal conflicts'. The tools of strategic and war studies seemed increasingly irrelevant to explain ethno-nationalism, religious militancy, environmental degradation, resource scarcity, preventive diplomacy or humanitarian intervention.

The increase in opportunities for peacemaking by the UN, regional organizations and political activists in war-torn societies (Gurr et al. 2000: 11) must also be considered. In particular, the renewed opportunity and willingness of the United Nations Security Council to act resulted in an exponential growth in intervention by the international community – interventions that faced considerable challenges as regards the best ways to operate in conflict environments. And these conflict environments were a far cry from the structured conduct of conventional war – leading several authors, in fact, to put forward the proposition of a structural transformation of war. Martin van Creveld, Kalevi Holsti and Mary Kaldor, among others, have devoted considerable attention to these 'low intensity conflicts', 'wars of the third kind' or 'new wars' respectively. The conduct of war in contexts characterized by poverty and underdevelopment (often weak states), and in particular the specific targeting of civilians, the multitude of different conflict parties (ranging from locally based warlords to irregular cells), the aetiologies invoked (usually revolving around identity politics), or the cohabitation with organized crime and dependence on war economies with links to the global economy, gave these conflicts a particularly complex nature.[10]

Whether as peacekeeping or humanitarian relief operations working *in* a conflict environment, non-governmental organizations trying their very best to work *around* conflict or peace-building and conflict resolution projects trying to work directly *on* conflicts, these actors faced challenges of a similar nature, for which specific analytical tools were required. How best to analyse conflicts that occur in contexts characterized by a myriad of actors and often very complex factors of a political, ethnic, military, economic and humanitarian nature? Is it likely that interventions may in fact exacerbate or escalate these conflicts? Inversely, what is the potential impact of a conflict's eruption, escalation or de-escalation on development interventions? Ultimately, what tools, analytical and programmatic, are available so that interventions effectively contribute to conflict prevention, management or resolution, reducing risks and maximizing impact? These questions prompted a new dialogue between policy-makers, practitioners and academics in an effort to devise methods and frameworks that could increase the chances of success in both direct conflict prevention, management and resolution activities and indirectly through development and humanitarian assistance. Central to the approach taken in these analytical frameworks is what became known as 'conflict sensitivity' – the acknowledgement that aid can also produce negative consequences. In fact, stemming from Mary Anderson's *do no harm* proposition,[11] the realization that 'humanitarian assistance sometimes feeds conflict rather than alleviates it, and that development aid sometimes exacerbates tensions', has elevated *conflict sensitivity* – the notion of systematically taking into account the positive and negative impact of interventions, and, conversely, the impact of these contexts on the interventions – into a fundamental principle of assistance.[12] As noted by Barbolet et al.,

> The idea of conflict sensitivity owes a great deal to diverse literature and thinking on Peace and Conflict Impact Assessment (PCIA), though PCIA is not the only intellectual and, importantly, experiential source that has influenced the development of 'conflict-sensitive approaches' (CSA). Mary Anderson's 'Do No Harm' work; the macro conflict assessment work undertaken by DFID, USAID, the World Bank and other donors; the writings of Jonathan Goodhand; and over thirty years of peace and development academic discourse have also provided significant insight. (Barbolet et al. 2005: 3)

In the pages below, I will specifically focus on the macro-conflict assessment work referred to above, largely because I share the authors' belief that 'the foundation of conflict-sensitive practice is a thorough and regularly updated conflict analysis; it is the base rock to which all project planning, implementation, monitoring and evaluation should be linked' (ibid.: 9). The importance of conflict analysis, increasingly recognized as a central component of conflict-sensitive practice (International Alert et al. 2004), as a basis for a series of policy processes is highlighted in no uncertain terms by the United Nations: 'it is critical

Mainstreaming of conflict analysis

that the recommendations [from conflict analysis] feed into other planning frameworks that are available to the UN system in transition countries, such as the CAP (Consolidated Appeals Process), UNDAF (Common Country Assessment and Development Assistance Framework) and PRSP (Poverty Reduction Strategy Process) as well as into national development plans' (UNDG-ECHA 2004). After all, conflict research academics had for quite some time highlighted the importance of adequate conflict analysis as an 'essential pre-requisite for normative conflict resolution' (Miall et al. 1999: 65). As highlighted by Dennis Sandole,

> ... In order to prevent or otherwise deal with violent conflict and war, we must know something about the underlying factors: their identities, sequences, relative weights, combination, and interaction. We require, in other words, theory which would enable us to explain these processes, not only as an otherwise noteworthy academic objective, but as a prerequisite to attempting to manage, control, prevent, or otherwise deal with them. (Sandole 1999: 4)

At this stage a caveat is required: while current debates tend to focus on the theory and practice of conflict sensitivity, the assessment of impact or method versus approach, for the purposes of this chapter we focus very specifically on one set of tools, those of conflict analysis.[13] We find it necessary to make this caveat as a result of a considerable degree of confusion between conflict analysis methods and conflict-sensitive practice. In this regard we share Dan Smith's thoughts to the effect that

> The issue of analysis is clouded by the common eliding of two different terms and concepts – peace and conflict impact assessment (PCIA), and conflict analysis (or conflict assessment) (CA) ... CA and PCIA are related, and any PCIA should include a rigorous CA, but they are different and it is not always necessary for CA to include PCIA. (Smith, D. 2004: 45)

A shared conflict analysis method? Examples of conflict analysis frameworks include, *inter alia*, the *Strategic Conflict Assessment Methodology* developed by Jonathan Goodhand, Tony Vaux and Robert Walker for the UK's Department for International Development (DfID); the *Guidelines for Conflict Analysis for Project Planning and Management* produced by Manuela Leonhardt for the German Technical Cooperation Agency (GTZ); the *Conflict Analysis Framework* produced by the Conflict Prevention and Reconstruction Team of the World Bank; and the UN's Inter-Agency *Framework for Conflict Analysis in Transition Situations* (Leonhardt 2001; DfID 2002; UNDG-ECHA 2004; World Bank 2005). As noted by Leonhardt, the experiences of organizations actively engaged in the reduction and transformation of violent conflicts, such as UK-based International Alert and Responding to Conflict, contributed significantly to these efforts (International Alert 1996; Fisher et al. 2000).

The conflict analysis frameworks referred to above are strikingly similar, demonstrating that a consensus of sorts has emerged at a policy level – to what extent this mirrors (in fact stems from) developments within peace studies and conflict research will be the focus of our next section. Three analytical clusters are normally suggested by these frameworks, comprising: (1) conflict analysis; (2) analysis of ongoing responses; and (3) strategic and programmatic recommendations. Following Leonhardt, we should note that these methodologies are action oriented and therefore there is considerable attention attached to stages two and three (outside the scope of this chapter), which focus on ongoing responses and the formulation of policy and operational options. As noted by this author, 'the purpose of conflict analysis is to gain a good understanding of the problem areas in which external organisations can make a meaningful contribution to reducing the potential for conflict and advancing the peace-building process' (Leonhardt 2001: 16).

Whether our focus is analysing the current situation in Darfur, the so-called 'post-electoral crisis' in Kenya, the attempted coup in Chad or the crisis in Zimbabwe, phase one or conflict analysis proper should focus on three main interlinked clusters: a critical analysis and review of the structural dimensions of conflict (multi-level and thematic) in tandem with an analysis of the proximate sources of conflict (equally multi-level and thematic); an analysis of actors or conflict stakeholders; and, finally, an analysis of conflict dynamics. The identification and mapping of structural factors and conditions considered relevant for a comprehensive yet critical understanding of the underlying dimensions of a particular situation – whether at a political, economic, social, military and security, cultural or religious level, as well as at different levels of the social spectrum: local (community), regional, national, subregional or international – are therefore undertaken concomitantly with an analysis of the proximate factors that may have caused the eruption of violence. In the case of the post-election situation in Kenya at the end of December 2007, this would entail both an assessment of the immediate precursors to the eruption of violence (including but not limited to the elections and the electoral dispute) and, equally important, a critical investigation into what Jonathan Goodhand et al. consider 'the long term factors underlying violent conflict' or 'the key sources of tension that have led to, or are likely to lead to, open conflict' (DfID 2002: 11). These conditions are variously termed in the academic literature 'underlying causes' (e.g. Brown 1996b), Dennis Sandole's 'conflict-as-startup conditions', Charles King's 'structural components' (King 1997: 29) or Kenneth Waltz's 'permissive or underlying causes of war'. They are regarded as 'cleavages' in the political, economic and social realms upon which the mobilization of individuals and groups for violent conflict is often undertaken.

These 'key sources' of tensions may be found in security, political, economic, social and religious structures in the society in question. The structuring of the analysis around the conceptual distinction between structural and proximate causes (often artificial but to this author no less useful) owes a great deal to reflections stemming from peace studies and conflict research over several decades, not least Galtung's often cited differentiation between positive and negative peace and the pivotal concept of structural violence (Galtung 1964b). Significantly, and perhaps more than a simple exercise at conflict sociology, the identification of structural 'cleavages' in society has the potential to uncover priority areas of intervention – in particular as regards conflict prevention and peace-building.

While at a political level, for example, the structural sources of conflict and tension may include, *inter alia*, a weakly institutionalized/unrepresentative political system, lack of independent judiciary, corruption, weak political parties, lack of popular participation in governance, or political exploitation of ethnic religious differences (DfID 2002: 12), at an economic level these may include poverty, underdevelopment or discriminatory economic systems (e.g. Brown 1996b: 14). In order to manage the complexity of possible structural sources, approaches may be thematically divided around clusters, such as the ones put forward by the World Bank, which include social and ethnic, governance and political institutions, human rights and security, economic structure and performance, environment and natural resources and, finally, external factors. If we take as an example the 'governance and political institutions' cluster of variables, the analysis of structural issues must entail an evaluation of 'equity of governance and political institutions', 'stability of political institutions', 'equity of law and judicial system' and 'links between government and its citizens'.[14]

Of relevance for several of the frameworks is the suggestion that the mapping of structural sources of conflict be done not only according to different issue areas but also according to different levels of analysis (local, national, regional, international) and that the exploration of linkages between levels and types of tensions is a critical component of the analysis. As will be discussed below, not only is there a theoretically important set of arguments in favour of multi-level analysis, but it should also be recognized that because implementing agencies tend to operate at different levels simultaneously (for example, national and local) this is required for programme implementation purposes. Furthermore, if structural factors may be considered to be 'pervasive and long standing factors and differences that become built into the policies, structures and culture of a society and may create the pre-conditions for violent conflict', proximate conflict factors can be seen as those 'likely to contribute to a climate conducive to violent conflict or its further escalation, sometimes symptomatic of deeper problems' (UNDG-ECHA 2004: 5). In this sense, while illegitimate government or lack of political participation may be considered structural factors, a surge in human rights abuses, refugee flows or massive population movements, or a stolen election, may be considered proximate factors. As will be discussed below, this forces us to recognize that the presence per se of structural conflict conditions is a necessary but not sufficient condition for the outbreak of violence.

As an example, consider the serious socio-economic (and often political) cleavages produced by skewed patterns of land distribution in southern Africa – often in situations where many of the same economic and social conditions of poverty, underdevelopment, inequality and lack of opportunities pertain. Why does violence occur in certain countries around land tenure and land use but not others? The same applies for proximate factors: although critical, they are not sufficient to explain the occurrence of violence. Why did violence erupt in Kenya to the extent that it did – ostensibly because of a stolen election – but not in Zimbabwe following the parliamentary elections of 2005? Once violence erupts the tendency is to focus on the events that immediately preceded the escalation, that are given by actors involved to justify their actions, that are amenable to quick rationalizations with proximate causes receiving considerable attention as sources of tension and conflict. Yet the implications of this for the day-to-day practice of organizations and individuals involved in conflict prevention, management and resolution are considerable. This is precisely the reason for incorporating both proximate and structural factors in the analysis of any one situation, as adequately recognized by the UN: 'understanding *proximate* conflict factors is critical to ensure that transition programming strategies militate against the impact of violent conflict over the short-term. At the same time, transition programming *should be informed by an analysis of structural conflict factors, in order to ensure that its inputs become assets for long-term peace building and development* [emphasis added]' (ibid.: 4).

Once a situation is mapped out in terms of its structural vulnerability and the identification of proximate conflict factors is completed, the next step is the analysis of actors or conflict stakeholders. Different actors' interests and agendas, incentives, resources and capacities are defined and their interrelationships discussed. Leonhardt distinguishes between primary stakeholders (parties engaged in the conflict and their active units – political or armed, for example); secondary stakeholders (those that play the part of intermediaries and have various means of influencing the course of the conflict); and external stakeholders (not involved directly in the conflict but having certain interests – for example, neighbouring states, donor governments, etc.).[15] By understanding the individuals, groups and institutions engaged in, as well as affected by, conflict, the 'potential risks associated with engaging with internal and external actors' may 'help address the issue of "interlocutors" and "partners" with whom support agencies interact, both in humanitarian and development terms' (UNDG-ECHA 2004: 8, 9). This is closely tied to a concern about what UNDG-ECHA terms 'capacities for peace' – structures, mechanisms, processes and institutions that exist in society to peacefully manage conflict.

The final step of conflict analysis usually involves what is referred to as conflict dynamics analysis, where patterns and trends are identified, and possible accelerators and triggers for violence explored. The development of possible scenarios as regards conflict dynamics is now possible. Is the conflict likely to escalate, de-escalate or remain at the same level of intensity? Is conflict eruption more or less likely in relation to certain triggers? What are the long-term trends that can be observed as regards certain developments? The value of dynamics analysis and scenario development (short, medium and long term) is a direct function of the comprehensiveness of the two steps preceding it (structural/proximate analysis and actors analysis). Identifying possible triggers and scenario-building will each uncover a number of key indicators or factors, the monitoring of which becomes imperative. Which factors are likely to accelerate or slow conflict dynamics? Which institutions or processes may mitigate or manage tensions? Which scenario is most likely to happen and why?

Agencies involved in the development of analysis frameworks emphasize the need to tailor the method to specific situations and particular ends rather than its blind or context-insensitive application. UNDG-ECHA notes that 'the intention in applying this framework should therefore not be to "fill in the boxes" but, in view of the specificities of each transition situation, to organise a process, which will help arrive at some common understanding of the key analytical components' (ibid.: 4). Equally, DfID warns that the methodology should not be seen as a formula and that it should (1) adapt according to the needs and objectives of the end-user; (2) develop according to the nature and phase of the conflict; (3) develop dynamic forms of analysis; and, finally, (4) encourage 'joined-up' analysis. The UN emphasizes that the process should arrive at a 'common understanding of the causes and consequences of violent conflict' and that because of that their framework 'places a shared vision of the underlying causes and consequences of conflict as the entry point for developing a transition strategy and programming' (ibid.: 4).

Conclusions: challenges and dilemmas of application in Africa

Over the last half a decade, conflict assessments have been undertaken by a large number of organizations (most prominently perhaps by departments for international development operating in Africa, such as DfID, USAID, SIDA; technical cooperation agencies such as GTZ or UN system agencies; but also significantly by African regional organizations, think tanks and NGOs). The conduct of conflict assessments as precursors to development planning, humanitarian assistance and conflict management interventions (whether related to peacekeeping missions, to disarmament, demobilization and reintegration programmes, or as a tool for strategic risk assessment) has gradually become an integral part of the day-to-day operations of organizations in Africa. While the frameworks may seem at first hand deceptively simple in their 'how to' approach, as well as overly ambitious in the resources (time and human capacity) required, a glance through the increasingly large number of assessments for African countries (Nigeria, Mozambique, Rwanda, South Africa) and regions (Great Lakes, Horn of Africa) reveals the increased use and reliance on these instruments (e.g. SIDA 2004; Management Systems International 2002; CHF International 2006; Vaux et al. 2006). The approaches to conflict analysis discussed above raise a number of interesting questions as well as challenges of application in African settings, for which some discussion of the assumptions that underlie these frameworks becomes relevant.

The causes of conflict The first of these assumptions regards the issue of causality – at no stage is the researcher drawn to a specific line of enquiry according to a predetermined set of conflict causes or cause-based typology. The fact that the operative concepts given are those of structural and proximate causes, the issues to be addressed are varied and complex and the terrain is that of multi-level analysis frees the individual from the straitjacket imposed by predetermined aetiologies. This represents an important departure from the immediate post-cold-war obsession with single-cause explanations of conflict. The 'tyranny' of the single cause has seen permutations across what David Singer has termed the 'usual suspects': territory, ideology, religion, language, ethnicity, self-determination, resources, markets, dominance, equality or revenge (Singer 1996: 38).

As we pointed out elsewhere, examples of single factor explanations and conflict types have included, at opposite sides of the aetiological spectrum, an 'ethnic conflict' type and a 'resource war' type (Porto 2002: 1–50). Often these classifications are attributed simplistically, uncritically and a posteriori, with the consequence that they may hinder the development of appropriate conflict management, resolution and peace building options. While in 'Contemporary conflict analysis in perspective' we gave more prominence to the greed proposition at the root of the 'greed versus grievance debate', for the purposes of this chapter we will briefly focus on 'ethnic conflict' as a conflict type – and in fact one which became in the early 1990s 'the most fashionable term and last resort to explain contemporary social conflicts'.[16]

Are there implications for analyses that explain the recent events in Kenya, the civil war in Burundi, the violence in Ituri (eastern DRC) or the civil war in Angola, which ended in 2002, as ethnic conflicts? And if so, to what extent do analyses differ according to different views on ethnicity? What are the implications for an understanding of conflict situations termed 'ethnic' if 'ethnicity' is seen as a primordial or inherited group characteristic which is biologically based? (e.g. van den Berghe 1981). On the other hand, what are the implications if ethnicity is approached as a contextual, fluid and negotiable aspect of identity, 'a tool used by individuals, groups, or elites to obtain some larger, typically material end'?[17]

Although the distinction between these two seemingly opposing views may at first appear academic, 'the extent to which scholars see ethnicity as immutable and innate versus socially constructed influences beliefs about the type of political systems that can best ameliorate conflict along ethnic lines' (Sisk 1996: 13). For the primordialist approach ethnicity is taken as 'a fixed characteristic of individuals and communities'.[18] An essential extension of the bond that unites kinship, ethnicity is inescapable and inevitable in the sense that 'ethnic group identities flow from an extended kinship bond, sharing common behaviours and transmitting across generations basic norms and customs, or ethnic culture'.[19] This leads authors within the primordialist approach to consider that ethnic identity is a distinct and superior form of identity. The consequences of such an approach are powerful: ethnic conflicts become a very specific type of conflict whose characteristics are typically not relevant to other social, political or economic conflicts. Taking ethnic divisions as inevitable, rooted in inherited biological traits and reinforced by centuries of past practice now beyond the ability of individuals or groups to alter, the primordialist approach sees 'conflict as flowing from ethnic differences and, therefore, not necessarily in need of explanation' (Lake and Rothchild 1998). This is because, for primordialists, 'few other attributes of individuals or communities are fixed in the same way as ethnicity or are necessarily as conflictual' (ibid.).

The instrumentalist view approaches ethnic identity in a very different light. Far from primordial, ethnicity is here conceptualized as 'a tool used by individuals, groups, or elites to obtain some larger, typically material end'.[20] This instrumentalist view of ethnicity, according to Sisk, argues that ethnic identity 'is socially constructed, often created or de-emphasised by power-seeking political elites in historically determined economic and social arrangements' (Sisk 1996: 12). As far as conflict analysis is concerned there are of course two critical components to this equation: the role of power-seeking elites in mobilizing people around ethnic identity (which can only be properly understood through a comprehensive analysis of actors and their networks) and, equally important, the reference to economic and social 'arrangements' – for our purposes here, structural and proximate causes. The instrumentalization of identity by actors (the basic tenet of instrumentalist approaches) presupposes that more than an immutable factor, identity is amenable to social construction and manipulation and is therefore influenced by the same patterns that characterize group mobilization at other levels and for different purposes. In fact, as Jabri points out, identity is the essential link between the individual and mass mobilization for conflict, whether it is identity with the group, community or state, where representatives decide on the use of force as a means of handling conflict.[21]

For this author, and following Sisk, identity, and particularly its relation to the eruption of so-called 'ethnic conflicts', is best understood midway between primordialism and instrumentalism (Sisk 1996: 13). In this sense, by conceptualizing ethnic identity as both primordialist and instrumentalist we are better placed to understand its role, importance, development and dynamic nature in armed conflict situations. For example, such an approach forces us to be critical about the 'ancient hatreds' type of explanation, which often appears collated to the explanation of genocide, such as in Rwanda and Burundi. It also places the current violence in Kenya, the ongoing low-intensity conflicts in Ethiopia or the attempted coup in Chad in a more nuanced perspective. Consequently, it becomes crucial that the conflict researcher critically analyses situations that may be described by participants and outsiders as 'ethnic conflicts'. This entails understanding that although a basic human need, identity and by extension ethnic identity is fluid, malleable, constructed and negotiable. Yet, perhaps more importantly, as noted by Gurr, while cultural identity may be stronger and more enduring than most other collective identities (i.e. ideological or class), it is most likely to provide the basis for political mobilization and conflict when it provides the basis for invidious distinctions between peoples (inequalities among cultural groups in status, economic well-being, access to political power) that are deliberately maintained through public policy and social practice.[22]

And here the classic works of James Davies (1962: 5–19, 1973) and Ted Robert Gurr[23] on relative deprivation become relevant. The relative deprivation approach was developed to explain individual and group violence. This approach places the relative sense of deprivation as the most important factor in creating grievances and mobilizing people for conflict behaviour. At the heart of individual and group grievances is the idea of unrealized expectations. In Davies's view, political violence results from an intolerable gap between what people want and what they get: the difference between expectations and gratifications.[24] This discrepancy is a frustrating experience sufficiently intense and focused to result in either rebellion or revolution.[25]

In this regard, the application of structurationism to conflict analysis by Jabri in her book *Discourses on Violence* points us in the right direction. She notes that it is precisely in the relationship between actors, their discourses and their actions that the question of identity and therefore of ethnic identity recurs. If identity, and by extension ethnic identity, is above all characterized by opposition or difference, meaning that *my* identity(ies) is (are) formed in opposition to what it is (are) not, we must locate the understanding of this type of agency through the practices that constitute and reinforce such interpretations.[26] What this implies is that the focus of enquiry should not be on an unmediated, uncritical and transparent notion of the 'ethnic group' (the subject) as the author of social practice (for our purposes *ethnic* conflict). But equally, it should not imply the abandonment or abolition of the ethnic group as a subject. This is particularly relevant in conflict analysis because it allows for a dynamic interpretation of events and is particularly useful in terms of understanding the formation and evolution of conflict groups and the crucial role and patterns of mobilization.

By requiring the evaluation of causality at different levels of the social spectrum and its relation with different issue areas, the methods under discussion allow for a more comprehensive approach to the causes of war, one grounded on the fact that any one conflict will have more than one cause and that causes can be found in more than one type of location. Consequently, single-cause or single-factor explanations of war which oversimplify a very complex and multilayered phenomenon are avoided, a requirement emphasized by Vivienne Jabri, who notes that 'the history of human political violence has shown that we cannot produce monocausal explanations of war' (Jabri 1996: 3), while Michael Brown considers that 'the best scholarly studies of internal conflict are powerful precisely because they do not rely on single-factor explanations. Instead they try to weave several factors into a more complex argument.'[27] This is exactly the point made by Jonathan Goodhand et al.:

> Underpinning the conflict assessment methodology, therefore, is the supposition that there is no single explanatory framework for looking at such complex conflict systems and the challenge is to blend different conceptual elements ... The value of the analysis is in the process of recognising connections and overlaps between sources of tension in different sectors and at different levels. (DfID 2002: 9, 11)

Levels, actors and mobilization The shift in focus implied by a turning away from the systemic level towards analyses that focus on local actors and local situations partly explains the importance of multi-level analysis in the frameworks discussed above. In fact, within the field of international relations, discussion of the causes of war has generally tended to follow what is termed a 'level-of-analysis' orientation.[28] 'Levels-of-analysis' were originally proposed by Kenneth Waltz in his very influential *Man, the State and War*.[29] Waltz suggested that an appropriate way to discuss and critically evaluate the multitude of approaches and theories on the causes of war was to divide them in terms of where along the social spectrum they locate the fundamental nexus of war causality. Within the vast literature on the causes of war, Waltz identified three main orientations as regards what for each of the authors discussed was the critical cause of war. Terming these orientations 'images of international relations', Waltz divided the extensive literature under discussion into three headings: the 'individual image', the 'nation-state image' and finally the 'state-system image'.[30]

The critical contribution of *Man, the State and War* concerns Waltz's proposition that all three images are crucial for an understanding of the causes of war. In his own words, 'some combination of our three images, rather than any one of them, may be required for an accurate understanding of international relations ... in other words, understanding the likely consequences of any one cause may depend on understanding its relation to other causes' (Waltz 1959: 14). That a consideration of all three images is of critical importance is clearly revealed by the following passage: 'so fundamental are man, the state, and the state system in any attempt to understand international relations that seldom does an analyst, however wedded to one image, entirely overlook the other two'. In fact, he says that 'the vogue of an image varies with time and place, but no single image is ever adequate', and that the result of a focus on a single image may 'distort one's interpretation of the others'.[31] Waltz recognized the fact that war and armed conflict have more than one cause and that 'causes can be found in more than one type of location' (Buzan 1995: 198). While the analyst may start from one of the levels identified, the need to take into account all three images is critical in that 'the prescriptions directly derived from a single image are incomplete because they are based upon partial analyses. The partial quality of each image sets up a tension that drives one toward inclusion of the others' (Waltz 1959: 230).

Because for the majority of groups involved in contemporary wars identity is pivotal in their struggles for self-determination aiming at independence, autonomy, secession or participation in government, for some authors the analysis of contemporary conflict should begin at unit level by looking at conflict groups themselves.[32] This focus follows the tradition of Edward Azar, a conflict research pioneer, for whom 'the most useful unit of analysis in PSC [protracted social conflict] situations is the identity group – racial, religious, ethnic, cultural and others' (Azar 1986, 1990b: 147, 148). Azar expands on John Burton's approach to the centrality of 'basic human needs' in conflict theory (e.g. Burton, John W. 1987), considering that basic needs such as security, communal recognition and distributive justice are primordial and therefore non-negotiable, emphasizing the fact that these needs are expressed in terms of religious, cultural or ethnic communal identity. He clearly recognizes that the problem resides in framing contemporary conflicts in terms of material interests, such as commercial advantages or resource acquisition, while empirical evidence suggests that 'they are not just that'.

It is crucial therefore to understand the way in which groups organize themselves as they become aware that they are in opposition to another group or groups. In this sense, a group is not defined by common interest alone. Definition must rest on communication and interaction. In order to understand the processes by which groups form some sort of collective entity and become conscious of that through sharing a measure of grievance and dissatisfaction,[33] a behavioural or interactional approach to conflict dynamics is needed. As Mitchell points out, '... conflicts are not static phenomena, and hence the dynamic aspects of conflict which alter both structure and interplay relationships over time, are essential aspects of any satisfactory analysis' (Mitchell 1981: 33).

Incorporating dynamics into the analysis of conflicts is therefore essential. In this respect, the now classic work by Louis Kriesberg entitled *Social Conflicts*[34] introduces a behavioural perspective by looking at 'social conflicts as social relationships':

... at every stage of conflict the parties interact socially; each party affects the way the others act, not only as each responds to the others but also as each may antecipate [sic] the responses of the others. Even the ends each party seeks are constructed in interaction with adversaries. (Kriesberg 1998: 21)

Furthermore, Kriesberg emphasizes that any particular conflict situation will be the result of many interlocking conflicts. The existence of multiple interlocking conflicts produces the interconnections between different stages in the sense that each conflict is part of a larger one and each is accompanied by several others, so that every conflict unit may be at a particular stage in the main conflict, but at a different stage in other related non-focal conflicts. For example, processes of anticipation and feedback affect each conflict stage, creating interconnection and interdependence between stages. Processes of anticipation and feedback in conflict cycles are the vehicles for what Sandole termed self-stimulating/self-perpetuating conflict processes. In this way, defensive actions may be interpreted as a threat (so-called 'security dilemma'), which helps create counteractions and conflict spirals.[35] Furthermore, a permanent characteristic of conflict processes is what is known as 'misperception', particularly regarding, as Levy points out, 'misperceptions of the capabilities and intentions of adversaries and third states'.[36]

The size, composition and in particular ideological outlook of conflict groups are critical, helping explain their choice of a particular approach to conflict. A group's size, its norms of participation and its experience in previous efforts at redressing grievances are important characteristics. Conflict groups exhibit different degrees of organization and boundary clarity. In this sense, while a state will have clear and demarcated boundaries, an ideological or ethnic group may present a lesser degree of boundary clarity. This is relevant in terms of understanding how and on what basis participants in different conflict groups are mobilized and organized for conflict behaviour. The same applies to the degree of organization, which varies immensely from one group or potential conflict party to the next. In fact, the degree of organization of a conflict group also helps explain recruitment, both actual and potential, as well as variations in the position of leaders.[37] It is therefore critical to understand how conflict groups are formed, what their perceived grievances are, how they formulate their goals and finally how they pursue their goals.

Moreover, it is critical to look at the decisions and actions of elites. Brown considers that 'although many internal conflicts are triggered by internal, mass-level factors, the vast majority are triggered by internal, elite-level factors', adding that 'in short, bad leaders are the biggest problem' (Brown 1996b: 575). Whether leaders based their actions on ideological beliefs (concerning the organization of political, economic and social affairs in a country), whether their actions are essentially a result of power struggles that may or may not result in assaults to state sovereignty, the role that individual leaders and elite groups play in the onset and escalation of disputes is undeniable. This line of reasoning looks at the ways in which political elites often promote conflict 'in times of political and economic trouble in order to fend-off domestic challengers' (ibid.: 18).

Relations between adversaries in a violent conflict are strongly affected by socio-psychological mechanisms such as fear, hatred and suspicion. As parties suffer the consequences of conflict behaviour they become increasingly suspicious of the adversary, and raise barriers of communication. In fact, '... as a fight escalates, the means of waging the struggle tend to become more and more removed from the underlying conflict. In this sense, the conflict may be considered to have increasingly "unrealistic" components' (Kriesberg 1998: 174).

Once violence has started issues in contention tend to be magnified and awareness of other potential conflicting issues also comes to the fore. Kriesberg considers that this expansion in issues may result in the upgrading of sub-goals that assume an added relevance for parties in contention: '... once conflict behaviour proceeds to the point that severe coercive threats and actions are employed, there is an interactive dynamic that expands the issues in contention'.[38]

Another major variant in the relations between conflict groups is the social system that they constitute or to which they belong. In fact, because the social context in which the parties to a conflict exist is both a source of their discontent as well as the channel for their actions, it is important to move up one level from the conflict groups' level. One should recall that for Azar 'protracted social conflicts' have as preconditions four sets of variables: communal content, deprivation of human needs, governance and the state's role, and, finally, international linkages.[39] Moving a level up in the analysis of conflict to considering the role of the state is necessary for 'it is the relationship between identity groups and states which is at the core of the problem' (Miall et al. 1999: 73).

We must now turn to the state level in order to understand both the underlying as well as the proximate conditions of conflict occurrence. The vast majority of contemporary armed conflicts occur in underdeveloped countries that may be undergoing rapid modernization processes or political transitions, as well as in countries characterized by state weakness and state decay.[40] The problem of weak and failed states should be looked at from the perspective of political legitimacy as well as whether they possess institutions of government capable of exercising control over the population and totality of the territory under their jurisdiction.[41] The questions of legitimacy and efficiency are particularly acute. As pointed out by Van de Goor, Rupesinghe and Sciarone, 'the phenomena of weak or failed states in the "Third World" should thus be related to the intra-state relations and the capacity of the state – the central government – to keep to the path of state-formation'.[42] In addition, problems of state weakness seem to be endemic to underdeveloped, former colonial countries. Countries with colonial backgrounds, arbitrary setting of boundaries by external powers, lack of social cohesion, recent emergence into juridical statehood and underdevelopment are potentially vulnerable to conflict. In such situations, processes of state-building are inevitably conflictual and the potential for conflict is furthermore exacerbated by attempts at nation-building.

Situations characterized by colonial legacy and what Azar termed 'weak societies' (disarticulation between state and society) are viewed by Miall et al. as 'associated with the prevalence of conflict, particularly in heterogeneous states where no overarching tradition of common and juridically egalitarian citizenship prevails' (Miall et al. 1999: 86). Explanations focusing on colonial legacies highlight the fact that the post-colonial predicament, as expressed by attempts at post-independence nation-building, is among the main causes of contemporary warfare. This predicament would, for example, include power structures devised by former colonial rulers, usually reliant on unified structures controlling a diversity of regional peoples or ethnic and tribal groups; situations where the former colonial power actively supported a particular ethnic group; or the power vacuum created after hasty decolonization leading to competition for power, control of natural resources and territory among rival parties, peoples or ethnic groups (see Holsti, K. 1996: 61–81).

In situations where state structures are unable to provide for the satisfaction of basic needs (physical security, access to political, economic and social institutions, acceptance of communal identity), individuals tend to revert to alternative means for their fulfilment. We have seen above that self-awareness as a collectivity, a predeterminant of group formation, depends on the existence of cleavages that serve as the basis for collective self-identification and organization. In addition we discussed how these cleavages and divisions may be based on nationality, ethnicity, ideology, class, religion, age or gender, etc. Whether or not a conflict escalates to the point where violence is used is more related to the political system, and in particular to the degree to which institutions of government are discriminatory or based on exclusionary ideologies. As Edward Azar points out, '... most states in protracted social conflict-laden countries are hardly neutral' in that 'political authority tends to be monopolised by a dominant identity group or a coalition of identity groups' and 'these groups tend to use the state as an instrument for maximising their interests at the expense of others ... the means to satisfy basic human needs are unevenly shared and the potential for PSC increases' (Azar 1990b: 10).

An analysis of the political system is therefore crucial if a complete understanding of a conflict situation is to be achieved. The type of regime and political system, its ideological underpinnings, the legitimacy and representativeness it enjoys, strongly affect patterns and types of relations with other societal actors. Authoritarian, repressive, exclusionary regimes are naturally more likely to create dissent and therefore increase the propensity for conflict. The ideological underpinnings of a regime affect the way in which it relates to the various societal groups as well as the way in which conflicts are resolved. Exclusionary regime ideologies based on ethnic, religious, political and class distinctions contribute to the discrimination of sectors of society, by preventing the 'state from responding to, and meeting, the needs of various constituents' (ibid.: 11), and therefore increase discontent.

Economic factors are also crucial for an understanding of proximate causes of conflict. As Miall et al. rightly point out, 'in the economic sphere, once again few would dispute Azar's contention that PSC tends to be associated with patterns of underdevelopment or uneven development' (Miall et al. 1999: 86). Rapid transitions amid poverty and social exclusion, high unemployment and at times heavy dependence on single-commodity exports, potentiate vulnerability to armed conflict. In addition to distributional conflicts within societies associated with resource scarcity, the existence of natural resources that may be easily extracted and traded (timber, minerals, oil) may potentiate the vulnerability to conflict. As Michael Brown points out,

> ... unemployment, inflation, and resource competitions, especially for land, contribute to societal frustrations and tensions, and can provide the breeding ground for conflict. Economic reforms do not always help and can contribute to the problem in the short term, especially if economic shocks are severe and state subsidies for food and other basic goods, services, and social welfare are cut. (Brown 1996b: 19)

Economic factors are particularly acute when they are associated with patterns of discrimination between groups. The perception by some groups that there are strong inequalities of economic opportunities and access to resources, as well as vast differences in standards of living between groups, will contribute to a sense of grievance. In addition, rapid modernization processes may increase the conflict vulnerability of a particular society by causing profound structural changes – migration and urbanization, among others.[43] These patterns of discrimination also affect groups culturally and socially. Access to education, recognition of minority languages and costumes, social stereotyping and scapegoating based on cultural and social characteristics of groups – all contribute to deterioration in the relations between different social groups and increase the propensity for conflict.

Finally, conflict analysis must also take into account the regional as well as international levels and the ways in which they affect particular conflicts. This is what Edward Azar called 'international linkages', one of the four main clusters of variables contributing to the occurrence of protracted social conflicts.[44] As Michael Brown points out, 'although neighbouring states and developments in neighbouring countries rarely trigger all-out civil wars, almost all internal conflicts involve neighbouring states in one way or another' (Brown 1996b: 590). Third-party involvement leading towards escalation or de-escalation is therefore critical as regards the analysis of the vast majority of contemporary armed conflicts. In this way, third parties may escalate a fight by supporting contending parties, or de-escalate a fight through attempts at a peaceful or cooperative resolution of the situation. In this sense,

> ... outside parties are not merely potential and then actual partisans. Their intervention and active involvement is much more complex than making a simple choice of sides. Their intervention changes the dimensions of the conflict and the possible pay-offs for all parties ... outside parties have their own interests and these affect their conduct in any given conflict. If the outside party is sufficiently powerful relative to the contestants, it may be able to impose its terms upon the contending parties ... (Kriesberg 1998: 244)

What about the international level? Miall, Ramsbotham and Woodhouse highlight three interlinked trends that at a global level point to systemic sources of contemporary conflicts:

> ... deep and enduring inequalities in the global distribution of wealth and economic power; human induced environmental constraints exacerbated by excessive energy consumption in the developed world and population growth in the undeveloped world, making it difficult for human well-being to be improved by conventional economic growth; and continuing militarisation of security relations, including the proliferation of lethal weaponry ... (Miall et al. 1999: 78)

Final words

> ... the research has clearly indicated which factors are important in the study of violent conflict. Conflicts are historical, dynamic and multi-dimensional, they have multiple causes and consequences of which a number are unexpected and unintended. They also involve a multitude of actors and have to be approached from different levels of analysis and intervention ... (Douma et al. 1999)

The development and increased application of conflict analysis and assessment frameworks are a significant achievement, evidencing the benefits of multi-disciplinarity as well as of a strengthened dialogue between academics and practitioners. Many of the assumptions underlying the creation of these frameworks have been part of the literature of several disciplines for some time, and yet their application in practical settings, in particular in Africa, was until recently minimal. We would like to conclude these pages by looking at one additional challenge of application. As developed by different organizations in different settings, conflict analysis for the purposes of strategic assessment, peace and conflict impact measurement or adequacy of development interventions should not be regarded as one-off exercises but be built in to the day-to-day operations of organizations. This is particularly the case for institutions directly involved in conflict prevention, management and resolution – and here we refer to the continental dimension (African Union) as well as the subregional dimension (Regional Economic Communities). As the situations in Darfur, Somalia and eastern DRC (North Kivu in particular) have made patently clear, there is a need for constant monitoring and analysis of volatile situations.

Yet if the analysis of day-to-day events in these areas, and in particular the development of appropriate response strategies, is to transcend the tendency for 'firefighting' and engage more directly with the conditions for the promotion of durable and sustainable peace, then an understanding of structural conditions underlying the occurrence of conflict is critical. It is my belief that these frameworks play an important role in this regard, as they promote a deeper reflection on the interaction between what Sandole has termed 'conflict as start-up conditions' and 'conflict as process'. The delicate balance between the two at any stage of a conflict's development can only be gauged through careful and comprehensive analysis. As Sandole poignantly noted *'it is not only the static identification of what variables might be worth looking at – conflict-as-startup conditions – but also the identification of dynamic processes that might overtake these static startup conditions: conflict-as-process* [emphasis added] ...' (Sandole 1999: 109–10). While as far as phases of conflict are concerned I tend to agree with Sandole's suggestion that 'once process comes to characterise conflict, it does not matter how (or when) the conflict started' with the result that 'different startup conditions can lead to the same process (initiation, escalation, controlled maintenance' (ibid.: 129), to this writer there should be no doubt that positive peace can be achieved only once the structural dimensions that characterize any one situation of violence are addressed – and for that to materialize they have to be understood. It is necessary therefore to concentrate on process as much as on start-up conditions, and 'in a way which connects it to startup conditions'. Structural and cultural peace-building in a Galtungian sense remain therefore paramount.

5 | Understanding conflict resolution in Africa

KENNETH C. OMEJE

The study and practice of conflict resolution are of huge importance to Africa, not least because the multiplicity of armed conflicts and wars on the continent in post-colonial times has earned notoriety for Africa as one of the world's most turbulent and poorest regions. The end of the cold war, especially the 1990s and the early 2000s, coincidentally witnessed an accentuation in Africa of the incidence of intra-state conflicts – horizontally between different socio-ethnic and cultural aggregates within a national territory, and vertically, between groups who feel excluded and marginalized from existing power structures on the one hand, and the central authority on the other (Egwu 2007: 406). As experiences of the Tuareg rebellion in the Sahel region and conflicts in the Mano River Basin and the Democratic Republic of Congo (DRC) have shown, many conflicts that have started as internal revolts or civil wars have inadvertently spread to other neighbouring countries or ended up provoking some form of intervention or complicity from neighbouring states and ethnic nationalities across international borders.

The tragic history and cycle of state breakdown, wars and armed conflict in different parts of Africa – albeit in recent years there has been considerable improvement on the situation at the dawn of the new millennium – have enlivened the debate on how to prevent, manage, settle, resolve and transform violent conflict on the continent. This chapter explores the concept and practice of conflict resolution in Africa. What are the different methods applied in trying to resolve, manage or prevent armed conflicts in Africa, and what practical challenges and opportunities do they throw up?

Theoretical discussions on conflict resolution

Conflict resolution, in particular the traditional or mainstream paradigm, comes with a basic assumption about the theory and causality of conflicts. It is an assumption rooted in the classical realist and behaviouralist (especially behavioural psychology) notion that human behaviour – and by corollary the behaviour of human organizations, institutions and states – is chiefly motivated by self-interest. Incompatible interests among actors inevitably result in conflicts, and where restraints are not exercised – which, depending on the issues at stake, underlying social context and disposition of actors is often the case – in the pursuit of driving interests, the conflicts could turn nastily violent. For realists, the behavioural regression to violent conflict is aggravated by asymmetries in the equation of power, which provides actors with the ultimate opportunity to explore coercive means in the pursuit of their interests. From this realist standpoint, violent conflicts are therefore viewed as rational choices of rational actors in a world of limited resources and competitive interests. They are a logical psychological response (subjective choice) to an interest-driven competitive world of finite resources (objective reality). Proponents argue that the psychological tendency of social actors to resort to conflict is often reinforced by both nurture (experiences of socialization) and nature (inherent aggressiveness and genetic inclination to violence over denial of certain existential needs) (cf. Morgenthau 1960; Burton, J. 1990).

(Neo)realists and behaviouralists largely believe that violent conflicts are inevitable, but exponents tend to be divided on the meaning and objective of conflict resolution. Most exponents tend to believe, however, that given the corresponding inexorability of competition for scarce resources and the asymmetrical structure of power in society, (violent) conflicts can only be controlled, managed, contained, mitigated, but not completely resolved, or are simply almost impossible to resolve. According to Hugh Miall (2004: 3): 'Conflict management theorists see violent conflict as an ineradicable consequence of differences of values and interests within and between communities. ... Resolving such conflicts is viewed as unrealistic: the best that can be done is to manage and contain them, and occasionally to reach a historic compromise in which violence may be laid aside and normal politics resumed.'

Articulating a behaviouralist discourse, Zartman (2001a: 299) posits that:

> Conflict can be prevented on some occasions and managed on others, but resolved only if the term is taken to mean the satisfaction of apparent demands rather than the total eradication of underlying sentiments, memories and interests. Only time really resolves conflicts and even the wounds it heals leave their scars for future reference. But short of such ultimate healing, much can be done to reduce conflict and thereby reduce needed energies for more productive tasks.

Assumptions about the irresolvability and ineradicability of violent conflict have influenced many proponents to channel their energies to what they tend to see as a more realistic alternative, conflict management – a term often used to describe the related phenomena of mitigation and containment of conflict through constructive methods which aims at promotion of dialogue, positive behavioural change, de-escalation of violence and political settlement (see Lewer 2002; McCandless 2006).

Critical theory of conflict resolution articulates an alternative view that challenges the assumptions of realists and behavourialists about the inevitability and irresolvability of violent conflicts. Contending that the realists and behaviouralists' conflict management agenda privileges status-quo-oriented asymmetries in power distribution and correlated interests, critical theorists argue that conflict resolution is not only possible in certain conflicts, but also necessary and desirable for change, emancipation and transformation. The discourse of 'emancipatory transformation' (see Fetherston 2000: 12), in fact, leads to the crucial distinction that many critical theorists make between conflict resolution and conflict transformation. Conflict resolution aims to address causes of conflict and seeks to build new and lasting relationships between hostile parties by helping them to explore, analyse, question and reframe their positions and interests; it moves conflicting parties from the destructive patterns of zero-sum conflict to positive-sum (win-win) constructive outcomes (Miall 2004: 3–4). Conflict transformation, on the other hand, is a process of engaging with and transforming the wider social, economic and political structures underlying a conflict, including transformation of the relationships, interests, discourse and, if necessary, the very constitution of society that supports the continuation of violent conflict (cf. McCandless 2006: 5; Miall et al. 1999: 4). While conflict resolution is mostly suitable for solving open conflicts, conflict transformation is appropriate for addressing both open and latent/surface conflicts. Critical theorists emphasize the role of a skilled and powerful third party as crucial for helping parties achieve constructively desirable outcomes in conflict resolution/transformation.

For definitional clarity,

> *open* conflict is deep-rooted and very visible, and may require actions that address both the root causes and the visible effects; *latent* conflict occurs underground or below the surface and may need to be brought into the open before it can be effectively addressed; and *surface* conflict has shallow or no roots and may be only a misunderstanding of goals that can be addressed by means of improved communication. (Fisher et al. 2000: 6)

The above typology of conflict (open, surface and latent conflicts) can also be recast in the context of Johan Galtung's (1990) famous differentiation of 'structural violence' from the more open and visible forms of direct violence or violent conflict, such as war and civil unrest. Galtung uses the term structural violence to refer to violence of an insidious nature, such as exploitative and oppressive relationships typically built into the diverse social structures and institutions of a society. Different types and levels of conflict require different methods of resolution. For instance, direct violence can be resolved by changing conflict behaviours, structural violence by removing structural contradictions and injustices, and cultural violence by changing attitudes (Miall et al. 2004: 15). By emphasizing transformation of embedded conflict-generating structures in society, such as unwholesome economic, social, legal and political structures, critical theorists incorporate political economy explanations of the causes of deep-rooted divisive and violent conflicts.

The nature of conflicts in Africa: some conceptual perspectives

To gain conceptual insight into the nature of conflicts in Africa, this section will basically explore and interrogate the analysis of African conflicts as articulated in dominant theories and explanatory discourses. Based on the analyses of principal causalities and catalysts, many recent studies and leading schools of thought have highlighted conflicts of varied significance and consequences both within and across a range of proximate African states.

Primordialism An influential and largely Western-centric paradigm perceives the proliferation of armed conflicts and wars in Africa as a primordial inevitability or an atavistic tendency rooted in the underlying phenomenological features and differences among the 'heterogeneous' communities and ethno-cultural/regional groups arbitrarily bunched together by colonial diktat to form sovereign states. Some of Africa's federated ethnic communities and groups, primordialists argue, are age-old hostile adversaries with historical animosities that date back to the unrestrained pre-colonial wars of conquest and supremacy among various African tribes, chiefdoms, clans, kingdoms and empires. Contemporary wars and armed conflicts in Africa are therefore interpreted by proponents as a resurgence of the unrestrained warrior spirit, instincts and mentality of the past and, given the patrimonial tendency for political mobilization and competition in most African states to build on underlying primordial features, violent conflicts become seemingly inevitable and virulent (cf. Geertz 1973; Llobera 1999).

Instrumentalism Another leading school of thought, which could be branded the instrumentalist approach, focuses on the place of primordial identities in African conflicts, but in their relationships with domestic political structures and the role of human agencies. While acknowledging the existence of the so-called primordial features – tribalism, ethnic culture and religion – instrumentalists argue that these features on their own do not naturally result in violent conflicts. Primordial factors instigate and affect conflicts only to the extent that they are deliberately manipulated and politicized by political actors and local elites, usually for their self-seeking advantages. In other words, it is not the 'subjective differences' of tribal, ethnic or religious groups which inevitably translate into primordial or identity conflicts but rather the 'subjective choice' of the hegemonic power players and local elites (Barth 1969; Olzak 1986; Nnoli 1995). The sentimentalization and politicization of primordial identity via the conscious actions and rhetoric of the observed intermediaries serve an expedient instrumentalist purpose in the sense that they help the latter to win cheap popularity and electoral victories, as well as to set and dominate the discursive agenda of politics within their various constituencies. Scholars like Lewis (1996) and Grugel (2002) blame this tendency on the neo-patrimonial nature of politics in most African states, which reflects the outward features of institutionalized administrative states, while operating along patron–client networks and trajectories rooted in historical patterns of authority and social solidarity. Neo-patrimonial politics blurs the modernist distinction between the secular and sacred, formal and informal, and, most significantly, between public and private resources. In fact, patrimonialism essentially blurs the contemporary statutory distinction between public office, the office-holder and public resources. Hence, state officials have little or no inhibition against using public offices for personal aggrandizement and to privilege cronies, kinsmen and ethnic loyalists usually placed in strategic positions to ensure regime survival. From the instrumentalist perspective, conflicts arise as local politicians and elites compete and struggle for state power and resources, often by recruiting militias and private armies from their ethno-national constituencies to challenge, unseat (by whatever possible means) and replace the 'prebendal state' (see Joseph 1987), but not necessarily to improve or transform it. Depending on how they are played out and the virulence of the key players, low-, medium- or high-intensity conflict could ensue, ultimately culminating in the phenomena of failed state, collapsed state and societal fragmentation.

Political ecology and conflict goods theories Focusing on the lopsided extractive structure and fragility of most post-colonial economies, some theorists have tended to emphasize competition for control of natural resources by various local political factions as a major factor that instigates and/or exacerbates armed conflicts and wars in Africa. The cases often cited by exponents to buttress their theory include the Jonah Savimbi-led rebel war in Angola, especially the post-cold-war phase of the campaign, the Revolutionary United Front (RUF) war in Sierra Leone, the National Patriotic Front of Liberia (NPFL) rebel war in Liberia, the Niger Delta conflict in Nigeria and the long-drawn-out internecine war in the DRC. It is common knowledge that most African economies are weak rentier economies built around the exploitation and export of one or a combination of strategic natural resources such as diamonds, gold, uranium, cobalt, copper, rock phosphate, timber and oil. Protagonists of the resource-based conflict school like Homer-Dixon (1994: 5–25; 1998), Karl (1997), Watts (1999), Collier and Hoefller (2000) and Ross (2003) essentially conceptualize African conflicts as predatory conflicts while the politics of who controls the strategic natural resources and the accruing revenues functions as either the conflict-instigating factor or principal catalyst. Homer-Dixon, in a neo-Malthusian structural ecologist explanation, for instance, emphasizes the virulence of inter-group and interstate competition for 'scarce environmental resources' and how it precipitates conflicts. Collier and Hoefller argue that 'greed and [economic] opportunities' rather than 'genuine grievances' account for the proliferation of predatory and militant groups in many conflict-affected countries of Africa and the Third World, and that the prevalence of lootable natural resources like diamonds, cobalt, etc., is likely to increase the duration and intensity of armed conflicts, as well as the chances of a relapse into war in the post-conflict dispensation. Ross expands the conflict goods theory by arguing that natural resource-dependent rentier states are more likely to be authoritarian than democratic because public expenditure is based not on taxation but on rents, and as such the government is not obligated to embrace the principles of representation and accountability, which are the hallmarks of democratic governance. Offering a post-structuralist account, Karl and Watts, on the other hand, highlight the role of global corporations and extraverted structures of capital accumulation in contributing to instigating and, to a greater extent, aggravating conflicts in Africa and the global South.

A critique of dominant explanatory theories

There are both merits and drawbacks in these explanatory paradigms. The instrumentalist approach, for instance, offers a thoughtful account of the dys-functionality of the political economies of many post-colonial states of Africa and the role of the local elites in the systematic deterioration of inter-group relations (albeit not only primordial groups but also social classes and gender) and escalation of violent conflicts. The primordialist approach and conflict goods – greed versus grievance – theory, on the other hand, tend to offer a largely essentialized pathological view of African states as inherently predis-posed to 'irrational' and predatory conflicts. It is this discursive paradigm which has in many years made Africa a flashpoint of 'tribal and communal wars' in the international media. While manifestations of predation and ethnic feud exist, it is important to stress that these are secondary factors encouraged by and, for the most part, epiphenomenal of neo-patrimonial decline and state failure. Principal proponents of the greed versus grievance theory such as Col lier and Hoefller have been particularly criticized for developing a neo-elitist, 'rebel-centric' theory that tends to ignore the often decisive role of the state's irresponsible behaviour (massive corruption and repression) in provoking rebel movements and insurgencies in the first place (see Kabia 2008). Hence, if African wars and armed conflicts have a greed dimension, as exponents have claimed, the greed (aggrandizement of power and public resources) of the elites prob-ably has a greater explanatory value that the so-called greed of the subalterns intrinsic to dominant theories.

The real problem with the theories attributing causality to primordialism/predation and similar Western-centric constructions is that given the embed-dedness of the so-called primordial features in Africa, for instance, coupled with the inability of most African states to conform to neoliberal notions of statehood using the conventional Westphalia benchmark, these theories entertain the tendency to castigate all African states as irredeemably conflict prone and conflict ridden. More significantly, analyses of this nature can hardly inform constructive or appropriate conflict intervention policy remedies. Little wonder some of the

Western neoliberal scholars and protagonists of pathological constructions of African conflicts, such as Linklater and Helman and Ratner in reference to the failed states in Africa, have made proposals for 'benign recolonisation'. Linklater (1996: 108) advocates a 'reformation of decolonisation' through 'new instruments of global stewardship' or 'some forms of international government' akin to the mandate system of the defunct League of Nations over 'failed states and failing states and weak states', 'not able to stand on their feet in the international system'. Helman and Ratner (1997: 12) argue that these forms of 'guardianship and trusteeship' are 'a common response to broken families, serious mental or physical illness or economic destitution', and thus should be invoked over the plight of failed states, preferably by the UN.

It suffices to say that African conflicts are part of the challenges of state formation and state-building and, given the peculiar and limited history of sovereign statehood in Africa, the transformation of African states from the original 'client state created by the colonialists for conquest' (cf. Ayoob 1995; Mamdani 1996) to a people-centred 'developmental state' (see Evans 1995) could not have been a smooth ride. Arguably, the history and transition could have been much smoother in many states. It is important to recognize in this context that while state-building has evolved over centuries in Europe, the Westphalia project of juridical statehood (as opposed to empirical statehood) imposed on Africa at independence is not yet six decades old and has evolved in a very different and changed international environment (Francis 2005: 8). Contemporary forces of globalization and imperial supervision and governance that define the international environment in which post-colonial states operate have in diverse ways contributed to the political and economic malaise of these less privileged states.

Another relevant point is that most of the contemporary wars and armed conflicts in Africa are a lot more complex than portrayed by some of the dominant theories, not least because of the multi-causal, multidimensional and interconnected nature of these conflicts. Mary Kaldor (2006: 1–2) describes African wars of the post-cold-war dispensation as the 'new wars' characterized by a blurring of the distinction between (conventional) 'wars', 'organised crime' and 'largescale violation of human rights', or, to use Robert Kaplan's (1994) hyperbole, 'criminal anarchy'. Early in the 1990s the UN described the 'new wars' as 'complex political emergencies' (CPEs). CPEs is a concept enunciated by the UN to describe the proliferation of major crises in transitional societies, the majority of which were intra-state conflicts, characterized by multi-causality, and requiring multidimensional international responses, including a combination of military intervention, peace support operations, humanitarian relief programmes, high-level political intervention and diplomacy (see Francis 2005: 14). Even though there might be some commonalities in terms of the nature and dynamics of African wars and armed conflicts, the notion of CPEs recognizes the need to understand the conflicts in both their context specificities and regional resonance as a necessary condition for enunciating appropriate intervention and resolution measures.

Conflict resolution practice in contemporary Africa

Attempts have been made in the preceding sections to conceptualize conflict resolution and the nature of conflicts in Africa. In this section, we shall focus more on the practice of the art in Africa – how real-life conflicts are managed, mitigated, settled and, most importantly (if applicable), resolved. It is significant to note that much of what is termed conflict resolution in practice is actually arbitrary contraptions and devices emanating from mainstream conceptions. Intrinsic to these conceptions, as already observed, is the notion that it is difficult, if not impossible, to completely resolve conflicts; that conflicts can at best be controlled, managed, mitigated and settled, but rarely resolved.

There are two dimensions to contemporary conflict resolution practice in Africa, the modern and traditional, albeit the two are not mutually exclusive. For analytical convenience, we can examine the two strands separately while pointing out complex intersections. To accomplish this in an effective way, it is important to appraise and analyse some of the contemporary conflicts in Africa and efforts to resolve them.

State-centred conflicts and dominant approaches to conflict management

It is observable that most of the major conflicts in contemporary Africa are state-centred, implying that these are conflicts that tend to challenge the sovereignty of the state (i.e. in both territorial and juridical terms) or the legal and moral authority of the government in power – i.e. crises of legitimacy. The state is a key protagonist in these conflicts and therefore cannot be trusted to play the role of a third-party umpire capable of bringing an effective resolution of the conflict. The vast majority of recent state-centred conflicts in Africa, especially since the end of the cold war, have been insurgencies and civil wars. Typical examples of the latter include the civil wars in Liberia, Sierra Leone, Côte d'Ivoire, DRC, Mali, Sudan, Somalia, Guinea Bissau, Angola, Rwanda, Burundi, Chad, the Casamance region of Senegal and northern Uganda, as well as the insurgencies by ethnic militias in the Niger Delta, Nigeria, and by Islamists in Algeria. Contestation of territorial and juridical sovereignty has often taken the form of separatist campaigns, a typical example being the protracted Eritrean war of independence from Ethiopia, which culminated in statehood for Eritrea in 1993. By and large, most of the state-centred armed conflicts in Africa are generally related to poor economic performance and underdevelopment, prebendal corruption, bad governance, political exclusion and marginalization (real, imagined or exaggerated) of salient groups and the arbitrariness and artificiality of colonial state structures and boundaries.

Conflict control through military reprisal A major feature of the initial attempts to tackle state-centred conflicts in Africa is violent conflict control – the use of military reprisal by the state to suppress protest and crack down on insurgents who are usually dismissed as disgruntled 'dissidents', 'rebels' or 'criminal elements'. This initial tendency by the state to resort to a military crackdown and to dismiss insurgents' motives as baseless has almost invariably aggravated the conflict by maintaining local and external support for the plight of helpless populations the 'persecuted insurgents' claim to represent. Consequently, the state's conflict control measure has often been shabbily prosecuted, with the result that it leaves a trail of avoidable civilian casualties, which further exacerbates the despair of sections of the local populations, and international opprobrium.

When Charles Taylor crossed the Ivorian border and invaded Liberia from the north-eastern Nimba County with fewer than two hundred rebel fighters in December 1989 with the purported mission to liberate Liberians from the despotic regime of Samuel Doe, President Doe's response was swift and ruthless (Global Security 2005):

> Liberian troops and provincial security forces were dispatched to Nimba County to counter the insurgency and indiscriminately killed Liberian civilians without regard to the distinction between combatants and non-combatants. ... President Doe launched an unrelenting wave of violence against the inhabitants of Nimba County. Media reports and international human rights organizations estimated that at least 200 persons, primarily members of the Mano and Gio ethnic groups, were killed by troops of the Government of Liberia during the counter-insurgency campaign.

Samuel Doe's murderous attacks on the Mano and Gio ethnic groups were premised on the grounds that they purportedly comprised the initial recruits of Taylor's rebel movement, the National Patriotic Front of Liberia (NPFL). The Mano and Gio (both groups comprise about 15 per cent of the Liberian population) were motivated to join the rebellion against the Doe regime because both suffered disproportionately during the 1985 putsch that brought Doe to power (Tellewoyan et al. 2000). Doe's ruthless response and the killing of many innocent ethnic Mano and Gio aggravated the grievances of many local people and inflamed hostile international reaction. Consequently, large numbers of jobless and hopeless Liberian youths defected to the rebel side.

The militaristic method of conflict control is widespread in African post-independence political history. A cursory discussion of a few cases will suffice.

1 Ex-President Mobutu repeatedly clamped down on protests of popular discontent against his regime and separatist uprisings in the mineral-rich Kasai and Katanga provinces during his thirty-two-year dictatorship in the DRC (1965–97).

2 The Senegalese government's crackdown on peaceful protesters (mostly women) in Ziguinchor in December 1982 saw the culmination of regionalist sentiments in the Casamance region and degeneration of affairs into a fully blown secessionist war that lasted for twenty-two years (1982–2004). The minority ethnic Diola protesters in the relatively geographically isolated Casamance region embarked on a peaceful demonstration against the government's agrarian reform that undermined traditional land rights and helped to encourage the heightened migration of wealthy ethnic Wolof (Senegal's largest ethnic group) agricultural investors from the arid northern part of the country to the fertile countrysides of the Casamance. During the 2004 peace talks that led to the end of the civil war, President Abdoulaye Wade acknowledged that the government's crackdown on the peaceful women's protest of December 1982, killing over two dozen people and arresting hundreds, was a 'mistake' that set the stage for the subsequent insurgency (Harsch 2005: 14).

3 President Paul Biya has repeatedly used military violence against growing discontent and protests from the minority anglophone region of Cameroon, especially since the widely flawed first multi-party elections of 1992 in which the opposition Social Democratic Front (SDF) of John Fru Ndi, significantly supported by the anglophone region, was prevented from dominating the polls through widespread irregularities masterminded by the state. Incidents and feelings of collective exclusion, popular protests (including secessionist agitations) and state repression have all intensified in anglophone Cameroon in the aftermath of the colossal 1992 electoral fraud. Subsequently democratic elections in Cameroon have all been marred by violence and irregularities, further compounding the political tension in the country, and the pressure for greater autonomy from the anglophone community, with the more radical sections calling for complete secession as the Republic of Ambazonia.

4 A civil war was triggered in Algeria in 1992 after a military coup that ostensibly had Western support annulled the parliamentary elections won by the radical Islamist party, which was also poised to win the presidential polls. The military government and the civilian regime of Abdelaziz Bouteflika that it installed in the widely flawed elections of 1999 have used military violence to crack down on the Islamist party, which, in turn, quickly resorted to guerrilla warfare. More than 150,000 people have been killed in Algeria in the high-intensity civil war that followed the annulled elections (1994–99), down to the current phase of low-intensity guerrilla attacks against high-level state officials, the Algerian military and Western targets/tourists (since 2000).

5 The Nigerian military government resorted to military crackdown against peaceful pro-democracy campaigners who protested against the annulment of the June 1993 presidential elections supposedly won by a south-western Yoruba business tycoon, Moshood Abiola. The elections were apparently annulled to prevent the emergence of a southern president in a country

where both the state and military apparatuses were structurally controlled by a powerful northern ethno-military oligarchy. Similarly, the inception of peaceful anti-oil protests in Nigeria's Niger Delta region in the early 1990s provoked the ruthless crackdown of the military government, the climax of the process being the arrest, trial and execution of the renowned Niger Delta environmentalist Ken Saro-Wiwa and eight of his co-activists from the Movement for the Survival of the Ogoni People (MOSOP) in 1995. Without doubt, it was this violent crackdown which set the stage for the defiance of the oil-bearing communities, including the present proliferation of heavily armed ethnic militia movements that menace oil operations and security in the volatile oil region.

6 The anti-Structural Adjustment Programme (SAP) riots that swept across different African countries like a hurricane in the late 1980s and 1990s, in which a coalition of civil groups (students, trade unions, women's groups, professional associations, etc.) led popular anti-establishment demonstrations and mass rallies to protest against the accelerated decline in living standards and rising inflation following the adoption of the stringent World Bank/IMF SAPs by their governments, invariably provoked states' military reprisals.

The practice of trying to control conflict through military reprisal and suppression has almost always accentuated the conflict. African opposition groups have increasingly proved defiant to the state's intimidation and authoritarian control, not least when their protests are informed by legitimate grievances and brazen acts of injustice on the part of key state officials. The usual trend of resorting to military reprisal to repress opposition by the state amid circumstances of brazen injustice against (sections of) the populace is akin to trying to use gasoline to put out fire.

Elite co-optation

Elite co-optation is one method of conflict regulation and settlement that many neo-patrimonial states in Africa use effectively to weaken opposition and rebuild a form of consensus aimed at more or less preserving and perpetuating the status quo. By elite co-optation African political regimes aim to placate, disorganize, silence or weaken salient pressure groups by luring vocal and influential members of the groups into the ruling circle with offers of strategic appointments, government contracts and other tangible benefits designed to incorporate them into the state patronage network. In turn, the co-opted activists are expected to mellow their antagonism against the state and possibly also appeal to their members to follow suit. Elite co-optation is partly an externality of the intolerance of opposition (for which many African states are known) and it is not always born out of a spirit of conciliation and consensus. Sometimes, the driving motives are based on expediency, treachery and regime survival.

In the dark years of military dictatorship in Nigeria (1984–99), co-optation of dissidents and leaders of vociferous pressure groups (labour union, bar association, medical association, the academy and other professional bodies) became an institutionalized political practice. The practice was colloquially branded 'politics of settlement' (implying the dishing out of conciliatory patronage) under Babangida's regime when the phenomenon was driven to a Machiavellian climax (see Omeje 2006: 50). Co-optation of vocal elites was used to achieve three important purposes by the military governments in Nigeria. The first was to silence and weaken credible opposition and defuse any correlated grievances. The second was to win much-needed legitimacy, as most of the co-opted social critics and activists were greatly respected individuals held in esteem both at home and abroad. One major example was the appointment of the renowned social critic and Nobel Prize laureate Professor Wole Soyinka as director of the Federal Road Safety Corps by the Babangida administration. The third aim was to seek to taint the moral integrity of targeted reputable critics by deliberately setting them up or simply exposing them to temptations of prebendal corruption. Some of the highly reputed opinion leaders and critics hired by the Babangida regime were later blackmailed and sacked with ignominy on charges of corruption (both real and fabricated). Adebayo Williams (1998: 287) attributes the marked scoundrelism demonstrated by many intellectuals and social critics appointed into top government positions under the military and the disingenuous tendency of the political regime to set up, blackmail and disparage these appointees to 'postcolonial anomie'.

Aili Mari Tripp (2004) demonstrates how the semi-authoritarian government of President Musuveni in Uganda has tried to use co-optation to appease and weaken the women's movement, by measures including the appointment of visible and vocal women to top government positions, the reservation of seats for women in parliament and local governments for women, and the creation of women's councils as 'administrative structures' (but critics describe them as pro-government 'political structures') for tackling women's affairs. In a related study, Gisela Geisler (2004), in her analysis of the key strategies employed by women's movements to gain a foothold in politics in various southern African countries (South Africa, Zambia, Zimbabwe, Botswana, Namibia), has underscored the uneasy relationship between the women's movements and the state, and between women activists and women politicians as they have negotiated co-optation, integration and exclusion. Co-optation, the author argues, has been particularly instrumental in the opening of the political space to women, and the appointment of many vocal women activists in top government positions, either by democratic election (mostly by conceding some parliamentary seats in party primaries to women) or political appointments.

Wagona Makoba (1999: 67) observes that by 1990, when the majority of the African countries were in profound political and economic decline, and popular agitation for political change was giving rise to a new wave of democratization, a few incumbent governments (e.g. in Kenya and Cameroon) had managed to prevent the democratization process by relying on the co-optation, repression and manipulation of opposition movements to their advantage. In Kenya, for instance, the authoritarian government of Arap Moi held on to a single-party constitution between 1979 and 1990, while the government continued to use a combination of co-optation, repression and manipulation to sequestrate the opposition well into the multi-party era of the 1990s, which helped Moi to further hold on to power. It was not until the 2002 elections, when Moi was barred from standing, having exhausted his two-term maximum limit under the new multi-party constitution, that Nwai Kibaki was elected president under the banner of the opposition National Rainbow Coalition. In the case of Cameroon, President Paul Biya's ruling Cameroon People's Democratic Movement was the only legally registered political party in the country until December 1990, but has, since the introduction of seven-yearly multi-party elections in 1992, retained power by co-optation, repression and manipulation of the opposition, as well as ballot-box rigging. The result is that despite mass discontent and a low popularity rating, President Biya has remained in power since 1982 and may probably continue for a long time to come.

In Zimbabwe, the merger of the ruling Zimbabwe African National Union (ZANU) of President Robert Mugabe and the opposition Zimbabwe African People's Union (ZAPU), led by the late Joshua Nkomo, to form ZANU-PF (PF stands for Patriotic Front) following the Unity Accord of 1987 that marked the end of the low-intensity civil war between the two groups following independence was a form of grand consensus. A few scholars have, however, interpreted the phenomenon as being tantamount to 'grand co-optation', which soothed President Mugabe's desire to silence opposition, maintain elite cohesion and exercise unitary control under a one-party state (cf. Stedman 1991; Moyo 2004). The one-party state of ZANU-PF was, however, short-lived, given the emergence in 1999 of the new opposition Movement for Democratic Change (MDC), led by former trade unionist Morgan Tsvangirai. The relationship between ZANU PF and the MDC has witnessed very limited co-optation (into the ruling party) and cooperation, but in contrast has exhibited extensive acrimony, recrimination and violence.

Generally, co-optation of some agents of the opposition – often tempered with persecution and repression in practice – is a form of 'negative peace' settlement that helps African ruling and governing elites to minimize threats to their hold on power, threats of revolutionary upheaval and fragmentation of the political elites. But being largely an instrument for elite politics, it cannot address the legitimate needs and grievances of the masses. This is why a large number of seemingly intractable low-intensity conflicts and incidents of urban violence in Africa today are led by aggrieved militant youths, lawless guerrillas and ragtag militias, who, to a large extent, articulate the discontent and hopelessness of the bulk of the deprived and powerless subalterns.

Third-party intervention in large-scale armed conflicts and wars

Third-party intervention occurs when conflict goes beyond the resolution capacity of the direct disputants or warring parties to involve an external intervener (e.g. a mediator, facilitator, observer, arbitrator, peace enforcement team, etc.). Third parties bring additional resources, skills and perspectives to the conflict process and too often their presence rubs off on and changes the relational structure, physical dynamics and outcomes of conflicts. In both theory and practice, the entire facilitative projects of conflict mediation, prevention, management, resolution, settlement and transformation are essentially a third-party phenomenon. The myriad of armed conflicts and wars of varying intensities in African post-colonial history has provided a theatre for diverse shades of third-party interveners and stakeholders – regional state actors, ex-colonial powers and other international state actors, regional and international (intergovernmental) organizations, local and international civil societies, private military/transnational corporations, multilateral institutions, and eminent non-governmental individuals and agencies. The intervention methods are varied and mixed, ranging from negotiation and arbitration to mediation, peacekeeping, humanitarian support, peace-building and preventive diplomacy (Tracks I, II and III).

For clarity, preventive diplomacy can be broadly defined as a set of political and diplomatic actions aimed at preventing violent disputes from arising between parties, aiming to mitigate or prevent the likelihood of existing conflict escalating into open violence, and to limit the spread of violent conflicts when they occur (Boutros-Ghali 1995). Preventive diplomacy has historically evolved along three tracks involving different sets of actors. Track I, which is the oldest model, applies to state-based or interstate diplomacy and initiatives to mitigate conflict. Track II is the diplomacy applied by intergovernmental organizations such as the Economic Community of West African States (ECOWAS), Inter-Governmental Authority on Development (IGAD) in the Horn of Africa and the Southern African Development Community (SADC), the African Union (AU) and UN agencies. Track III is the diplomacy of local and international civil societies (e.g. Greenpeace, Environmental Rights Action, Oxfam, International Alert, Saint Egidio, etc.), a growing number of which are increasingly active in the conflict resolution industry in Africa. A constructive application of the three strands, which tends to be the preferred practice in most contemporary armed conflict, is known as multi-track diplomacy. The practical challenge of multi-track diplomacy is usually how to coordinate and reconcile the activities of the different third-party interveners – a challenge that often becomes more problematic if intervention involves some powerful external actors representing hidden national, institutional or corporate interests.

The outcomes of third-party intervention in African conflicts have been mixed. Some of the factors that could positively or negatively affect the outcome include the nature of the conflict and how well the intervener understands it, the motive and credibility of the intervener and how acceptable he is (and continues to be) to the conflicting parties, the timing and suitability of intervention methods, the availability/efficient use of (sufficient) funds and other logistical resources, as well as the role of other third-party agents and how an intervener relates to them.

A plethora of literature exists on various aspects and ramifications of third-party intervention in African conflicts (cf. Helman and Ratner 1997; Jackson, H. R. 2000; Moundi et al. 2007). In this section, it suffices to focus more on the activities of African regional organizations and the UN, with special reference to peacekeeping, not least because of the likely effects of the changing dynamics of peacekeeping since the early 1990s (notably the involvement of regional organizations and the evolution of multidimensional peacekeeping) on conflict resolution practice in Africa.

It is significant that, since the early 1990s, African Regional Economic Communities (RECs) have taken the *de facto* lead in expanding the regionalist project into the peace and security domain. This observation is evident whether one is looking at the politics of regionalism in ECOWAS, IGAD or SADC. The larger continental body, the AU, is comparatively a late starter in this respect. Various factors account for the expanded regionalist projects, but they are generally related to such phenomena as the specific political, historical, socio-demographic and ecological contexts of the different regions.

ECOWAS In the West African region, expansion of the regionalist project into the peace, security and conflict management domain was mainly necessitated by the succession of disruptive civil wars and armed insurgencies in such countries as Liberia, Sierra Leone, Mali, Guinea Bissau and Côte d'Ivoire. Given the complex ethno-demographic and geopolitical linkages of West African states, most of the recent armed conflicts have had far-reaching regional resonance in terms of refugee flow, use of mercenaries, proliferation of small arms and light weapons, exploitation of 'war economies', etc. Hence, under the subregional hegemony of Nigeria, the ECOWAS Ceasefire Monitoring Group (ECOMOG) was formed and deployed to some of the conflict zones as a regional peacekeeping and intervention force. ECOMOG's conflict resolution mechanism has mostly involved multidimensional peacekeeping (i.e. traditional peacekeeping through monitoring implementation of peace agreements reached between conflicting parties, peace enforcement or 'robust peacekeeping'; Disarmament, Demobilization and Reintegration of rebels and other non-professional combatants, the protection of civilian populations, safe havens and humanitarian aid delivery, etc.), depending on the mandate given at any given circumstance by the Abujabased regional body. ECOMOG is significant in the sense that it was the first major peacekeeping deployment by a regional economic community globally.

In addition to the deployment of ECOMOG, ECOWAS has also been instrumental in most of the conflict mediation diplomacy and peace settlement agreements in almost all the recent civil wars in West Africa. Although it originally started with an under-resourced ad hoc firefighting approach in August 1990, ECOWAS peacekeeping has in recent years evolved into a more coherent security architecture with the adoption of the 1999 Protocol relating to the Mechanism for Conflict Prevention, Management, Resolution, Peacekeeping and Security by ECOWAS member states. The 1999 Protocol, which is the main constitutional framework for the new ECOWAS peace and security architecture, provides for the establishment of various organs and institutional mechanisms for collective conflict prevention, management, resolution and peace-building in West Africa. ECOWAS has undergone and continues to undergo significant transformation with regard to collective security issues since the 2000s (cf. Malu 2003; Francis et al. 2004).

IGAD The origin, development and progressive expansion of IGAD have all been linked to the need for a concerted regional response to the environmental (famine, drought, desertification), political and developmental challenges of member states within a regional framework. The protracted civil conflicts in Sudan, Somalia, Uganda and the Ethiopia–Eritrea war have, since the mid-1990s, increasingly forced IGAD to develop and implement regional peace and security programmes, including structures for Conflict Early Warning and Response Mechanism, known as CEWARN. In fact, since the early 1990s IGAD has developed a number of political structures to deal with conflict prevention, management and resolution in the highly beleaguered Horn. The regional body faces enormous challenges given the worrying circumstance that 'in this region there are thirty potentially threatening inter-communal conflicts; a collapsed state due to internal conflicts; a recent interstate war between two member states; a great number of endemic violent cross-border pastoral conflicts; and, the continued threat of interstate wars arising from cross-border inter- and intra-communal conflicts' (IGAD 2007). Two major conflicts, those of Sudan and Somalia, have more than any other greatly tested and challenged the initiatives and capacity of IGAD and the ability of its members to act independently. The organization has been actively involved in attempts to resolve the two conflicts, albeit with a range of daunting challenges. In the case of Sudan, IGAD has organized several mediative meetings, which resulted in the consensus on the Declaration of Principles in which the conflicting parties, namely the central government in Khartoum and the Sudanese People's Liberation Movement (SPLM/A – 'A' stands for 'Army', referring to the guerrilla/military wing), agreed on the principle and conditions for self-determination for the southern Sudan (Ghebremeskel 2002).

The implementation of this is ongoing even though there are fears as to whether the central government in Khartoum will acquiesce to a referendum on full independence and also be favourably disposed to the outcome of any such referendum, as proposed in the fragile Comprehensive Peace Agreement of January 2005. Much of Sudanese oil and other vital mineral resources are found in the SPLM/A-controlled territory of southern Sudan.

Similarly, IGAD has convened and taken part in a multiplicity of peace talks to resolve the conflicts in the collapsed state of Somalia. Perhaps IGAD's boldest conflict resolution initiative with regard to Somalia was the proposal in January 2005 to deploy 10,000 peacekeepers to be known as the IGAD Peace Support Mission to Somalia (IGASOM). This proposal received the express endorsement of the African Union and the UN Security Council. But IGASOM was never realized for a multiplicity of logistical reasons, notably lack of funds, the absence of a decisive regional hegemon in the Horn, and the divided concentration of some of IGAD's members on overlapping regional communities such as the East African Community and COMESA. Consequently, many IGAD members support insurgencies and different warring factions in other member states, and as such their vested interests in specific conflicts cloud and undermine their political will for radical collective action, such as peacekeeping intervention.

SADC Originally founded in 1980 as the Southern African Development Co-ordinating Conference (SADCC) to help address some of the security and development challenges in southern Africa, the regional body was transformed into SADC in 1992 with a common market objective. Following the intervention of the East African states of Uganda, Rwanda and Burundi in the civil war in the DRC, three SADC members, Zimbabwe, Namibia and Angola, deployed the SADC Allied Armed Forces (SADC-AAF) to the war-torn country in August 1998. Given the controversial and horrific nature of the deployment, many critics have described SADC-AAF as 'a coalition of willing states in pursuit of strategic security, military and economic interests' (see Francis 2006b: 17). It is significant to note that the leading economic power in the SADC region, South Africa (often described as a reluctant hegemon), was not part of the peacekeeping deployment to the DRC. South Africa chose to advocate for 'a negotiated settlement in the DRC', but barely a month after the SADC-AAF deployment South Africa and Botswana deployed about six hundred and two hundred troops respectively to Lesotho to quell a mutiny by a faction of the country's defence forces and prevent chaos, anarchy and a creeping military coup in the small southern African quasi-city state (Santho 2000). The mutiny was part of the disorder precipitated by the controversial multi-party parliamentary elections of 1998, widely believed to have been rigged by the ruling party to retain power. Both the joint South Africa–Botswana intervention in Lesotho and the Zimbabwe–Namibia–Angola military deployment to DRC were authorized by SADC, albeit the DRC intervention received only a retroactive mandate from the regional body. Both interventions were believed to have been at the invitation of the embattled governments of the two countries. The South African-led intervention was able to quickly restore order and political stability in Lesotho, but the war in the DRC, being a more convoluted affair, provoked a range of other external peacekeeping interventions, not least from the French and the UN.

AU For its part, since the late 1990s the Organization of African Unity (OAU), transformed into the African Union (AU) in 2002, has developed and proposed a number of institutional mechanisms and structures aimed at expanding its development and security profile. These include the Peace and Security Council, the New Partnership for African Development (NEPAD), the African Peer Review Mechanism, and the Peace and Security Directorate. The repealing of the non-intervention clause in the defunct OAU charter and subsequent empowering of the AU to intervene in a member state's internal affairs in cases of genocide, war crimes or crimes against humanity is a significant development in the recent transformation of the OAU to the AU, as well as in the evolution of regional conflict resolution and peacekeeping in Africa.

Under the defunct OAU, the efforts of the continental body in conflict resolution were mostly based on mediation, arbitration and conciliation, relying on both the institutional mechanisms of the organization and the good offices of influential member states and statesmen. The creation of the AU coincided with the already evolving transformation of the peace and security framework of the regional body to, among other things, take on board multidimensional peacekeeping. The first peacekeeping mission of the AU – the African Union Mission in Burundi (AMIB) – was deployed in April 2003 to sufficiently stabilize the conflict situation for a UN intervention. At full capacity, AMIB consisted of some 3,335 troops from South Africa, Ethiopia and Mozambique, with additional military observers from Burkina Faso, Gabon, Mali, Togo and Tunisia (Powell 2005). AMIB was later to be officially absorbed into the UN Mission in Burundi (ONUB – its acronym in French) in June 2004.

The African Union has also made recent peacekeeping deployments in the Sudanese war-torn region of Darfur – African Union Mission in Sudan (AMIS), deployed since July 2004 – as well as in Somalia – the African Union Mission in Somalia (AMISOM), authorized in January 2007 to replace and supersede the IGAD peacekeeping mission that did not effectively take off as envisaged. The AU peacekeeping missions in Sudan and Somalia have been fraught with far-reaching challenges, not least because of the complexity of the conflicts involved, competing local, regional and international interests, and the extreme financial and logistical constraints facing the Union.

The expansion of the different regionalist projects into the peace, security and conflict management domain has created a range of challenges and opportunities that form the basis of constructive international and regional cooperation and partnerships. The emerging partnerships are expected ultimately to help in further developing and strengthening the institutional, technical and operational capacities of regional organizations in Africa for conflict intervention and peace support operations.

UN Peacekeeping was first developed by the UN in 1948 following the creation of the United Nations Truce Supervision Organization (UNTSO), deployed to monitor the ceasefire between the Israelis and the Arab states in the war that followed the creation of the new state of Israel. From its UN origin, 'traditional or first generation peacekeeping', as it was later retrospectively reconceptualized by scholars, entailed deployment of a multinational intervention force based on the consent of conflicting parties to assist in monitoring of ceasefires and implementation of comprehensive peace settlements, and to ensure safe delivery of humanitarian aid. The UN charter, which gives the Security Council responsibility for initiating collective action for the maintenance of international peace and security, provides the necessary statutory framework for the creation of peacekeeping operations by the world body. The first UN peacekeeping operation in Africa was the United Nations Operation in the Congo (ONUC, July 1960–June 1964), established, *inter alia*, to avert a civil war in the then Congo-Brazzaville and ensure the withdrawal of all non-UN foreign military personnel whose presence complicated the civil conflicts in the newly independent state. An earlier UN mission was deployed around the Suez Canal to monitor the ceasefire of 1957 in the war between Egypt (backed by the Arab countries) and the UK/France/Israel over access to the Canal.

The end of the cold war and the subsequent proliferation of complex multidimensional wars and political turmoil in Africa between the late 1980s and 1999 challenged the UN to make a radical transition from traditional peacekeeping to multidimensional or 'second generation' peacekeeping to meet the changing imperatives of conflict intervention. The more ambitious and diversified operation of multidimensional peacekeeping involves a large number of military and civilian personnel deployed for a variety of functions including:

> the supervision of cease-fires, the *regroupement* and demobilization of forces, their reintegration into civilian life and the destruction of their weapons; the design and implementation of de-mining programmes; the return of refugees and displaced persons; the provision of humanitarian assistance; the supervision of existing administrative structures; the establishment of new police forces; the verification of respect for human rights; the design and supervision of constitutional, judicial and electoral reforms; the observation, supervision and even organization and conduct of elections; and the coordination of support for economic rehabilitation and reconstruction. (Boutros-Ghali 1995: 6)

Between 1989 and 1999, a total of thirty wars of varying intensities (mostly civil wars) occurred in Africa, to which sixteen UN peacekeeping missions were sent (USIP 2004: 4). A considerable number of the 1990s missions were either from the outset or at a later stage multidimensional peacekeeping operations (e.g. the missions to Namibia, Mozambique, Angola, Burundi, Sierra Leone, Liberia, etc.). One of the most challenging UN peacekeeping operations in Africa is that in the DRC, where the conflict at its peak in 1998 involved the armed forces of nine different intervening regional and international state players, and about twenty-five rebel and civil militias groups (Ngoie and Omeje 2008: 140). Given the intensity of the conflict and interest in the conflict goods, as well as the diversity of warring and intervening parties, many analysts have described the conflict as 'Africa's first world war' (cf. Vlassenroot 2003: 339; UN 2001; Hoyweghen 2005).

The UN has been widely criticized for its peacekeeping and conflict intervention failures in the civil war in Somalia in 1993 and the genocide in Rwanda in 1994 – two disasters that later contributed to the setting up of the Expert Panel that reviewed UN Peace Operations and submitted its report (the famous Brahimi Report) to the Secretary-General in 2000 with major recommendations on how to fundamentally transform the institutional and functional capacity of the UN for peacekeeping. UN peacekeeping in Africa is further affected in an adverse way by the reluctance on the part of the advanced Western countries to commit their national troops in Africa under a UN mandate. This development emerged after the disastrous peacekeeping in Somalia in 1993, in which sixteen American soldiers were killed by local militias, leading to a backlash in public opinion in the USA and Washington's withdrawal of American troops. The USA's abrupt withdrawal of its forces unravelled the UN mission in the war-torn country and has since remained an unsavoury emblem of the failure of UN peacekeeping and the strategic indifference of the West to participating in UN peacekeeping in Africa. Since Somalia, some of the leading Western powers have resorted to a rather ambiguous mechanism of conflict intervention as 'lead nations' independent of the UN mission. This trend has occurred in the form of the UK bilateral peacekeeping intervention in Sierra Leone, the French intervention in Côte d'Ivoire, the US involvement in Liberia and the Belgian/ French intervention in the DRC. It is remarkable that the noticeable failures in Somalia and Rwanda tended to overshadow the achievement of the world body in countries like Namibia and Mozambique, where UN multidimensional peacekeeping proved effective in restoring and building peace in the two war-ravaged countries in the 1990s.

Presently, there are six UN peacekeeping missions in Africa: the United Nations Mission in Sudan (UNMIS), United Nations Operation in Côte d'Ivoire (UNOCI), United Nations Mission in Liberia (UNMIL), United Nations Mission in the Democratic Republic of Congo (MONUC), United Nations Mission in

Ethiopia and Eritrea (UNMEE) and the United Nations Mission for the Refer-endum in Western Sahara (MINURSO) – the oldest of all the UN missions on the continent.

It is significant to note that the UN has in various missions been involved in cooperative peacekeeping (military observer missions included) with African regional organizations, notably ECOWAS (in Liberia, Sierra Leone and Côte d'Ivoire) and the AU (in Burundi and Sudan) (see Francis et al. 2004). Cooperative peacekeeping between the UN and African regional organizations raises chal-lenges of coordination and subsidiarity, command and control of forces, division of labour, and joint operations, as well as issues of harmonization in the ultimate absorption of regional forces into UN missions – colloquially known in military parlance as 'rehatting' of regional troops to UN troops.

Traditional African approach to conflict resolution

Dating from pre-colonial antiquity, various African societies have had their own traditional and customary approaches and methods of conflict prevention, management and resolution. The traditional approach and correlated methods were (and still are) deeply embedded in the people's cosmology and culture, which in turn had a profound religious content – the philosophy about God, life, community and being. Prior to Western contact, African traditional religions and Islam largely shaped the culture, world-view and civilization of various parts of the continent, albeit pockets of orthodox Christian tradition that date back to the first century AD existed in Egypt and, to a larger extent, Ethiopia. Similarly, the early conquest and settlement of Dutch merchants in the coastal region of South Africa prior to late-nineteenth-century colonialism led to the establishment of the Dutch Reform Christian church in this part of Africa.

The incorporation of Africa into the global system through Western colo-nialism has had sweeping effects on the nature of conflicts in Africa, as well as the traditional approach and methods of conflict resolution. The result is that the traditional African approach has been significantly battered, while some of the related methods have been displaced or significantly transformed by the countervailing imperatives of Western civilization and its concomitants of multifaceted liberalism and cultural secularization (see Almond and Powell 1966). Given the radical nature of Western cultural influence on African states and societies, many contemporary critics contest the relevance and place of traditional African approaches in the face of the complexity of modern social structures and the conflicts they generate in Africa. There are others who argue that traditional approaches and methods of dispute resolution should be con-fined to local communities while the modern Western alternatives should be applied to the cities, formal-sector institutions and state systems. Such a categori-cal distinction seems both conceptually and empirically problematic because of the immense diversity and overlapping dynamics of the African heritage.

Post-colonial Africa subsumes and reflects a diversity of cultural and religious world-views, traditions and practices, including a vast range of traditional patterns that survived the onslaught of colonialism and Westernization. The African cultures that underpin the traditional approach and methods of conflict resolution are vastly heterogeneous and dynamic. There are, however, still a wide range of cross-cutting and overlapping tendencies and practices across a large number of communities and regions.

The most important philosophy underlying traditional African approaches to dispute resolution seems to be captured by the Swahili (originally Bantu) concept of *Ubuntu*. *Ubuntu* is a humanistic philosophy (which has no English synonym) and connotes 'collective personhood', and is best captured by the Zulu maxims: 'a person is a person through other persons'; 'my humanity is inextricably tied to your humanity' (Masina 2000: 170). It is an overarching, multidimensional philosophy that invokes the idiom and images of group cooperation, generosity, tolerance, respect, sharing, solidarity, forgiveness and conciliation (ibid.; Mbigi and Maree 1995).

Ubuntu subsumes the African interpretation of both 'negative' and 'positive' peace, and as an indigenous conflict prevention and peace-building concept it embraces the notion of acknowledgement of guilt, showing of remorse and repentance by perpetrators of injustice, asking for and receiving forgiveness, and paying compensation or reparation as a prelude for reconciliation and peaceful coexistence (Francis 2007: 26). Beyond the concept and practice of conflict resolution, *Ubuntu* conveys the African philosophy of 'humanness', and it is a notion that has cultural resonance in diverse African societies, even though the concept is most widespread in southern, central and eastern Africa. To a large extent, the *Ubuntu* philosophy runs counter to the notion of the irresolvability of conflict intrinsic to some mainstream Western-centric theories, notably realism and behaviouralism.

It is significant that the transitional justice system implemented in post-apartheid South Africa – the restorative justice-oriented 'Truth and Reconciliation Commission', subsequently adopted in varying degrees by different post-war and deeply divided African societies (e.g. Sierra Leone, Liberia, Nigeria, Burundi), was philosophically informed by the *Ubuntu* tradition. Similarly, the *Gacaca* transitional justice system enunciated in post-genocide Rwanda, which combines both punitive and restorative justice and African customary and Western civil laws, is in concept an expression of *Ubuntu*.

It is within the philosophical context of *Ubuntu* and comparable practices in other parts of Africa that traditional African methods of conflict resolution are essentially situated. With regard to methods, it is pertinent to mention that negotiation, mediation, adjudication and reconciliation have, since pre-colonial history, been developed to different levels and practised in various African communities (see Zartman 2000). In many communities, especially but not exclusively the centralized and relatively hierarchical political systems, the practices usually involve the intervention of reputable elders, either on their own initiative or by the invitation of a concerned third party or the disputant(s). This method of dispute settlement is highly context specific and disputants are expected to honour the outcomes and decisions, which could be more or less binding, depending on the power relations at play and the customs of the community. There are also semi-formal and more formal litigations in which one party could sue another in a royal or customary court, as the case may be. In this case, adjudication is handled by a presiding traditional ruler with or without the support of legal counsellors. It is remarkable that under most African traditions elders are respected as the communities' repository of functional wisdom and experience and therefore assigned a prime place in community leadership and dispute settlement. This traditional philosophy is the logic behind the creation of the AU Panel of the Wise, comprising a team of five to seven highly distinguished African personalities constituted to support the conflict intervention efforts of the regional body through preventive diplomacy and peacemaking.

In many local communities of sub-Saharan Africa, especially among the relatively less centralized political systems (e.g. the Masai of Kenya, the Ibo of Nigeria, the Kpelle of Liberia, the Fanti of Ghana, the Oromo of Ethiopia, etc.), there exists the tradition of 'palaver hut' settlements of dispute. This is a traditional republican method of active dialogic settlement involving negotiation – sometimes tempered with mediation and arbitration – in which all parties in a conflict take part in deliberation until consensus is reached (Brock-Utne 2001). The dispute settlement is not necessarily in a 'hut' as the name suggests, but could, as the case may be, take place in a community hall, village square or under the shade of a sprawling tree. In communities like the Kpelle of Liberia, the palaver hut method of mediated settlement in ad hoc local meetings is operated side by side with informal adjudication and/or arbitration in which some institutionalized courts make and enforce arbitral verdicts (Malan 1997: 26). Among the Ndendeuli of Tanzania, the two methods of mediation and arbitration are combined into one: mediators play an active role by suggesting an agreement and even pressurizing the parties to accept it (ibid.: 26).

A more exclusivist form of 'palaver hut' method of dispute settlement is the *guurti* (literally implying 'traditional elders') governance structure in Somaliland, in which supreme authority in decision-making, peacemaking, adjudication and reconciliation of disputants rests with a council of community elders that as a matter of rule excludes women, youths and social minorities within the clan. The *guurti* system has been incorporated into the political governance structure of the de facto sovereign state of Somaliland. Through a series of traditionally styled *guurti* conferences, and with insignificant help from the outside world, the war-affected former British protectorate of Somaliland succeeded in resolving tribal conflicts, disbanding tribal militias and establishing a primordial but working system of government – a feat that could not be achieved in war-torn Somali in the south (Khalil 2000: 321).

Finally, even though many disputes might end in amicable settlement, confession of guilt and forgiveness, there are instances in which both minor and heavy sanctions are applied in accordance with the norms of the community concerned. Sanctions may range from restoration of a coveted or stolen item (in the case of theft) to a fine, ostracism, a vendetta, banishment, death, invocation of the wrath of the gods on the guilty and sundry forms of dishonour. In some communities, satire is used to shame and ridicule a person guilty of antisocial and conflict-causing conduct, especially in contexts where the cause of the dispute is self-evident and the tradition of poking fun at offenders is acceptable (ibid.: 26). Traditional African approaches and methods of conflict resolution have often been criticized for the arbitrary nature and disproportionality of their sanctions relative to the offence. But in general, the traditional approach and methods underscore the significant role of culture in conflict management and resolution.

Conclusion

It is evident from this chapter that conflicts in Africa are a lot more complex than many conventional discourses portray. The instigating and aggravating factors of most contemporary armed conflicts and wars in Africa are multidimensional, in the same way that the actors, interests and stakeholders are diverse and dynamic. As the study reveals, the practice of conflict resolution in Africa, especially with regard to incidents of large-scale armed conflicts and wars, is, to a large extent, dominated by the mainstream realist and behaviouralist perspectives of conflict analysis, which are built on the assumption that conflicts can at best be controlled, managed, mitigated and settled, but hardly resolved. These dominant perspectives, however, run counter to critical theory and African traditional approaches to conflict resolution, which are partly inspired by the philosophy that conflicts can be constructively and permanently resolved. Viewed from the perspective of dominant paradigms, the practice and strategies of conflict management in Africa are profoundly nuanced, reflecting not only the complex nature of the conflicts, interests and actors, but also the complexity of post-colonial systems and politics on a world stage dominated by the powerful industrialized Western countries.

6 | Context of security in Africa

NANA K. POKU

The Millennium Development Goals (MDGs), which were set almost eight years ago, include halving poverty and hunger, arresting diseases and environmental degradation, helping newborn babies survive infancy, and educating them in childhood. At the present rate, Africa south of the Sahara will not meet any of these noble goals by the expected date of 2015. The reasons are many and familiar: despite decades of structural adjustment pressures, the promised advantages of economic restructuring have not been borne out on the continent; foreign investments have failed to flow in, the debt burdens have continued and commodity prices go on fluctuating amid declining industries. The domestic economy, at macro and sector levels, remains fraught with a wide range of problems which have existed since colonialism but have been compounded with the passage of time. As regards links with the global economy, dependence on external resources, even for budgetary support, continues to increase, but the actual flows have fallen short of requirements.

When weak political systems are added to this catalogue of socio-economic ailments, the outcome is insecurity of ordinary people in circumstances where states – and the international system of states – are either unable to provide protection or are themselves the principal sources of violence. This chapter offers a frankly eclectic analysis of the context of security and insecurity in Africa. The subject is a moving target, developing – or underdeveloping – like everything else on the continent, so that the concept differs not only from the pre-colonial to the colonial to the post-colonial periods but also from immediate post-independence to the present period. A central argument is that though differences in internal construction have had a substantial impact on how states on the continent define threats and vulnerabilities, and therefore on the whole construction of the security problematic, the *context of security* is bound in complex ways to the continental struggle to consolidate states. The chapter stresses the importance of the unforeseen actions of the colonial regimes and the poor policies of post-colonial leaders. It is, however, with a broader conception of the notion of the state and security that I begin my analysis.

A historical sociology of the state, security and colonialism

It is perhaps necessary at this stage to offer a working framework of the state and security. Elsewhere, Raymond Aron ascribes a 'collective personality' to the state, which, like the individual personality, 'is born and dies in time ... asserts itself only by consciousness, being capable of [rational] thought and action' (Aron 2001: 750). Thomas Hobbes, however, offers the most robust definition. In *Leviathan*, he defines the state as an 'Artificial Man' characterized by prominence and sovereignty, the authorized representative giving life and motion to society and the body politic (Hobbes 1968). Importantly, Hobbes describes a social contract between the sovereign and citizenry, in which the latter confer on the former the right to control a definable territorial space and, in the process, the right to make and enforce such rules or laws as are deemed necessary in exchange for political, economic and military security by the former. The contract between individuals and the state is carried out on the condition that every individual does the same. The result is the creation of a powerful sovereign, which cannot be limited in its authority since the sovereign requires considerable power to formulate laws, enforce agreements and ensure contracts: in other words, to bring order to the previously natural condition of disorder.

For the Hobbesian state, the security problematic has two faces, internal (domestic) and external (foreign). States can be just as thoroughly disrupted and destroyed by domestic contradictions as they can by foreign forces. These two environments may function more or less separately; a good example is when internally coherent Zimbabwe was threatened by an aggressive neighbour – South Africa – during the apartheid era. Equally, an unstable state can disintegrate on its own initiative – post-apartheid Zimbabwe, Somalia and Sudan. Any attempt to construct a historical sociology of security has, therefore, to take into account both the changing characteristics of the internal construction of states and the nature of the external environment formed by their relations with each other. It would be convenient if one had to hand a coherent orthodoxy about the history of the state on which to draw. It would be even more convenient if this orthodoxy came as an evolutionist account in which a clear pattern of developmental stages offered a framework within which to explore the security issues.

In reality, neither is the case, but states of western Europe offer significant insights for understanding the challenges facing Africa in its pursuit of security. European states were mostly formed after the overthrow of monarchical or colonial regimes or by the merger of smaller states whose existence had become unrealistic, as in the case of the early-nineteenth-century German Confederation of states. Revolutionaries espoused a mix of liberal, republican and, later, Marxist (proletarian) values in defining the ideological underpinnings of new states. Key to these revolutionary processes was the concept of mass action. Such ideologues also had to be pragmatic, however, and careful not to threaten the new regimes that had come into existence. Thus, revolutionaries had to adapt their ideas to prevailing ethnic, racial, religious, gender and class sensibilities. These new European states were, then, in part, the result of a certain set of historical processes that formed an evolutionary path. They were also imbued with what R. M. Smith refers to as 'constitutive stories' of ethnicity, race, religion, gender, culture and class in order to define the national identity upon which citizenship status could be defined (Smith 2002: 109). Even the United States shares this type of political history, although the resulting post-revolutionary state became polyethnic (not dominated by one ethnic group) and lacked the same historical emphasis on class.

The evolution of these states, therefore, has taken place within the framework of territorial sovereignty under what Anderson rightly referred to as the 'absolutist state' (Anderson, P. 1974). A substantial majority of the current states have not completed this process, and some have barely begun. In this sense, Jackson is right – almost all African states are still 'quasi-states', enjoying external recognition but not yet having succeeded in establishing internal sovereignty – a point to which we shall return (Jackson, R. 1990). At least four major additions to the basic absolutist state can be identified. One was the development of an administrative bureaucracy to manage the state. The second was the rise of an independent commercial class. This increased the resource base of the state, but also created a more complex class structure, as well as centres of power and interest within the state that were separate from the traditional dynastic ruling establishment. Third was the invention of nationalism as an ideology of the state. This transformed the people from subjects into citizens. It welded government and society together in a mutually supportive framework, and it strengthened the bond between a state and a particular expanse of territory (Mayall 1990). Fourth was the introduction of democracy. This institutionalized the transfer of sovereignty from ruler to people implicit in nationalism, and made the state actually as well as notionally representative of its whole citizenry.

R. B. J. Walker rightly reminds us that externally the state has to be strong because the 'ahistoric moment of utilitarian calculation informed by reason and fear that gave rise to social contract has no counterpart in international relations' (Walker 1989: 174). As a result, domestic order became the mirror image and necessary condition of international disorder, thus making anarchy the axiomatic and unalterable principle of global politics. Again Hobbes offers insight; in Chapter 10 of *Leviathan*, he opens with the proposition that 'The Power of a Man is his present means, to obtain some future apparent Good' (Hobbes 1968). Harmless enough, it would seem, until this power is put into relation with other men seeking future goods. Conflict inevitably follows, 'because the power of one man resisteth and hindereth the effects of the power of another: power simply is no more, but the excess of the power of one above that of another' (Hobbes 1928: 26). A man's power comes to rest on his eminence, the margin of power that he is able to exercise over others. The classic formulation follows in Chapter 11: 'So that in the first place, I put a generall inclination of all mankind, a perpetuall and restless desire of power after power, that ceaseth onely in Death' (Hobbes 1968).

The implications for interpersonal and interstate relations are obvious.

Without a common power to constrain this perpetual struggle there can be no common law: 'And Convenants, without the Sword, are but Words, and of no strength to secure a man at all' (ibid.: 223). In the state of nature there exists a fundamental imbalance between man's needs and his capacity to satisfy them, with the most basic need being security from a violent and sudden death. To avoid injury from one another and from foreign invasion, men 'conferre all their power and strength upon one Man, or upon one Assembly of men, that man reduce all their Wills, by plurality of voices, into one Will' (ibid.: 227). As was noted earlier, the constitution of the Leviathan, the sovereign state, provides for a domestic peace, but at a price. Hobbes's solution for civil war displaces the disposition for a 'warre of every man against every man' to the international arena. Out of fear, for gain or in the pursuit of glory, states will go to war because they can. Like men in the pre-contractual state of nature, they seek the margin of power that will secure their right of self-preservation and run up against states acting out of similar needs and desires.

The result is a decentralized system where conflict is endemic and security is managed by self-help. Each state has to provide for its own security, and as a result each is forced to arm itself. Within this world-view economic considerations are subordinate to military considerations because, although states engage in international exchanges (such as trade), this engagement is fragile because they must worry about the relative gains accruing from such exchange, gains that could directly affect their relative position of strength and power. Thus, there can be no permanent friendships or enmities but only constantly changing alliances dictated by no other sentiment than the survival of the state. In this sense, the logic of international society is supportive of state security. It provides the legitimization of external sovereignty and some legal protection against aggression. It also provides ways for states to deal with some of the threats and opportunities arising from increased interaction capacity. Participation in frameworks of rules and institutions gives states some power to shape their environment, and provides a greater element of stability and predictability than would otherwise be the case. But international society can also threaten states. It limits their freedom of action, seems to subordinate them to larger bodies, and may erode their distinctive identities.

The sovereign state and territoriality become the necessary effects of anarchy, contingency and disorder that are assumed to exist independent of and prior to any rational or linguistic conception of them. Hence, the search for security through sovereignty is not a political choice but the necessary reaction to an anarchical condition: order is man made and good; chaos is natural and evil. Out of self-interest, men must pursue this good and constrain the evil of excessive will through an alienation of individual powers to a superior, indeed supreme, collective power. Seen from this perspective, the state is a concept whose content has undergone a remarkable expansion (Migdal 1988). The most advanced states have steadily fused government and society, in the process becoming much deeper, more complex and more firmly established constructs than either their predecessors or contemporary 'weak' states (those with low levels of socio-political cohesion). They have expanded not only to incorporate, but also to represent, an ever-widening circle of interests and participants. Their functions and capabilities have expanded along with their constituency, until the state has become involved in all sectors of activity, and responsive to all sectors of society. Because of their broader constituencies, powers and functions, the security interests of such 'strong' states are much more extensive than those of their absolutist ancestors. They share the basic worries about independence and integrity common to all states but, in addition, they have concerns about territory, citizens, welfare, economy, culture and law that would hardly have registered with the absolute monarchs of yesteryear (Buzan 1991).

On closer scrutiny, therefore, the older states appear to have grown much more solid and deeply rooted. Moreover they are altogether more developed entities, much better integrated with their societies, much more complex and internally coherent, much more powerful (in terms of their ability to penetrate society and extract resources from it), and much more firmly legitimized. Along with this development, and stemming from it, is a much more comprehensive security agenda. As a result, these states worry not just about their military strength and the security of their ruling families or elites, but also about the competitiveness of their economies, the reproduction of their cultures, the welfare, health and education of their citizens, the stability of their ecologies, and their command of knowledge and technology.

Colonial roots of Africa's security problematic

By contrast, states on the African continent are new; their boundaries lines drawn on maps by colonial governments, generally with startling unconcern for the people whom they casually allocated to one territory or another (Poku 1996). Their bureaucracies, however much expanded since independence, still bear important traces of their colonial origins – not least in the language they use and the structure of government machinery they possess. Few have a population large enough to rank as middle sized by the standards of Europe, Asia or South America. Moreover, despite the demographic explosion of recent decades, only Nigeria reaches the 100 million mark, and of the others only Ethiopia, South Africa and the Democratic Republic of Congo reach 30 million. Given Africa's legacy of ethnic fragmentation, moreover, size can only be purchased at the price of internal division. All of Africa's large states – Sudan and Angola, as well as those noted above – have been riven by conflict. Almost all of them are desperately hard pressed to extract the resources needed for their maintenance from their inadequate economic base, and even Nigeria, the giant of the continent, has a gross domestic product only a little larger than the Republic of Ireland's;

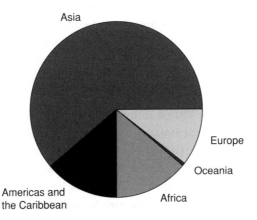

Asia

Europe

Oceania

Americas and
the Caribbean

Africa

Source: United Nations (2007): World Population Prospects.
The 2004 Revision, UN/DESA Population Division, New York

Figure 6.1 World population by region 2007

while the gross domestic product of the whole continent is about equal to that of the Netherlands.

The Congress of Berlin in 1884 offers an important starting point. It was there that the political map of modern Africa was drawn, not by Africans themselves, but by Europeans intent on staking out their claims to what James Mayall described as 'the last great land mass still awaiting enclosure'. The resultant extension of the European notion of sovereignty brought with it a near-total compartmentalization of political space in which there were very few uncolonized areas on the continent (Mayall 1991). Only 10 per cent of the continent was under direct European control in 1870, but by the end of the century only 10 per cent remained outside it. Superimposed over the continent were highly divergent and artificial geographical forms and the distortion of traditional social and economic patterns.[1]

Nigeria is a good case in point. It comprises over 280 different ethnic groups. Three major ethnic groups account for roughly 66 per cent of the total population of 130 million people: the Igbo in the south-east; the Yoruba in the south-west; and the Hausa/Fulani in the north. A number of practical challenges are associated with the maintenance of such a state; how does one, for example, communicate effectively across the entire territory? The British imposed English as the language of administration, but only a minority of the population was fluent in the language at independence. The most notable challenge associated with the creation of these artificial colonial states was the potential clash between highly diverse political cultures. In the case of Nigeria, this was highly conflated with religion: does one adhere to the Islamic traditions and laws of the Hausa/Fulani or the Christianity of the Yoruba? The political ramifications of these differences, especially when one multiplies them by the over 280 ethnic groups that comprised Nigeria, were enormous. The worse-case scenario emerged on 30 May 1967 when the Igbo formally seceded from Nigeria and created an independent Igbo country known as Biafra. The brutality of the three-year civil war that followed marks one of the darkest chapters in African history.

At least two legacies of the way modern Africa was brought into global politics have shaped the security problematic of the continent until this day. The first is the construction of the *nation-state*. Unlike in Europe, where nation-builders sought to replace the older empires with states comprising some combination of cultural, linguistic and patriotic unity, African states emerged from the authoritarian structures of their colonial past. Thus the ability of these states to produce 'constitutive stories' was severely constrained by lack of a revolutionary process that had led to their coming into being – a problem further compounded by the lack of mass action, except in the case of wars of liberation such as those in Angola, Mozambique, Zimbabwe and Namibia. But even in these cases, after independence ethnic and class divisions rapidly split any overwhelming sense of unity in the new state. As a result, African states have suffered from a paucity of history or, at least, of evolutionary historical processes akin to the European experience from which the nation-state emerged there. Consequently the parallelism between statism and nationalism has had a limited role in contemporary African politics; making the Hobbesian social contract impossible to formulate on the continent.

In truth, various approaches have been tried to meet this challenge. In some states, the dominant traditional nation became the core of the new nation, as other ethnic groups were assimilated into it or marginalized. Wolof in Senegal, American-Liberian in Liberia, Hutu in Rwanda, Shona in Zimbabwe, Baganda in Uganda and Amhara in Ethiopia were the key elements in defining the new nations as the cultural basis of the new state. In other states, an artificial creation was decreed and all traditional nations were dissolved in it; those who could or would not fit were excluded. The Ivoirité of President Henri Konan Bedie defined a new nation of essentially southern ethnic groups 'native' to the land within Côte d'Ivoire's boundaries, and the rest were decreed non-nationals and non-citizens But in all these cases, the social experiment failed to produce a unified nation upon which a strong state could be built. Partly the failure derives from an inability to construct 'constitutive stories' such as those associated with a 'freedom struggle' that are inappropriate to large sections of the population who did not participate in or understand such dynamics, although they were all affected by them. In such situations, people, particularly in the rural areas, received or are 'subjected' to citizenship that they have not chosen and are not convinced of the value of, simply because they or their community happen to live where a new state was born. As R. M. Smith asserts, 'Even today ... most people acquire their political citizenship through unchosen, often unexamined, hereditary descent, not because they explicitly embrace any political principles ...' (Smith 2002: 110).

The second legacy of colonialism is the *division of traditional ethnic groups among numerous colonial states* (Herbst 2000: 233). The arbitrary nature of the demarcation of the state boundaries at the Berlin conference resulted in a large number of diverse identities, ethnicities and cultures being grouped into new states; while at the same time separating nations with rich and unified histories into separate states. The division of the Somali people of the Horn of Africa is a notable example (Clapham 1990, 1998a). Previously united by a common culture, history and identity, this group was divided by the colonial powers into five different states. The north-western portion of the Somali nation became part of the French empire and later (1977) the Republic of Djibouti. The Western Ogaden region was annexed by the Ethiopian empire and remains part of modern-day Ethiopia. The south-eastern part of the Somali nation became part of the British colony and subsequently independent state of Kenya. Two final portions, the British Somaliland Protectorate and Italian Somaliland, became what is now the Republic of Somaliland. The primary long-term problem associated with the division of one people among many states is the potential emergence of irredentism: the political desire of nationalists to reunite their separated people in one unified nation-state. In the case of Somalia, irredentism emerged during the 1950s as the cornerstone of a Somali nationalist movement, which called for the redrawing of inherited colonial boundaries in the Horn of Africa. The nationalist movements have sought reunification by force of arms. As a result, they have funded guerrilla movements in Djibouti, Ethiopia and Kenya.

The outcome is that Africans became citizens of new states by default – that is to say, by being born in a certain territory nominally controlled by a state within borders defined by a departed exogenous power. These new states took the place of the colonial regimes whose histories were based in Europe, not Africa. Meanwhile, colonial regimes had themselves only partially deconstructed the political communities they found on arrival in Africa. In rural Africa, which constituted most of the continent and its people, pre-existing political communities including thousands of nations and primitive states were simply overlaid, either within the same colony or divided by new colonial boundaries. Thus, when colonial regimes made way for new nationalist states that attempted to form states based on the artificial land borders of departing colonialists, the governments of these new states were faced with multifarious political communities whose ethnic, racial, religious and cultural underpinnings had not been modified since the pre-colonial era. Separately, these pre-colonial political communities all had history and 'constitutive stories' that were firmly entrenched.

Accordingly, many states in Africa are not able to claim the legitimate monopoly of force in the Hobbesian sense, because the ostensible monopoly is contested, as is its legitimacy. Elsewhere William Zartman notes how there are large areas where security is challenged by both rebellion and internal lawlessness in Senegal, Guinea Bissau, Liberia, Côte d'Ivoire, Ghana, Nigeria, Chad, Sudan,

Ethiopia, Somalia, Kenya, Uganda, Rwanda, Burundi, Congo, Angola, Zimbabwe, South Africa and perhaps others – a list that includes all of Africa's largest states (Zartman 2007). In all these states, though government is accepted, the political institutions through which its powers are exercised are treated with remarkable indifference by large sections of the citizenry. While this passive acceptance might not be problematic in other contexts (one often hears about the disenfranchised or disenchanted electorate in western Europe and North Africa), in the African context it serves to deepen insecurities by alienating people from the apparatus of the state.

The security problematic in post-colonial Africa

The assurance of Ghana's first president, Kwame Nkrumah, in 1954 that 'with self government, we'll transform the Gold Coast [read Africa] into a paradise in ten years' was one of his more extreme, but not markedly out of line, descriptions of the anticipated fruits of African freedom. For Nkrumah's generation, independence was a unique opportunity to prove, in the words of Habib Bourguiba, Tunisia's head of government in 1961, that 'the African was capable of running his own affairs; fighting his own battles and developing his own people'. The key was the control of the state; what Nkrumah termed the political kingdom. 'Seek ye first political kingdom,' he exclaimed at independence, 'and all else will follow.' As we celebrate Ghana's fiftieth anniversary, it is painfully clear that 'all else' has not followed; the aura of 'optimism' has largely faded, while the debilitating effects of decades of misguided policies assume new realities. The political norm in the interim has been near-absolute power in the hands of Africa's political elites, who tolerate no opposition, manipulate elections and regard state revenues as their personal income. Meanwhile, ordinary Africans lurch between an alien superstructure (the remnant of the colonial state) and a decaying traditional African past, their loyalties stretched between predatory elites and disintegrating tribal systems as many of them head to the melting pots of ever expanding cities in pursuit of the elusive dividends of independence.

The ongoing conflicts over the remains of Somalia, for example, give a poignant reminder of the plight of ordinary folk on the continent who are without protection from any state – some falling prey to the remnants of the very state that was once supposed to be their protector. Similarly, the periodic descent of countries like Sierra Leone, Côte d'Ivoire, Liberia, Chad, Somalia and Rwanda, to mention but a few, into anarchy or something close to it demonstrates in the most dramatic way the exposure of vast numbers of people not only to the dangers of violence from marauding hordes of warriors and bandits, in a manner reminiscent of medieval times, but to hunger and disease on a cataclysmic scale. Hence, if we remove territorial space from our cognitive maps, the inescapable image we are left with is of a people across the continent deprived of their basic needs in conditions of extreme adversity as state managers and continental leaders fail to advance (or apparently are incapable of so doing) policies and programmes that would alleviate the plight of ordinary Africans, prompting the late Claude Ake to conclude that 'African leaders have presided over a pervasive alienation, the delinking of leadership from followers, a weak sense of national identity, and the perception of the government as a hostile force' (Ake 1987).

The problem is that, though independence brought an extraordinary opportunity to establish something resembling the Hobbesian social contract in Africa, it was severely flawed (Zartman 2005). The colonial system functioned on the conviction that the administrators (the white Europeans) were sovereign; that their subjects neither understood nor wanted self-government or independence. Indeed, such were the ambiguities in which rulers and the ruled were involved, and of which they were generally only vaguely, if at all, aware. If there was any training of the native, it was a schooling in the bureaucratic toils of colonial government; a preparation not for independence, but against it. It could not be otherwise. Colonialism was based on authoritarian command; as such, it was incompatible with any preparation for self-government. In that sense, every success of administration was a failure of government. With good reason, then, both Africans and Europeans usually approached problems of governance circumspectly. What emerged from the post-colonial settlement, therefore, was above all an agreement between nationalist elites and the departing colonizer to receive a successor state and maintain it with as much continuity as possible (Zartman 1964). Herbst also makes a very valid point about the agreement being explicitly about how nationalist elites allocated the 'Golden Eggs of independence', not an agreement involving the body politic as the idea of a social contract implies (Herbst 2000).

In this sense, the real political inheritance of the African state at independence comprised the authoritarian structures of the colonial state, an accompanying political culture and an environment of politically relevant circumstances tied heavily to the nature of colonial rule. Imperial rule from the beginning expropriated political power. Unconcerned with the needs and wishes of the indigenous population, the colonial powers created governing structures primarily intended to control the territorial population, to implement exploitation of natural resources and to maintain themselves and the European population. For all European colonizers – British, French, Belgian, Portuguese, German, Spanish and Italian – power was vested in a colonial state that was, in essence, a centralized hierarchical bureaucracy. Under this circumstance, power did not rest in the legitimacy of public confidence and acceptance. There was no doubt where power lay; it lay firmly with the political authorities. Long-term experience with colonial states also shaped the nature of ideas left at independence. Future African leaders, continuously exposed to the environment of authoritarian control, were accustomed to government justified on the basis of force. As a result, notions that authoritarianism was an appropriate mode of rule were part of the colonial political legacy.

The disconnection between state and citizenry has resulted in a position where the idea that governments and their institutions are in existence to serve the people is treated with apprehension and suspicion at best, and cynicism and contempt at worst. Individuals tend to consider themselves to be citizens and subjects of more than one socio-political community, and these communities are more communitarian and less associationist in nature, although they can be just as 'peelable'. Thus, people often consider themselves to be of their ethnic groups or tribes (which may cross national boundaries) first and of the post-colonial state second. Religion, which also knows no national boundaries, becomes another major identifier, articulated by lifestyle, mode of worship, type of church building and the appearance of the followers of each faith when engaged in religious activity. Thus, the streets of an average town in eastern or southern Africa are likely to be adorned with smartly dressed people wearing the colours of their respective faith, scurrying in different directions to different places of worship, often to spend a whole morning or entire day engaged in services and cultural activities associated with the church. Indeed, people are often defined first by their ethnic group and second by their church.

Consequently, power does not reside in the legitimacy of public confidence and acceptance; instead, it resides firmly within political authorities. This has given rise to a position where individuals have greater attachments to their localities (or local communities) than to the overarching state. Hence, though the notion of the state is accepted, the political institutions through which its powers are exercised are treated with remarkable indifference. Until recently, multi-party systems have been replaced by single-party states, and in turn by military regimes, without raising much more than a flicker of interest from any but those who were immediately affected by the change. For the great majority, life simply goes on; and while passive acceptance of this nature certainly has much to be said for it, it provides no assurance of political stability and no more than a resigned and probably temporary acquiescence to whatever policies the government pursues. Meanwhile, it would not be true to assume disillusionment with the state as normative and universal across Africa. As Miles and Rochefort (1991: 401) discovered, Hausa villagers on the Niger/Nigeria border 'do not place their ethnic identity as Hausas above their national one as citizens of Nigeria or Niger and express greater affinity for non-Hausa co-citizens than foreign Hausas'.

State effectiveness, therefore, has continually waned as a result of ongoing parochialization of the public realm. Resource allocation by government and other state institutions has typically come to follow ethnic or religious lines. The segmentation of society that has followed has impeded the many reforms of the political structures that could possibly have enhanced the security context of ordinary Africans, thereby limiting political tensions on the continent. The reverse has led to a litany of conflicts strung across the continent. Between 1970

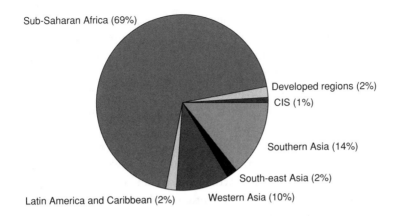

Sub-Saharan Africa (69%)

Developed regions (2%)
CIS (1%)

Southern Asia (14%)

South-east Asia (2%)

Latin America and Caribbean (2%)   Western Asia (10%)

Source: World of conflict review, special papers for
Security Council session 2247

Figure 6.2 Deaths from conflict 1994–2006, world regions

and 2006, more than forty-two wars were fought in Africa, with the vast majority of
them intra-state in origin. In 2006 alone, fourteen out of the fifty-three countries
of Africa were afflicted by armed conflicts, accounting for more than half of all
war-related deaths worldwide and resulting in more than eight million refugees,
returnees and displaced persons – see Figure 6.2.

Across the continent, the motivation to earn an income is strong, exacerbated
by poverty and by low and declining civil service salaries. Opportunities to engage in corruption are numerous. Monopoly rents can be very large in highly
regulated economies. In transition economies, economic rents are particularly
large because of the amount of formerly state-owned property that is essentially
up for grabs. The discretion of many public officials is also broad, and this
systematic weakness is exacerbated by poorly defined, ever changing and poorly
disseminated rules and regulations. Accountability is typically weak. Political
competition and civil liberties are often restricted. Laws and principles of ethics
in government are poorly developed, if they exist at all, and the legal institutions
charged with enforcing them are ill prepared for this complex job. The watchdog
institutions that provide information on which detection and enforcement are
based – such as investigators, accountants and the press – are also weak.

Artificiality and the weakness of legitimacy then raise the central question of
how African states keep going. There are, it seems to me, two linked elements
which go some way towards providing an answer. The first is the commitment
to the state of those who benefit from it, expressed through the institutions of
government of which they form part. So long as the state's own hierarchy and
the social groups that form it continue to hold together, it is very difficult for
anyone else to challenge it. The collapse of the state, or the mounting of any
secessionist movement dedicated to its dismemberment, has invariably been

prompted by deep divisions within the governing class or elite: the fragmentation of the Nigerian officer corps under the stress of coups and massacres in 1966; the destruction of the old Ethiopian government, and the bloody struggle for succession, after the 1974 revolution; the dissolution of the Somali Republic into clan rivalries; the shattering effects of despotic military rule in Liberia or Uganda; and the inability at any time to create a unified governing community in such states as Sudan, Chad and Angola.

The second element of Africa's state survival is due to its contacts with the outside world. In an ironic reversal of nationalism, it was the international community which maintained the external appearances of an often virtual state (Jackson, R. 1990). Lacking a positive definition of what their nation was, African elites agreed on what it was not – the Foreigner – just as in the absence of a fully functioning state, it was the international community which asserted its sovereign existence. When the African state has been challenged – as was the case with Sierra Leone – it is the international community which has come to its defence, often under the guise of the protection of national sovereignty. Interestingly, the international community has actively embraced the goal of boundary stability established by the Organization of African Unity (OAU) to effectively prevent the application of the norm of self-determination to a group of people once their country has become independent (Herbst 2000: 109).

Africa's security problematic: the challenge ahead

Black-ruled Africa has fallen farther and farther behind the rest of the world on almost every indicator of development. Today, the continent is the least developed in the world. According to the 2007 United Nations Development Programme (UNDP) data, in 2006 some 80 per cent of the Low Human Development Countries – these are countries with high population growth rates, low income, low literacy and low life expectancy – were located in Africa (UNDP 2007a). There are only ten African countries in the middle category – Algeria, Botswana, Egypt, Gabon, Libya, Mauritius, Morocco, Seychelles, Swaziland and South Africa, five of which have a combined population of just 4.6 million Mauritius, Seychelles, Botswana, Gabon and Swaziland. The remaining forty-three countries on the continent are in the Low Human Development category. This, however, does not tell the entire story. There are fifty-five countries in this category, which means African countries account for a staggering 76 per cent of the category. Even more telling is that, of the thirty countries with the lowest human development indices, twenty-six (or 87 per cent) are African.

The latest economic indicators from the African Development Report 2007 underline the extent of the continent's socio-economic condition. The report's celebrated headline growth of 3.5 per cent in GDP in 2007 compared to 3.2 per cent in 2006 belies the systematic decline observable in real per capita GDP growth from 1.0 per cent to 0.8 per cent in the same period. In develop-

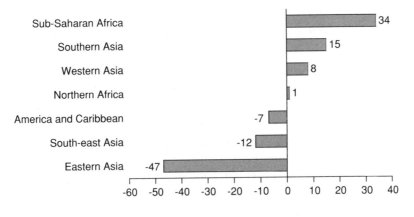

Sources: United Nations, *Millennium Goals Report 2005*;
Millennium Goals Report 2006

Figure 6.3 Increase in proportion hungry 1990–2006, global

mental terms, this means that the combined economies of Africa actually shrank by 0.2 per cent in the twelve months up to the end of 2006. To put this in context, all other regions in the world are already outperforming Africa, and efforts to redress this poor performance over the past two decades have not been successful. In 2006, for example, the average gross national product (GNP) per capita in the Organisation for Economic Co-operation and Development (OECD) countries was $28,086, compared with $528 in Africa (OECD 2006). This means that the industrialized countries are roughly fifty-one times wealthier than African states. Assuming that the OECD countries could stop stretching this development gap further, and hoping that African economies could grow at an annual rate of 3.5 per cent over the coming years, it would still take the continent some 135 years to reach the level of wealth enjoyed today by OECD countries (World Bank 2006).

An outcome of Africa's poor economic condition is an increase in poverty across the continent; with a fifth of the world populations, the continent is home to one in three poor persons in the world and four of every ten of its inhabitants are living in what the World Bank classifies as 'a condition of absolute poverty'. More worrying still, Africa is the only region in the world where both the absolute number and the proportion of poor people are expected to increase during this millennium (UNDP 2004). Nearly half the population of Africa (300 million people) lives on less than $1 a day: if current trends continue, by 2015 Africa will account for 50 per cent of the poor of the developing world (up from 25 per cent in 1990). During the 1990s the region experienced a decline in GDP per capita of 0.6 per cent per annum, and because economic growth was highly skewed between countries, approximately half the total population is actually poorer in 2006 than they were in 1990. It is also the case that income and wealth

Context of security in Africa

105

distribution are extremely unequal in many countries, and with improved growth rates such inequalities are likely to increase rather than to diminish.

Political elites are growing increasingly cognizant of the realities facing the continent. They have, in the words of Nigerian president Olusegun Obasanjo, recognized that 'an unjust historical legacy will not change simply because of the euphony of their rhetoric'. As such, they have to stop blaming their problems on the legacy of colonialism, while acknowledging that their countries are bleeding from self-inflicted wounds. The adoption of the New Partnership for Africa's Development (NEPAD) and the commitment to improve economic and political governance, built on the substantial achievements of the last decade, is some indication that changes are taking place for the better. The Commission for Africa and the resultant focus of the 2005 and 2006 Group of Eight industrialized countries meeting on Africa reflect a renewed international soul-searching about how best to arrest the continent's underdevelopment. In all, the unprecedented confluence of global and domestic (read African) forces bodes well for a continent that for so many decades had seemed hell-bent on self-destruction. But a qualitative improvement in the context of security in Africa will depend on improving governance, attracting Overseas Development Assistance (ODA), addressing the debt burden and overcoming HIV/AIDS.

Improving governance Africa's leaders have undertaken major policy reforms over the past ten years. The World Bank's Country Policy and Institutional Assessment (CPIA) ratings for Africa have improved substantially over the last decade and moved closer to global averages. In 2005, the best CPIA ratings were in macroeconomic management and trade policy, both of which help to underpin improved growth performance. Recent data provide some evidence of governance improvements (World Bank 2007). Measures of bureaucratic capabilities or the quality of 'checks and balances institutions' improved in six African countries (Gambia, Ghana, Kenya, Madagascar, Senegal and Tanzania). Three of the seven countries worldwide that improved governance in a balanced manner over the last decade were in Africa. Four countries, however, suffered large declines in governance indicators (Central African Republic, Côte d'Ivoire, Eritrea and Zimbabwe). Conflicts have decreased.

But much more needs to be done: African governments need to improve transparency, accountability and efficiency in the provision of public services. Overall, progress has been mixed. Countries have made progress in strengthening the institutions needed to implement policies and programmes (UN Economic Commission for Africa 2005). The Africa Peer Review Mechanism (APRM) successfully completed peer reviews in Ghana and Rwanda, and both governments are implementing the APRM recommendations. Fourteen countries have endorsed the Extractive Industries Transparency Initiative (EITI), and Nigeria has led the way in developing fiscal rules for saving oil windfalls. Compared to the average for all developing countries, about a third of African countries have made more rapid strides in decreasing corruption, improving voice and accountability, and boosting government effectiveness since 2000. The remaining two-thirds, however, are not keeping pace.

Yet corruption remains the key challenge to economic growth. Corruption feeds on government policies that generate rent-seekers and allow some members of society to capture 'unjustified profits' by bribing government officials. By diverting resources from development and increasing inequality, corruption becomes a major obstacle to development. More than forty African states have ratified the UN Convention Against Corruption (UNCAC). The problem has deeper roots, however. To tackle corruption, African governments ought to proceed with public sector reforms, including ensuring appropriate pay for civil servants and enhancing accountability of all public administrators. They could also remove import and export quotas, some tax exemptions, non-targeted subsidies and other policies that grant privileges to special-interest groups. Anti-corruption efforts should include increased public–private collaboration as well as increased transparency through improved data collection and analysis.

There is a growing consensus on what the key elements of governance reforms in Africa should comprise. These include creating or strengthening institutions that foster predictability, accountability and transparency in public affairs; promoting a free and fair electoral process; restoring the capabilities of state institutions, especially those in states emerging from conflicts; anti-corruption measures; and enhancing the capacity of public service delivery systems. Addressing South Africa's National Assembly in 2001, President Thabo Mbeki made clear his vision for NEPAD in the following terms:

> This is a programme premised on African ownership, African control of the projects and programmes, with African leaders accepting openly and unequivocally that they will play their part in ending poverty and bringing about sustainable development ... we have to deal with corruption and be accountable to one another for all our actions. Clearly these measures of ensuring democracy, good governance and the absence of wars and conflicts, are important both for the well-being of the people of Africa and for the creation of positive conditions for investment, economic growth and development.[2]

Attracting Overseas Development Assistance At the Gleneagles summit, G8 heads of state committed to doubling development assistance to Africa – from $25 billion in 2004 to $50 billion in 2010 – and the Multilateral Debt Relief Initiative (MDRI) was launched. Except for debt relief, which has been a major achievement, promises of scaled-up aid have not yet been fulfilled. Despite a recent revival of interest, the Doha Round of trade talks has been a disappointment in terms of increasing market access for Africa. Non-OECD/DAC development partners, including new bilaterals, foundations and the private sector, are changing development finance in Africa. Between 2004 and 2005 non-special-purpose aid declined by 2.1 per cent in real terms. The OECD/DAC and the Strategic Partnership with Africa project means that for 2006–08 most of the growth in aid will continue to come from debt relief and special-purpose grants (such as disaster relief) (Development Cooperation Directorate 2006). As a result, a typical 'well-performing' African country has seen little or no increase in the resources available to support development projects and programmes.

In the short to medium term NEPAD's external capital expectations are tied more to official inflows in the form of ODA and debt relief than to private capital inflows, despite the continent offering the highest rates of return. This recognizes the historical fact that nowhere has foreign capital led economic transformation in a country and that prospects for private flows are weak relative to the continent's massive needs. 'From worldwide experience, private capital flows of more than 5 per cent of GDP are unlikely to be feasible or sustainable' (World Bank 2000). The removal of Africa's debt burden is critical to the continent's investment prospects – through releasing monies currently spent on debt servicing for urgent public investment and improving the image of the continent as an investment destination. Western creditor countries and institutions such as the World Bank have hitherto resisted calls for radical debt cancellation. The Heavily Indebted Poor Countries Initiative (HIPC), the ruling debt relief mechanism, is widely regarded as inadequate and criticized for tying debt relief to IMF/World Bank-supervised reforms. This policy is one dimension of the new directions in the tying of aid to policy choices of the donor countries. The Africa Action Plan adopted at the 2002 G8 meeting, with its highly conditional pledge to support NEPAD, has been hailed as signalling a new willingness to raise ODA to Africa, but it in fact confirms the trend.[3]

The bright spots of private inflows illustrate both what is possible and their limits. In 2002 foreign direct investment (FDI) inflows amounted to $11 billion, a drop of $6 billion compared to the previous year.[4] Outside the extractive sector the bulk of recent private flows have been for the purchase of privatized public assets rather than investment in new enterprises, and the 2002 slowdown is directly tied to trends in privatization.[5] The few African countries that have recently attracted FDI outside privatization and the extractive sector, such as Lesotho, have mainly done so in labour-intensive low-value-added manufacturing, mainly textiles. There is likely to be an expansion of this phenomenon as countries eligible under the USA's Africa Growth and Opportunity Act (AGOA) attract capital seeking to take advantage of the preferential US market access offered under the scheme. The opportunities under AGOA are, however, circumscribed by two factors. The first is the ending of the Agreement on Textile and Clothing with its quota limits on 1 January 2005, freeing all lower-cost developing-country manufacturers. Closely related to the preceding point is the evidence of the

TABLE 6.1 Africa's external debt, 1970–2006 (US$ billions)

	1970–79	1980–89	1990–96	1997–99	2000–06
Total debt stocks	39.3	180.5	297.2	317.3	303.6
Principal arrears	0.7	9.1	31.6	40.5	26.3
Total debt service paid	3.3	18.6	25.7	26.1	23.7
Total debt stocks/XGS	91.0	195.2	242.8	217.6	168.6
Debt service paid/XGS	7.8	20.1	21.0	17.9	13.7
Total debt paid/GDP	24.2	51.7	67.0	61.8	54.6

Source: UNCTAD secretariat computations based on World Bank, *Global Development Finance and World Development Indicators*, online data

Note: XGS = exports of goods and services, per cent

limits of such labour-intensive manufacturing in the form of declining terms for such exports (UNCTAD 2000). Even if exports of labour-intensive manufactures from Africa should expand, thereby creating jobs and incomes, the stabilization of commodity markets and prices would be important for the ability of millions of Africans to participate effectively in the global economy.

Addressing Africa's debt burden In 2006 sub-Saharan Africa's external debt stood at US$303.6 billion, equivalent to $958 per person, compared to the region's average income per person of just US$470. As shown in Table 6.1, the region's debt has grown dramatically in the last three decades. Only since 1996, the year in which the HIPC initiative was launched, have debt stocks exhibited a modest reduction. To address the debt burden problem, many African countries, at first, resorted to repeat debt rescheduling focused on debt service flows, resulting in steadily increasing debt stocks and related service payments.

As of July 2007, twenty-three African countries out of twenty-seven participants were benefiting from debt relief under the Heavily Indebted Poor Countries Initiative (introduced in 1996). These are Benin, Burkina Faso, Cameroon, Chad, Congo (Democratic Republic of), the Gambia, Guinea, Guinea Bissau, Ethiopia, Ghana, Madagascar, Malawi, Mali, Mauritania, Mozambique, Niger, Rwanda, São Tomé and Príncipe, Senegal, Sierra Leone, Tanzania, Uganda and Zambia (IMF/World Bank 2004: 7). The total amount of debt relief committed (for the fourteen completion- and the thirteen decision-point countries) under the original HIPC Initiative and the enhanced HIPC Initiative (launched in 1999) was US$54 billion in nominal terms, equivalent to a reduction of US$32 billion in Net Present Value (NPV) terms. In 2006 NPV terms the outstanding debt stock of the twenty-seven countries was expected to fall from about US$80 billion to US$26 billion after

'raditional debt relief by bilateral creditors, assistance under the
and additional bilateral forgiveness.

neagles summit in July 2005, G8 heads of state promised to double
ment assistance to Africa, from $25 billion in 2004 to $50 billion by 2010,
the Multilateral Debt Relief Initiative (MDRI) was launched. During the past
year and a half multilateral debt relief has been an important achievement.
Beginning in July 2006, sixteen countries benefited from the MDRI.[6] Another
seventeen will become eligible when they reach their HIPC Initiative completion
points. MDRI countries will face important challenges in using the space created
to contract new debt prudently and from a shift in the share of aid linked to
projects and programmes towards unrestricted budget support in the form of
debt service reductions.[7]

As argued in the MDG report, the appropriate amount of debt reduction should
be measured against explicit development objectives, such as these enshrined
in the MDGs themselves. The amount of debt relief would then be determined
on the basis of expected development assistance and the need to avoid a new
debt overhang. An approach along the same lines was taken by the US General
Accountability Office (GAO), which had calculated the amount of the overall
additional assistance needed to help achieve economic growth and sustainable
debt targets for HIPC countries. Similarly, the Commission for Africa reports
that criteria for relief should be similar to those applied for aid, and, thus,
focus on the utilization of the resources released for poverty reduction and
growth. In line with the growing consensus on the need for significant debt
reduction for African countries, as evidenced by the widespread support given
to the proposals of the UK government, the international community should
endorse, in the context of the MDGs, a comprehensive debt reduction to benefit
all heavily indebted countries in sub-Saharan Africa, and a substantial debt relief
for middle-income countries. In the past, as in the case of the debt write-offs
for Egypt (US$29 billion), Jordan (US$1.4 billion) and Poland (US$2.7 billion),
similar relief has been provided to support countries on their path to economic
restructuring and resumed growth.

Confronting HIV/AIDS Across Africa, the dominant mode of HIV transmission
is heterosexual contact. Yet many people, particularly among the high-level
leadership, are reluctant to openly admit that the continent faces a crisis of
shattered tradition, where poverty, social alienation and political disaffection
mean that sexuality is no longer guided by traditional norms. Moreover, historical reluctance to speak openly about sex and sexuality has resulted in political
and religious leaders struggling to acknowledge the deeper cultural crisis at the
root of Africa's AIDS epidemic. Leadership, consequently, has been narrowly
defined as simply making references to the epidemic in speeches and passing
laws that are neither monitored nor consistently enforced for efficacy. Yet, as

effective as laws are in offering the perception of protection, they do not stop generalized epidemics.

Advocacy is needed to ensure that political leaders include the fight against AIDS among their primary responsibilities, as well as to mobilize and support those willing to speak out against stigma and discrimination. More also needs to be done to tackle HIV-related stigma and discrimination in relation to other forms of inequality and exclusion through the promotion of multi-sectoral action, e.g. by means of broad-based alliances between organizations working in HIV prevention and care, and those working in other fields such as gender equality, sustainable development and rights. There is evidence that many NGOs are slowly but surely beginning to 'mainstream' HIV/AIDS in their work, but governments need to do more. In the struggle against HIV/AIDS, leaders are challenged to use their capacity to influence their people in a positive way – to create a national, social environment that hinders the spread of the disease and cares for people living with HIV/AIDS (PLWHA).

There are two further elements which go some way to providing an answer to addressing Africa's HIV/AIDS crisis. The first is the provision of treatment for PLWHA on the continent. The reduction in the cost of ARV and other drugs has significantly changed the possibilities for treatment of PLWHA. As treatment sustains health and prolongs the lives of those infected, increased access to treatment has the potential to reduce the socio-economic cost of the epidemic on the continent. The costs of the epidemic to societies and economies are much greater than those usually quantified by economists, and so the benefits from treating people will also be greater, once there is a full accounting for the losses. These costs are to a significant degree socio-economic, and are largely avoidable through increasing access to treatment. Thus the costs of inactivity in conditions of weak access to treatment are much greater than the UNAIDS estimate of losses of 2.6 per cent of GDP annually, once all of the direct and indirect costs of the epidemic are factored into the analysis. There is a separate and powerful case to be made in respect of access to ARV therapies for pregnant women, where HIV transmission can be reduced substantially through the provision of prevention of mother-to-child-transmission programmes that are relatively inexpensive and clearly beneficial to mothers and infants. The benefits are, of course, not confined to the direct beneficiaries but also accrue to society as a whole.

The second element is human capacity planning. National policy-makers must sustain and improve the pool of human resources in the face of HIV/AIDS. In most countries it is still the case that most workers are free of HIV infection and are productively employed. It follows that keeping the labour force free of HIV infection through an expansion of prevention activities must become everywhere a priority. It should not be assumed by the national planning process that public services can continue to be supported with the present establishments, and in-novative ways of delivering educational, health and other services that are less human resource intensive must be developed. If present losses of skilled and professional labour are to be addressed, it is clear that responding to losses through an expansion of existing training programmes will rapidly become too costly for national budgets. New ways of delivering essential public services need to be developed and implemented, and less costly ways of meeting the needs for skilled and professionally qualified labour need to be identified and delivered.

Conclusion

The context of security in Africa is interrelated in a complex fashion with state consolidation. It is a classic 'catch-22'; state instability in Africa has generated the conflicts that have merely served to intensify the conditions of underdevelopment and the economic and social injustices that lead to further conflict. Where to break the cycle? In the past the answers were sought at the level of the international community. But, as is often noted in commentaries, the international community has been much less part of the solution and rather more a major part of Africa's security problems. The signs of a shift in perspective to a people-centred approach, reified in the emergent structures and agencies of the African Union's institutional framework, in civil society initiatives and in discourses of Africa's intelligentsia, hold out some promise. But the challenges within sub-Saharan Africa to the tentative consensus of support for the current human developmental security focus clearly remain substantial and threaten to unravel the process of positive change. Pan-Africanism redefined in contemporary terms is promoting positive change. But this can take the process only so far. The international community's role in providing sustained support for the initiatives being promoted in Africa by Africans, grounded in the developmental needs of everyday existence faced by millions of Africans, therefore remains critical and inescapable.

7 | Peace-building in Africa

TONY KARBO

Since the end of the cold war, Africa has suffered its fair share of violent wars and armed violent conflicts. Liberia, Sierra Leone and Angola have just emerged from armed violent conflicts, while Chad, Kenya, Somalia and Sudan are embroiled in internal armed conflicts. Despite the variant nature of the wars and armed conflicts in Africa, a critical analysis of peace-building processes on the continent reveals some shared patterns and trends.

Peace-building is not new in Africa. History tells us that Africa is the cradle of humanity, an assertion that suggests the existence of rich and diverse indigenous resources and institutions of conflict resolution and peace-building dating back centuries (see Albert and Murithi, this volume).[1] What is new is the exportation and 'imposition' of peace-building and development interventions based on the 'Liberal Peace Project'. The idea of liberal peace, according to Mark Duffield (2008), combines and conflates 'liberal' (as in contemporary liberal economic and political tenets) with 'peace' (the present policy predilection towards conflict resolution and societal reconstruction). This view reflects the notion that war-torn societies can and should be rebuilt through the utilization of a number of interrelated, connected, harmonious strategies for transformation. The emphasis is on conflict prevention, resolution, institution-building and strengthening civil society organizations. A review of existing literature (Ali and Mathews 2004; Reychler 2001; Rupesinghe 1998) on the subject of peace-building in Africa, however, reveals a limited analysis restricted to the post-conflict phase of armed conflict, which has very limited short-term prescriptions for a return to order and stability in a country that has experienced violent armed conflict.

Such an approach, of course, offers a marked similarity to African efforts at peace-building (see Murithi, this volume).[2] Murithi writes: 'Early mechanisms of indigenous conflict resolution mechanisms in pre-colonial Africa had a significant degree of success in maintaining order and ensuring the peaceful coexistence of groups.' Quoting Derry Yakubu, Murithi observes that in most African societies 'the resolution of conflict was guided by the principle of consensus, collective responsibility and communal solidarity'.

A central question for this chapter, therefore, should be: is peace-building an end in itself or a means to an end? What does the end look like? Should issues of justice, peaceful coexistence, reconciliation and development be the ultimate outputs of peace-building? Are there any African approaches to peace-building that can be used to ensure that peace in post-conflict societies is sustainable?

How do we measure the success of peace-building activities and programmes in Africa?

The focus of this chapter is to provide a conceptual definition of peace-building, including the different theoretical debates and approaches. It will seek to identify peace-building approaches in Africa and how they have been utilized in building peace in transitional societies. To achieve this objective, the chapter will present an overview of the form and structure of peace-building strategies in Africa, present theoretical frameworks for such approaches and analyse the current nature of the field. In addition, the current challenges and opportunities for Africa in building sustainable peace will be examined.

The concept of peace-building

The term 'peace-building' was popularized after 1992, when Boutros Boutros-Ghali, then United Nations Secretary-General, presented the report *An Agenda for Peace* (Boutros-Ghali 1995). In his report, Boutros-Ghali defined peace-building as a range of activities meant to 'identify and support structures which will tend to strengthen and solidify peace in order to avoid a relapse into conflict' (ibid.). Prior to Boutros-Ghali's report, peace-building was restricted to activities designed to consolidate peace in *post-conflict countries* in order to avoid a relapse into conflict. Since then, 'peace-building' has become a broad and expansive term. In *Agenda for Development* (2004), then UN Secretary-General Kofi Annan said peace-building required 'sustained, cooperative work on the underlying economic, social, cultural and humanitarian problems' (Annan 2004). This report, like other empirical studies of peace-building, utilized a limited and narrow analysis with emphasis and focus on periods of transition which generally require short-term interventions in post-peace agreements. Taisier Ali and Robert Mathews (2004) agree with this assertion and suggest that 'the focus of this literature tends to be on the political negotiations and accommodation among leaders of the rival parties, with emphasis on such short-term tasks as the signing of a ceasefire, the demilitarization and reintegration of former combatants, the resettlement of displaced persons, the approval of a new or revised constitution, and the holding of elections' (ibid.). Hevia Dashwood (in ibid.) agrees. She writes: 'the literature and governments such as Canada tend to approach peacebuilding in post conflict situations as a short-term proposition spanning two to three years'. The shortcomings of such a short-sighted approach to peace-building have been widely documented. In a study of peace-building processes in Angola, Somalia and Sudan, for example, empirical data (see ibid.) have aptly demonstrated the weaknesses embedded in approaches limited to political aspects of the complex process of building sustainable peace. Peace-building should be much more than designing interventions at the political and economic levels; peace-building must be designed with a view to addressing the fundamental causes and conditions of the conflict. This requires sustained processes of designing programmes that address the security and political realities of the country as well as looking at measures that will transform the personal, social, economic and cultural relationships of that country. The ultimate goal of peace-building in the African context, or in any context for that matter, is the rebuilding of relationships, asserting communal responsibility and solidarity. In this volume Murithi and Albert talk about African conceptions of peace and approaches to peace-building. Lessons can certainly be drawn from these examples. In the examples cited, it is clear that the fundamental guiding principle in peace and peace-building activities in the African context is the precondition of relationship-building for effective peace-building. This offers a departure from the so-called liberal peace approaches to peace-building.

In the liberal peace project tradition, peace-building refers to the full spectrum of interventions designed to facilitate the establishment of durable peace and prevent the recurrence of violence. Such interventions include peacekeeping, peace support operations, disarmament, demobilization, rehabilitation and reintegration. Taking a Galtungian approach,[3] peace-building as a concept incorporates the goals of both negative peace, or the absence of physical violence, and positive peace, which refers to absence of structural violence. Peace-building seeks to address the root causes and effects of conflict by restoring broken relationships, promoting reconciliation, institution-building and political reform, as well as facilitating economic transformation (see Ramsbotham et al. 2005; Reychler 2001; Ball 2005). In this regard, peace-building aims to promote long-term stability and justice, as well as the promotion of good governance, rebuilding of state infrastructures and rehabilitation and reintegration of ex-combatants. Overall, peace-building is a long-term process that occurs before, during and after conflict has slowed down or abated. In Liberia and Sierra Leone, for example, there continues to be a sustained presence of numerous NGOs engaged in different peace-building processes.

External interventions in peace-building initiatives have been intrinsically linked to state-building efforts in developing countries. Post-conflict situations have arguably been viewed by Western actors as prime opportunities for reconstruction of the state, and most significantly its reform. Robin Luckham writes:

> The problem remains that reform tends to be conceived in terms dictated by the major donors and international agencies, prioritizing the usual formula of liberal democracy, good governance, and economic liberalization. Whilst elements of this formula are desirable in themselves, the entire package, and the manner [in which] it is promoted or imposed from the outside, tends to inhibit the fundamental rethinking that post-conflict states require about the nature and purposes of political authority. (Luckham 2004)

Luckham contends that state legitimacy is the key to building peace in post-conflict situations. External attempts to export replicas of Western liberal demo-cratic states, however, can in fact repress popular accountability of government and thus the states' legitimacy in the eyes of their citizens. By interlinking peace-building strategies with the wider project of state-building, Western intervention can have the adverse affect of undermining the sustainability of peace.

In contrast to this narrow view of peace-building, NGOs have often viewed the process of peace-building in a broader sense which includes long-term transformative efforts, as well as peacemaking and peacekeeping. In this view, peace-building includes early warning and response efforts aimed at violence prevention, advocacy work, civilian and military peacekeeping, military interven-tion, humanitarian assistance, ceasefire agreements and the establishment of peace zones. The purpose of peace-building according to this view is to facili-tate the establishment of sustainable peace by preventing the re-emergence of armed violence by addressing the fundamental causes and impact of conflict. This, according to NGOs, can be achieved through establishing processes of reconciliation (as was done in South Africa through the Truth and Reconciliation Commission, by the Special Court in Sierra Leone and the Arusha Process and the establishment of the *Gacaca* in Rwanda), institution-building, and political, social and economic transformation through initiatives that are anchored in state structures and form an integral part of the post-conflict reconstruction and rehabilitation. Overall, the goal for sustainable peace-building is to ensure that society moves towards addressing the core causes of the conflict and to changing attitudinal patterns of interaction of disputing parties.

Peace-building, therefore, may involve a number of activities, including con-flict prevention, conflict management, negotiation, mediation, peacemaking, advocacy, humanitarian assistance, emergency management, development work and post-conflict reconstruction. In other words, peace-building is concerned with the longer-term reconstruction and development of society so as to pre-vent deadly conflict or the re-emergence of armed conflict. It also looks at the structural conditions underlying the manifestations of violence, including the discrimination faced by vulnerable groups such as women and ethnic minori-ties in any phase during a conflict situation. Ultimately, peace-building aims to enhance and promote human security, a concept that includes democratic governance, human rights, rule of law, sustainable development and equitable access to resources (economic and environmental security). It is generally agreed that the central task of peace-building is to create positive peace, a 'stable social equilibrium in which the initiation of new disputes does not escalate into vio-lence and war, a situation where the structural and cultural forces of violence are addressed'.

'The current concern of global governance is to establish a liberal peace on its troubled borders: to resolve conflicts, reconstruct societies and establish functioning market economies as a way to avoid future wars' (Duffield 2008).

In essence, the liberal peace project is premised on the logic of inclusion and exclusion; a stark contrast with African conceptions of peace, where the primary concern is to rebuild social relations and communal harmony.

At the international level, David Chandler (2006) proposes that the International Commission on Intervention and State Sovereignty's (ICISS) 2001 report *The Responsibility to Protect* can be seen as an attempt to codify and win broader international legitimacy for new interventionist norms. He claims that the justification of the right of humanitarian intervention to protect 'human security' and human rights is more than a moral shift away from the rights of sovereignty. Rather, the dominance of the liberal peace thesis in fact reflects the new balance of power in the international sphere:

> Fundamentally, the Commission underestimates the problems involved in distinguishing international interventions which may be motivated by moral, humanitarian reasons from those which are motivated by traditional Realpolitik concerns of the Great Powers.

A major distinction, however, between the liberal peace project and African peace-building practices is the reliance on the African approach to conflict management, where, as stated earlier (see also Murithi and Albert, this volume), the focus is on rebuilding broken relationships and ensuring harmony. 'The relevance and applicability of the traditional strategies have, however, been greatly disenabled by the politicization, corruption, and the abuse of traditional structures, especially traditional rulership, which have steadily delegitimized conflict management built around them in the eyes of many, and reduced confidence in their efficacy' (Egosa, in Zartman 2000). Similarly, there is an inherent confusion regarding the meaning and concept of peace-building in an African context. In most instances, peace-building is equated with conflict management, which, as Egosa suggests, has been disenabled by the abuse of traditional structures. African approaches tend to focus on process rather than outcome. The goal is to minimize, contain and prevent conflicts from escalating. Although the liberal peace process has very strong tendencies to use a top-down approach to building peace, its strength lies in both process and outcome. African conflict management techniques, according to Zartman (2000), are based on the existence of a community of relationships and values to which they refer and which provide the context for their operations.

Approaches to peace-building

Conflict transformation approach The concept of peace-building has undergone theoretical examination from various scholarly perspectives. One such approach is the conflict transformation approach, which focuses on the transformation of deep-rooted armed conflicts into peaceful ones. Marie Dugan (1997), for example, sees peace-building as both processual and dynamic, like the social relationships it seeks to transform. Since peace-building is both processual and dynamic, conflict transformation must recognize the existence of irresolvable conflicts, and Maire Dugan therefore suggests replacing the term conflict resolution with the term conflict transformation (Rupesinghe 1995; Lederach 1998). This approach acknowledges the inevitability and ubiquitous nature of conflict, hence the desire to combine short-term conflict management with long-term relationship-building and transforming the root causes of conflict. The conflict transformation approach seeks to terminate an undesired situation by building something desired through the transformation of relationships and construction of the conditions for peace.

Lederach agrees with Maire Dugan's reasoning regarding the transformative nature of peace-building as it relates to rebuilding relationships. Lederach posits that peace-building involves the transformation of relationships, in the sense that peace-building includes processes of change within a more expansive view of context and time. For Lederach, peace-building is not limited to the so-called concrete markers of peace, such as the signing of agreements, or the cessation of hostilities. It is an ongoing, multifaceted and holistic concept that should be tied to society's social, cultural, political, spiritual, economic and developmental fabrics. Conflict transformation assumes that the consequences of conflict can be modified or transformed so that relationships and social structures improve as a result of conflict instead of being harmed by it (Lederach 1999: 35). In addition, Lederach sees the need to rebuild destroyed relationships, focusing on reconciliation within society and the strengthening of society's peace-building potential. He argues that one of the most important needs is for peace-builders to 'find ways to understand peace as a change process based on relationship building' (ibid.).

Understanding peace as a social change process requires designing interventions at various levels. Lederach's peace-building pyramid analyses three levels of interventions with players who can help to build peace and support reconciliation. The pyramid analytical framework provides a holistic overview of affected societies and their populations representing various stakeholders, including leaders of governments, armed groups (rebel groups) and grassroots leaders, all of whom play differing roles in conflict. Lederach's framework is a very practical tool, although viewed by some as a simplistic division of a complex web of relationships within a conflict context. The division provides areas and levels of interventions with suggested practical activities that can be used to begin the long process of peace-building. A departure from reliance on political settlements and short-term interventions after violent conflict, the framework offers doable and durable approaches to transforming conflicts emanating from political, economic, cultural, ideological and psychological causes. For example, empowerment of the middle level is assumed to influence peace-building at the macro and grassroots levels. The conflict transformation school has been influential in peace-building processes in most of Africa's protracted conflicts,

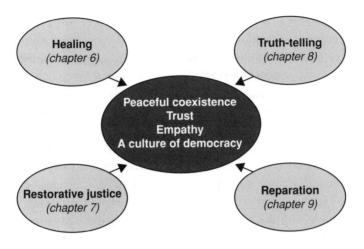

Source: Adapted from the work of John Paul Lederach

Figure 7.1 Reconciliation: the instruments

including northern Uganda and Sudan, where NGOs, traditional leaders and diplomats have been involved in various ways in peace-building efforts. For example, in 1999 different faith-based development and peace organizations joined hands to raise awareness of the conflict in Sudan and northern Uganda. A group from the Acholi Religious Leaders Organization has been and continues to be instrumental in the current efforts to bring lasting peace to northern Uganda. In Sudan different faith-based organizations have lobbied Western governments about the case of Sudan to put its conflict on the international agenda.

In Africa the rebuilding of broken relationships (reconciliation) in post-conflict societies is seen as a continuous process that evokes the spirits. The rebuilding process is seen as an interconnected web, the different strands of which cannot be dealt with in isolation. Lederach and Assefa, for example, examine relationship-building in different spheres and on different levels. For Lederach (1998) reconciliation is seen as the place where justice, peace, truth and mercy meet. He perceives reconciliation to be both a locus and a focus:

> As a perspective, reconciliation is built on and oriented toward the relational aspects of a conflict. As a social phenomenon, reconciliation represents a space, a place or location of encounter, where parties to a conflict meet. Reconciliation must be proactive in seeking to create an encounter where people can focus on their relationship and share their perceptions, feelings and experiences with one another, with the goal of creating new perceptions and a new shared experience.

The basis for this approach, according to Lederach, is anchored first on *relationships*, which form both the basis for the conflict as well as the solution. This sounds simple, but the consequences are profound since reconciliation is not fostered by minimizing affiliations between contending groups but rather by creating ways of engaging in 'relations with other human beings'. This involves the painful exercise of looking back and acknowledging a hurtful past (ibid.).

Second, reconciliation in essence represents a *place* for the encounter and engagement of contending groups where concerns about the past and the future can be aired. This involves looking at the future together without getting trapped in a vicious circle of blaming the other and excluding them from the process. Reconciliation is about envisioning an interdependent and shared future, and contending issues need to be dealt with in light of this 'higher goal' (ibid.).

Third, reconciliation requires a wider perspective than the international political traditions, discourse and operational modalities. Considering the characteristics of contemporary conflict, sustainable peace is not drawn up at the negotiation table with the heads of states. The immediacy of hatred, distrust, prejudice and racism as pivotal causes of conflict requires that the transformation of conflict is also grounded in social-psychological and spiritual dimensions, which have traditionally been regarded as irrelevant to and outside international diplomacy (ibid.: 29).

Hizkias Assefa (1999) views reconciliation as the restoration of relationships. He describes reconciliation as reconciling with God, the self, neighbours and nature. This can also be translated as reconciliation in four different but not separate dimensions, the spiritual, social-psychological, social and ecological.

Assefa also perceives reconciliation as a form of conflict management, in other words conflict resolution, and he distinguishes the following process elements:

a) Honest acknowledgement of the harm/injury each party has inflicted on the other;
b) Sincere regret and remorse for the injury done;
c) Readiness to apologize for one's role in inflicting the injury;
d) Readiness of the conflicting parties to 'let go' of the anger and bitterness caused by the conflict and the injury;
e) Sincere efforts to redress past grievances that caused the conflict and compensate the damage caused to the fullest extent possible;
f) Entering into a new mutually enriching relationship.

Reconciliation then refers to this new relationship that emerges as a consequence of these processes. What most people refer to as healing is the mending of deep emotional wounds (generated by the conflict) that follow the reconciliation process. (ibid.: 37, 42)

The methodology of reconciliation differs from other conflict-handling mechanisms (e.g. force, adjudication, arbitration, negotiation and mediation) in that the essence of reconciliation is the voluntary initiative of the conflict parties to acknowledge their responsibility and guilt (Bloomfield 2006).

Reconciliation after violent social conflict is the long, broad and deep inter-

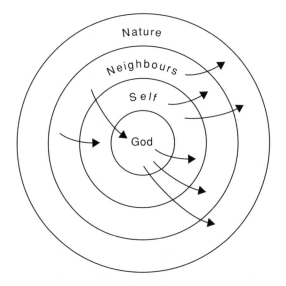

Source: Assefa (1999)

Figure 7.2 Basis of reconciliation

communal relationship-building process, whose constituent instruments include justice, truth, healing and reparations. These instruments 1) are reconciliation's main constituent parts; 2) thus have the potential to work in coordination in the same direction; 3) depend fundamentally on each other; and 4) contribute together to the overarching relationship-building process that is essential for progress towards the (perhaps idealistic) goal of a reconciled society (ibid.: 13).

Structural approaches 'Civil wars occur at different levels of political and economic development, with diverse political and social systems and varying physical and human resource endowment, culture and historical experiences' (Ball 2005). Structural dimensions of conflicts are generally characterized by weak political and administrative institutions, a repressive political system that does not allow for a diversity of voices, lack of legitimacy of political leaders and, more importantly, particularly in Africa, the idea of 'stayism'; the situation where leaders seek to perpetuate their irresponsive leadership. Parallel to these political realities of a country in conflict, the economic and social structures are also generally characterized by unique features that work to intensify conflict. These include weak and decaying economic infrastructures, high levels of international debt, poor and weak legal frameworks for taxation and its collection mechanisms, relatively high unsustainable military expenditures and high levels of human and capital flight. These political and economic anomalies require peace-building activities and strategies that will address these challenges at these systemic levels. For structural peace-building to occur, the focus should be on the systemic and structural conditions that foster violent conflict. This is based on the belief that stable peace must be built on social, economic and political foundations that are a response to the needs of the people. Structural factors relate to issues of governance and the functioning of the state, especially its relationship with the citizenry, legitimacy and ability to provide basic services and modes of governance. The root causes of poverty, corruption, discrimination, lack of political representation, environmental degradation and unfair distribution of resources such as land, as in the case of Zimbabwe during and after colonialism[4] need to be addressed.

Arguably, the Rwandan case is an example where causes of the conflict lie in the structures of society. One explanation for the cause of tension between the Hutus and Tutsis was the structural issues relating to the unequal distribution of resources between the two groups (Ramsbotham et al. 2005; Ali and Mathews 2004). These inequities required few proximate causes to trigger off the genocide. They were further compounded by the weakness of the state, unresponsive leadership, colonial legacies, constitutional inadequacies and age-old hatred between Hutus and Tutsis. Structural approaches to conflict also focus on institution-building, transformation of the social structure and infrastructure development, activities that typically require dismantling, strengthening or reforming old institutions in order to make them more effective. The linkages between poverty and conflict (Collier et al. 2003) have led development actors such as the World Bank to take an increased interest in peace-building by implementing various programmes aimed at reducing violence and consolidating peace. The World Bank, for example, now has a post-conflict unit which focuses on programmes that seek to prevent conflict as well as to help societies rebuild after violent armed conflict. This unit has been involved, for example, in the rebuilding processes in post-conflict Liberia and Sierra Leone.

Peace-building at the structural level should give priority to all of these issues to build a sustainable platform for the transformation of conflicts. Nicole Ball (2005) suggests that priority should be given to strengthening the capacity of the government to carry out key tasks, assisting the return of internally displaced persons and external refugees, rehabilitation of infrastructure and state institutions, conducting constitutional and judicial reviews, stabilization of the national currency, removal of landmines, termination of extralegal forms of recruitment to the security sector, restructuring of the security sector based on the principle of civil management, and oversight of the security forces.

Non-governmental organizations and peace-building

Africa has witnessed the proliferation of NGOs renowned for their involvement in peace-building. Such well-known NGOs include the African Centre for the Constructive Resolution of Disputes (ACCORD), the Centre for Conflict Resolution (CCR), the Institute for Security Studies (ISS), the Nairobi Peace Initiative

(NPI) and the West Africa Network for Peacebuilding (WANEP) among others. The sheer diversity and number of NGOs involved in peace-building reflect the growing continental and global concerns on issues affecting peace, such as proliferation of small arms, increase in child soldiers, trauma and poverty. Some of these NGOs are more effective than others because they make use of networking as a peace-building model, apart from taking a continent-wide approach. WANEP, using its network partners, was able to bring attention to the Liberian dilemma by mobilizing women and other citizens' groups in the peace talks that culminated in the Accra peace agreement between the Liberian government and two rebel forces, namely the Movement for Democracy in Liberia (MODEL) and Liberians United for Reconciliation and Democracy (LURD) in August 2003. In addition, NGOs have been at the forefront of developing early warning systems for regional blocs, such as the Economic Community for Western African States (ECOWAS) and the Inter-Governmental Authority for Development (IGAD).

Although NGOs and other civil society organizations have been instrumental in the implementation of peace-building programmes at the structural level, they have also been able to initiate implementation of the liberal peace project. In 1996, an estimated three thousand development NGOs from OECD countries controlled and dispersed up to US$5.7 billion per year in assistance to developing countries (Rupesinghe and Anderlini 1998). Working in concert with NGOs are the so-called community-based organizations (CBOs), sometimes also referred to as grassroots organizations (GROs). Conditions GROs imposed on the northern NGOs include a requirement to work with CBOs and GROs. This, according to Rupesinghe, is not accidental. 'For donor governments their support of such independent organizations falls in line with the belief that private initiatives are more efficient than government controlled programs. It is believed that private initiatives, either as GRO or NGOs, have always been better at reaching the poorest sectors of society' (ibid.). This approach, of course, promotes the end goal of the liberal peace project – that is, the process of liberalization. As examples in Somalia and elsewhere have illustrated, such an approach has destabilizing side effects, including a resort to violence when NGOs, GROs and CBOs do more harm than good, thereby exacerbating violence or leading to renewed violence.

NGOs have also been criticized for their inability to coordinate their efforts with governmental institutions in post-conflict societies. In many cases, NGOs are the preferred outlet for donor funds and support, and they end up 'competing' with the government. Such competition has exacerbated the adversarial relations between civil society and the state. It is important for the gap between NGOs and governmental institutions to be bridged in order to promote sustainable peace-building. Moreover, the continued burgeoning of NGOs at the peace-building frontier has led to duplication, commercialization of peace-building and reduced efficacy of the work of these players, a process resulting from what Orjuela (2004: 225) terms 'NGOization'.

Peace-building and DDR

The process of demobilization, disarmament and reintegration (DDR) is part of the long-term goal of peace-building. In this vein, there is an interwoven and symbiotic relationship between peace-building and the DDR processes (Berdal 1996). The process of demobilizing and disarming combatants and repatriating and reintegrating them into their communities is one of the most immediate and complex challenges faced in post-conflict situations. Collier (1994), Weiss-Fagen (1995) and Kingma (1999) assert that improperly demobilized combatants are likely to turn to crime, banditry and violence.

As examples from Mozambique, Angola, Liberia and Zimbabwe demonstrate, poorly conceived and implemented DDR processes increase the likelihood of a relapse into conflict. In Liberia, for example, the haphazard manner in which the DDR process was carried out in 1995 caused a re-emergence of the war since Charles Taylor and his LURD rebel group were not fully disarmed and reintegrated into society. This situation allowed Taylor and his men to quickly regroup when the ceasefire agreement was violated by Johnson and his rebel movement.

Sustainable peace can be achieved only through sustainable DDR programmes. DDR programmes are essential, not only for disbanding armed groups, but also in providing a transitional safety net for ex-combatants. DDR can enhance the capacity for durable peace by promoting the human security of ex-combatants through their long-term sustainable reintegration in secure post-conflict frameworks. The way in which DDR processes are implemented has a bearing on the long-term peace-building process in a country (Berdal 1996; Colletta et al. 1996; Kingma 2002). The UN Transitional Assistance Group (UNTAG) carried out a DDR process in Namibia in 1989–90, and this programme is regarded as one of the success stories in Africa. UNTAG's mandate was specific on the disarmament and demobilization of all armed groups. After DDR, UNTAG successfully supervised the country's transition to independence and exited when the new government had established a new and professional military and formulated a reintegration policy.

Similarly, Sierra Leone's post-conflict activities were arguably well implemented. Apart from payment of former fighters ($US300 to each person who returned their weapons), Sierra Leone's DDR process ensured that combatants were first sequestered, then demobilized, disarmed and camped for eventual reintegration into their respective communities. In contrast, Liberia's 1997 disarmament and demobilization programme was deeply flawed and half-heartedly undertaken, leading to the holding of a speedily organized presidential election which Charles Taylor won. Dissatisfied and still-armed factions were quick to return to war, however, leading the country into another conflict resulting in complete state failure.

In Zimbabwe, the DDR process may be accountable for the lack of sustainable peace which the country is currently embroiled in. Following the Lancaster House Agreement on Rhodesia of 21 December 1979, the Cease-Fire Commission (CFC) and a modest Commonwealth Monitoring Force (CMF) provided the institutional framework for the implementation of the Agreement, supervising Zimbabwe's ceasefire and monitoring transitional elections leading to majority rule and legal independence. In Zimbabwe, the economic reinsertion happened partially in 1979, when ex-combatants received a demobilization grant of Z$400. The limited monetary reintegration strategy resulted in the ineffective reintegration of these demobilized combatants, however, the majority of whom re-registered under the Demobilization Programme of 1981, and also demanded compensation in 1997 as a result of their poor economic plight. The discontent of war veterans in Zimbabwe culminated in their being awarded Z$50,000 as allowances.

Cash payments without long-term development perspectives, however, are often easily lost or misused for consumption and pleasure. In 1998, the same war veterans began demanding land for resettlement, culminating in a controversial land reform programme which has witnessed turmoil, violence and economic crises in Zimbabwe.[5] It is therefore important to involve other players such as NGOs, international agencies and the United Nations in the development arena in reinsertion phases to implement initiatives aimed at full and self-sustained social and economic reintegration with ex-combatants. Such initiatives must follow temporary reinsertion assistance programmes and should provide ex-combatants with financial independence through employment, education and professional training, public employment, encouragement of private initiative through skills development and micro-credit support, and access to land. The success of the Sierra Leone DDR process can be attributed to the holistic approach taken in the design and implementation of the strategies for DDR. CBOs, GROs, the government and other local actors were intimately involved in the design and implementation of DDR programmes.

Challenges to peace-building in Africa

The peace-building terrain in Africa is characterized by a significant number of challenges. Sadly, a sizeable number of armed conflicts relapse to war, resulting in renewed violence and 'new' wars, as proven by greater violence in Angola and Rwanda in 1992 and 1994 respectively, after the failure of peace processes. First, the conflicts in Africa are seemingly intractable and protracted. Most peacemaking agreements do not last, and a lot of countries have demonstrated a relapse into violence. Although the number of violent conflicts has decreased since the beginning of the new millennium, there is strong evidence of recidivism in many post-conflict countries, as witnessed in Eritrea-Ethiopia, Sudan, Uganda and Liberia. Collier et al. (2005) found empirical data that suggest that there is almost a 44 per cent risk of a country reaching the end of a conflict returning to conflict within five years. One reason for this, according to Collier et al. (ibid.), is that the same factors that caused the initial war are usually still present. If a country has a fairly low average income, rural areas that are well endowed with natural resources, is surrounded by a hostile neighbour and has a large active diaspora, after the war it is likely that these characteristics will persist (ibid.). Critics of Collier's view assert that violent armed conflict is fraught with complex dynamics and processes, including the idea of interventions that are made by a plethora of international actors who have no interest in seeing countries relapse into violence. Effective and sustainable peace-building is often based on the empowerment of communities. Effective peace-building moves away from what Ramsbotham et al. (2005) refer to as 'simple' one-dimensional peace-building to peace-building frameworks that take a longer and broader developmental approach; an approach that Lederach (1998) calls 'integrated peace-building'. In this approach, peace-building is carried out with a long-range view of trans-forming relationships within communities and their members, through conflict prevention, vision and transformation.

Another challenge with peace-building in Africa is that external players often attempt to engage in peace-building activities without seeking sustain-able solutions at the grassroots level. Very often, peace-building is managed by international NGOs and diplomats, who have no intimate acquaintance with the local environment. Peace-building programmes are designed by northern NGOs with specific strategies for implementation. This approach has problems in the sense that designers and implementers are not accountable to members of communities where such programmes are implemented. Funds are disbursed to CBOs, GROs and other implementing partners of the northern NGOs which, in equal measure, are not accountable to local communities. Communities have no ownership of peace-building processes designed in the North, minimizing the possibilities of anyone having to account to members of local communities.

In addition, the problematic of peace-building in Africa is compounded by the nature of conflicts in the region. Contemporary African conflicts tend to have a spillover effect, and they subsequently affect all the countries in the region, feeding into existing conflicts or generating new ones. The main protagonists of conflicts in Africa often operate across borders – notable examples include the Lord's Resistance Army, which operates from Sudan and more recently in the DRC. This poses a challenge to various actors in the peace-building process, including regional organizations, diplomats, NGOs and grassroots organizations.

The persistence of protracted internal conflict, increased cases of countries relapsing into war as well as the failure of major peace agreements in Africa are indications of the tricky ground on which peace-building stands. This challenge is exacerbated by the fact that the African state is usually fractured, failing or failed. Defined simply, a failed state is one in which the social, political and economic structures are fissured and shattered. Most failed or failing states in Africa experience severe economic decline, disintegration, social unrest and loss of state legitimacy, massive human and capital flight, absence of rule of law, poor governance structures and decline in public services. The state is increasingly divided along various cleavages, including ethnic, regional, linguistic and political divides. This is compounded by government corruption, which is usually very high in post-conflict countries. High rates of corruption are a repellent to external and domestic investment as well as Official Development Assistance. This has been the experience in Guinea Bissau, Zimbabwe and the DRC, where the government struggles with corruption to the extent of setting up anti-corruption commissions to address the problem in an apparent effort to reassure donors. Peace-building tends to struggle to mend such lines. The case of the DRC is illustrative of this. There, rebel factions, in spite of agreements and subsequent elections that international observers have proclaimed transparent, relatively free and fair and credible, continue to challenge the central government in Kinshasa. This is because the central government is relatively weak with almost non-functioning institutions and rampant corruption. It is imperative for sustainable peace-building to recognize and respond to this challenge.

The entire conundrum of peace-building in Africa is further complicated by countries' relations with the Bretton Woods institutions, namely the World Bank (WB) and the International Monetary Fund (IMF). Countries that default on loan repayments should be placed under prescribed sanctions, and therefore would not be eligible for further loans. Ostracism by Bretton Woods institutions cascades into a country's relations with other donors and international agencies. If the IMF programme is suspended, donors are generally reluctant to engage directly with such a country. This situation makes it more difficult for countries emerging from conflict to keep their reconstruction and peace-building efforts on course. Such a scenario makes it important for peace-building to go beyond peace agreements and the politics of consolidating peace by seeking to address the broader economic dimensions that support durable peace.

The World Bank's response to such needs is its Post Conflict Reconstruction Unit, as well as a special programme called Low Income Countries Under Stress (LICUS), which assists debilitated countries that are fractured and failing. Countries under LICUS are usually characterized by weak policies, absence of rule of law, weak institutions, poor governance, fractionalized relations and extended internal problems. The LICUS unit has worked with country teams to support strategy development in twelve focus countries in Africa, including Angola, the Central African Republic, Guinea Bissau, Liberia, Somalia, Sudan, Togo and Zimbabwe. Evidence of any significant successes for the LICUS programmes is yet to be recorded by the World Bank.

Against this background, peace-building operations should help countries emerging from conflict by building their capacity for good governance and effective public sector management. A similar programme runs in the United Nations, now transformed into the UN Peacebuilding Commission (PBC), created in 2005.

The PBC works closely with its related mechanisms, a Secretariat Peacebuilding Support Office and a Peacebuilding Fund (PBF) created in October 2006. The United Nations launched the PBF to respond to the needs of post-conflict countries in achieving durable peace. The PBF prevents a country from sliding back into conflict by establishing the initial crucial bridge between conflict and recovery. In essence, the PBF is an 'innovative mechanism aimed at extending critical support during the early stages of a peace process, immediately following the conclusion of a peace agreement, when sufficient resources from other funding mechanisms were not yet available'.[6] Currently the PBF supports Burundi and Sierra Leone, although it is also available to countries in similar circumstances. About $35 million each has been available for peace-building in Sierra Leone and Burundi.[7] Other countries are also able to access this fund, as deemed fit by the Secretary-General. For example, in 2007 the PBC approved $700,000 and $800,000 to support inclusive dialogue and political dialogue in Burkina Faso and the Central African Republic respectively.[8]

A much more difficult challenge for peace-building in Africa is the top-down approach taken by promoters of the liberal peace project. Peace-building programmes and activities designed by NGOs and Civil Society Organizations from the North are generally not suited to specific local contexts and do not address local problems. This is further compounded by the mere presence of many of these organizations, which, because of specific donor conditionalities and demands, do not take a long-range view based on developmental peace-building and do not utilize conflict-sensitive approaches in their programmes. Their goal is often to complete projects and programmes based on timelines stipulated by donors. In addition, implementers of peace-building programmes do not seek to address specific development challenges that might have been at the root of the conflict. They do not have a clear understanding of the type of development that countries and societies need to build sustainable peace.

Prospects for peace-building in Africa

More wars have ended than started since the beginning of the new millennium, reducing the number and intensity of armed conflicts in Africa (UNECA 2004). Only three (Chad, CAR, Sudan) of the fifty-three member states of the African Union are currently embroiled in violent armed conflict. The decrease in conflicts is encouraging because it reflects the success of peace-building efforts and interventions at the regional, continental and international levels. Africa has a goal of making the continent violence free by 2010. In addition, Africa is making a case for its role in peace-building by emphasizing its own efforts in various peace processes. The establishment of organizations such as the Economic Community of West African States Monitoring Group (ECOMOG) and the presence of African Union troops reflects ownership of the peace-building process by Africans. Since 2006, the African Union and a few regional organizations (IGAD in East Africa, for example) have been engaged in sustained efforts in mediating and resolving conflicts. ECOMOG played an important role in mediating the Liberian conflict in the late 1990s and early 2000. Recently, the African Union has made its determination to have its own peacekeeping force a reality. Currently, there are AU forces in Sudan, which have been designated to form part of a hybrid peacekeeping force. In addition, the African Union has come up with a novel approach to peace-building through the establishment of the Peace and Security Council (PSC); an African Standby Force (ASF); a Military Staff Committee (MSC); a Continental Early Warning System (CEWS) and a Panel of the Wise.[9] These institutions recognize the imperative to have a framework for promoting peace and security on the continent.

Furthermore, there is potential for sustainable peace-building in Africa that is rooted in strong and deeply embedded indigenous conflict resolution mechanisms. Many nations are taking a revised perspective on the role of local methods of conflict resolution, and Africa has proved to be the hub of these wonderful ideas of merging culture with peace-building. In Africa there are indigenous traditions for peace-building that facilitate healing, promote reconciliation and create foundations for re-establishing social solidarity (Zartman 2000). Such approaches include the *gacaca*[10] in Rwanda and *mato oput*[11] in Uganda. More often, traditional methods of peace-building in Africa encompass various features including restoration, reconciliation, national unity, truth-telling and redistribution rather than punishment and retribution. In South Africa, the Truth and Reconciliation Commission (TRC) process was characterized by the African concept of *ubuntu*, which can be interpreted as 'humaneness' and awareness of our interconnectedness. Literally translated, *ubuntu* means 'a person is a person through other persons', meaning that community peace and individual peace are codependent. *Ubuntu* aims to create an environment where people are able to recognize that their humanity is inextricably bound up in the humanity of others. *Ubuntu* then encourages people to see beyond the crimes of the perpetrators by seeking to integrate the evildoer back into the community.

The quest for sustainable peace on the continent is within reach because of the upsurge of 'gendered peace processes' in various African countries. A considerable number of African countries have made significant strides in mainstreaming gender into their peace processes and post-conflict reconstruction. Contemporary Africa is characterized by local, national, subregional and regional women's initiatives that are actively transforming the socio-economic and political spheres through peace-building activities. Kofi Annan, former Secretary-General of the United Nations, acknowledged that 'The Women of Africa have long borne the brunt of African violence and dislocation but they have always been a force of peace and development.'[12] Examples of women involved in peace-building efforts include the Liberian Women Mass Action for Peace (WMAP), which effectively mobilized for peace in a country that was besieged by fourteen years of civil war. WMAP held vigils and protests both in Monrovia and at the peace talks in Ghana, leading to the Golden Tulip Declaration of March 2003.[13]

In Rwanda, the government has gone beyond the 30 per cent quota in terms of representing female leadership. In Tanzania and South Africa, measures such as proportional representation, quotas and a percentage of women on lists of candidates have succeeded in enabling women to move ahead numerically, and transform parliamentary agendas. Although merely increasing women's numbers in positions is not enough to ensure a sustainable process, the call for increased women's participation in politics is in tandem with the realization that peace-building is a gendered activity. If peace-building incorporates gender, there will be more prospects for durable peace. This reflects the importance of increased women's participation in decision-making positions, gender mainstreaming and continued capacity-building for women in leadership.

Conclusion

The experience of peace-building in Africa is eclectic, although there are some unifying themes across the continent. Peace-building in Africa reflects various theories of social change, such as conflict transformation and structuralist approaches. In addition, many players are involved in this field, including NGOs, GROs and governments, regional and international organizations. A lot of effort is needed to strengthen peace processes in Africa. The words of Roland Paris (2004) aptly demonstrate the motives of so-called peace-building from the top, as proposed by the liberal peace project. Paris asserts, and rightly so in my view, that: 'Peace-building missons in [the] 1990s were guided by a generally unstated but widely accepted theory of conflict management: the notion of promoting "liberalization" in countries that had experienced civil war would help to create the conditions for a stable and lasting peace' (ibid.).

The basic assumption of the liberal peace project is the idea that peace-building in post-conflict situations would bring about democratization, which in turn would shift societies away from violence into peaceful electoral politics and the development of capitalist markets, which will promote sustainable economic growth – a specific kind of what Paris calls 'social engineering'. Of course, this kind of approach, although desirable, does not address the whole spectrum of contextual contemporary African issues for post-conflict societies. For sustainable peace-building to be achieved, peace-building activities must be scaled up to include, through processes of inclusion and empowerment, traditional mechanisms for conflict management and peace-building. My argument here is that both the liberal peace project and traditional endogenous mechanisms for peace-building have to be used simultaneously in order to achieve sustainable peace.

TWO | Issues in peace and conflict in Africa

8 | Understanding transitional justice in Africa

JANNIE MALAN

On the way towards understanding transitional justice, particularly in Africa, we should avoid the possibility of becoming satisfied with a partial or a popular understanding. The term is often used in a rather narrow ad hoc sense of *retributive justice*, as if the aim of transitional justice was merely the prosecution of perpetrators of injustice (see Boraine 2004: 67).

This widespread but restricted meaning is understandable, since the term 'transitional justice' has emerged precisely in situations following intra-state struggles waged against unjust systems of governance. That is when a more democratic system of governance is being phased in, but the newly empowered people feel obliged to make a case against key figures of the old dispensation (Crocker 1998: 1, 4).

There is, however, also the broader meaning of *restorative justice*, which is a very typical element in traditional African methods of resolving conflict and restoring social harmony. Such a restorative approach can form an important part of a comprehensive and inclusive transitional process, in which the focus is not only on punishment for past crimes but also on cooperation towards a future of 'political stability and socio-economic transformation' (Heyns and Stefiszyn 2006: 363).

As an obvious starting point on our way towards understanding as much as possible about transitional justice in Africa, not merely as a textbook topic but as a real-life undertaking, we may look at two significant examples: retributive justice in Rwanda and restorative justice in South Africa. In both these countries the urgent need for an appropriate form of transitional justice arose in 1994 – after Rwanda's genocide and after South Africa's first post-apartheid election.

Pursuing retribution through court procedures in post-genocide Rwanda: restorative

Justice and reconciliation In Rwanda, more than one version of history is found. Each of the two main groups, the Hutu and the Tutsi (85 per cent and 14 per cent of the population, respectively), has its own perspective and its own terms to describe the same historical processes and events (Sarkin 1999: 768). For many centuries these two groups have coexisted in the area of present-day Rwanda and Burundi. Each group seems to have had its socio-political organization, and its economic situation. The Tutsi apparently managed to put a feudal-type class system in place, in which they, as a minority, had control over land, cattle and the Hutu. In such a situation, the Hutu self-evidently saw themselves as the original inhabitants and the Tutsi as foreigners (ibid.: 774). Over time, the ethnic distinction was maintained, but also somewhat blurred – by intermarriage and by a custom of 'honorary membership' (History World 2007).

The history of the last century and a quarter included, as in the rest of Africa, the waves of colonial rule and independence. During the colonial period, the power of the Tutsi king was reduced and the feudal system modified. The United Nations required the Belgians to integrate the Rwandans into the political process. This was done in a way that 'granted the Tutsi minority political, economic and social domination over the Hutu majority' (African Studies Center 2007). Quite understandably, this preferential 'development' caused civil unrest that escalated until it led to an outburst in 1959. After further years of violence, Rwanda became independent in 1962, under a Hutu president whose party was oriented to 'Hutu Emancipation' (History World 2007). More violence followed when 'rebels invaded'/'exiles returned'. 'Massacres' occurred and large numbers fled (see Havermans 1999b: 247). A 'civil war'/'liberation conflict' erupted (Sarkin 1999: 768). Several rounds of talks took place between early 1991 and late 1993. Ceasefires and agreements were signed, one after the other.

At the same time, however, extremist Hutus became vehemently opposed to talking, negotiating and power sharing. The media began spreading false rumours and hate speech, and youth militias started their reigns of terror. In April 1994, the plane in which the presidents of Rwanda and Burundi were travelling was apparently shot down, probably by a group strongly opposed to Rwanda's Hutu president, who had, during his twenty years in office, been favouring both Hutus and Tutsis, allowing other political parties to promote democracy and making concessions towards actual power sharing.

What almost immediately followed was the organized elimination, in the capital and the rest of the country, of Tutsis and moderate Hutus who sympathized with the Tutsis. The slaughtering was ruthlessly carried out by the Interahamwe and other Hutus, wielding machetes normally used as agricultural tools. The conservative estimate of the casualties is usually given as 800,000.

The genocide was brought to an end in July 1994 when Rwandan Patriotic Front forces 'seized control from the ruling regime' (ibid.: 769). What then followed was that retaliation was feared and was indeed practised. Out of fear, some two million refugees, mostly Hutus, fled to neighbouring countries. And out of revenge, both sides carried on with brutalities and atrocities, in Rwanda and in refugee camps across the borders. Feelings and reactions could have been exacerbated by a previously existing hatred of the 'others', or mitigated by insight into the background and causes of such extreme atrocities.

Through intra- and inter-group communication and media, stories and reactions were shared and outcries and demands were made. What the country, through its leaders, had to find, urgently and rapidly, was a generally acceptable strategy of dealing with the masterminds and executors of the killings, and the entire aftermath of the genocide – in order to pave the way towards a future of reasonable tolerance and coexistence, a future in which the 'again and again' massacres of the past could be replaced by a concerted 'never again'.

At the same time, however, the international community was calling for appropriate action. Living up to its primary purpose of maintaining international peace and security (UN Department of Public Information 2003: 5), the United Nations Security Council established the International Criminal Tribunal for Rwanda (ICTR) in November 1994.

In Rwanda, in the same year, the new transitional government and parliament of national unity 'ambitiously embarked on a mission to bring every genocidaire to justice' (Wierzynska 2004: 383). This objective was understandable, but almost impossible to reach. More than 120,000 suspects were awaiting trial in overcrowded prisons, but Rwanda's judicial system was depleted to a 'mere five judges and fifty lawyers' (ibid.: 383).

Plans were therefore made to try to cope with the immense task that had to be undertaken. Already in 1994, 'the government decided not only to expand and strengthen the existing judicial capacity but also to make use of the *gacaca* system in the trial of genocide crimes' (Murithi 2000: 71). Restoring the collapsed judiciary was an obvious necessity, but an inadequate measure in the circumstances. The pragmatic decision was therefore to incorporate the *gacaca* system in an adapted form to cope with the post-genocide situation. *Gacaca* was an established tradition for resolving conflict and promoting reconciliation in families and local communities. Modifying it could of course be seen as an ad hoc co-optation of an ancient custom by the government. The matter therefore had to be properly discussed, and the *Gacaca* Law was eventually passed in 2001.

As in the original model, members of society could provide testimony and evidence against suspects and participate in hearings. In the adapted model, however, the elders who served as judges were granted the power to impose sentences up to lifetime imprisonment, 'thus substituting retributive characteristics for some of *Gacaca*'s rehabilitative ones'. Still, '[t]he *Gacaca* courts established by the government were put in place to serve two official purposes: Justice and reconciliation' (Wierzynska 2004: 384).

The availability of such a traditional custom for restoring justice and reconciliation was most fortuitous in Rwanda's post-genocide predicament. It had its time-proven name signifying 'justice on the grass', and it breathed the spirit of restoring social harmony. It had its inherent community friendliness, which allowed anyone to participate, and it could indeed be seen as a 'democracy-promoting mechanism' (ibid.: 383).

It is quite understandable, of course, that time was needed to implement the modified *gacaca* system. Thorough planning had to be done. The crimes of the planners, organizers and leaders of the genocide, as well as sexual crimes involving torture and rape, had to be tried by the ICTR and the Rwandan courts of justice. But all those suspected of homicide, serious assaults against persons and damage to property had to be dealt with by the *gacaca* courts. Some ten thousand of these courts were envisaged, but by 2003 only 10 per cent had held pre-trial hearings and none had begun to try suspects (ibid.: 384).

More interesting details could be added about the functioning of the ICTR, the Rwandan judiciary and the *gacaca* courts, but for the purposes of this chapter it may be more important to focus on the almost surprising way in which Rwanda and Rwandans seemed to have taken the interrelatedness of truth, justice and reconciliation seriously. One could have expected a vengeful retaliation by the Tutsi minority, perhaps with help from supporters from the international community, or a forceful suppression of all opposition to the Hutu majority. What happened, however, was that justice, particularly *retributive justice*, was indeed sought, and that the urgent need for *restorative justice and reconciliation* was also addressed.

This interrelating of the two types of justice may especially be expected from the *gacaca* project, but the president of the ICTR has recently emphasized that the challenging responsibility of the ICTR was not only 'to establish the guilt or innocence of the accused' and to 'bring justice to victims of the massive crimes that were committed', but also to 'establish a record of facts that can aid reconciliation in Rwanda' (Byron 2007).

Seeking reconciliation through commission hearings in post-apartheid South Africa

In South Africa, three and a half centuries ago, white, seafaring foreigners from Europe made their appearance. Initially they focused on producing food for passing ships, but before long they gave in to the temptation of colonizing. As scientifically and economically developed people, who took individual responsibility seriously, the Europeans regarded themselves as superior to the nature-loving, socially minded peoples of South Africa (Biko 1984: 29). Very soon, the threatened South Africans began protesting and raiding, and the Europeans took up their primitive guns.

Subsequent history contains innumerable accounts of suffering, exploitation and suppression. There were clashes and wars between white farmers appropriating more and more land, and black farmers trying to defend the land to which they belonged. The expansion of whites across large stretches of South Africa was accelerated when many Afrikaans-speaking whites moved away from the British government in the Cape and declared their own republics. The discovery of gold in one of those republics led to a war between the two groups of whites. Thereafter, however, the British were accommodating to their opponents and safeguarded white supremacy. British imperialism and Afrikaner nationalism were somehow patched together, but for the vast majority of South Africans an all-white 'Native Affairs Commission' drew up a 'native policy' which was a blueprint for a 'segregated' South Africa. The new 'Union' of South Africa (1910) was founded upon an old and widening rift between black originals and white colonials, and the scene was set for a century of struggle.

A joint forum for expressing African opinions and propagating African needs and aspirations was founded in 1912, and eleven years later its name was changed to the African National Congress (ANC). At first, the ANC leadership tried to win the acceptance of whites. A remarkable example of moderation and reasonableness was still found at the large All-African Convention of 1935. Owing to utterly unfair laws with regard to land allocation and voting rights, however, the separation and hostility between blacks and whites grew to alarming proportions.

In 1948, the Afrikaner National Party won the whites-only election on the policy of 'apartheid' ('separateness'), which was built on long-standing social practices, a belief in the racial superiority of whites and a fundamentalist 'theology' of divinely ordained separateness. In the same year, the ANC adopted a Programme of Action: boycotts, strikes and civil disobedience. The government implemented their policy through adding pivotal laws to all the segregation laws that were in place already.

An ANC ultimatum to repeal the laws was rejected with an urgent warning, and so a Defiance Campaign was launched. A Congress of the People adopted the Freedom Charter (1955), which envisioned a non-racial democracy, equal rights and opportunities, peace and friendship. After a non-violent Pass Law protest resulted in the Sharpeville massacre (1960), the ANC retained its commitment to non-violence, but allowed Nelson Mandela and other members to initiate an armed struggle. Umkhonto weSizwe ('Spear of the Nation') was formed and began focusing on sabotage and disruption.

The government responded with the first of many states of emergency, the banning of the ANC and other organizations, tighter legislation, numerous arrests and court trials. It tried to propagate 'separate development', a euphemism for 'apartheid', especially when South Africa began staggering under economic sanctions, disinvestment and sports boycotts. It took refuge in a tricameral parliament for whites, coloureds and Asians, independent states for African ethnic groups, and other cosmetic measures.

Eventually, however, early in 1990, Prime Minister F. W. de Klerk opened the parliament with an astonishing speech announcing the unbanning of the ANC and other organizations, and the release of Mandela and other political prisoners. A few days later, a dignified, smiling Mandela could leave twenty-seven years of imprisonment behind him and look forward to a promising future. Addressing the crowds in Cape Town, he expressed the hope that a climate conducive to a negotiated settlement would soon be created, so that the armed struggle would no longer be necessary.

The talks did get under way, and in spite of several problems a surprising degree of consensus was reached. An interim constitution was drafted in 1993, and the first democratic elections were held in April 1994. The ANC obtained just less than a two-thirds majority in parliament, and Nelson Mandela became the first president of a free South Africa. The new constitution was adopted in 1996, 'so as to heal the divisions of the past and establish a society based on democratic values, social justice and fundamental human rights ...' (Republic of South Africa 1996: 1).

That the new, democratic South Africa came into being without anything approaching a civil war, after the history of the preceding centuries and especially after the four decades of terribly unjust apartheid, was a miracle indeed!

For the challenging task of dealing with the past, in which such terrible social injustice had been inflicted upon black South Africans, and in which both the apartheid regime and the liberation movements had been accountable for horrendous events, a Truth and Reconciliation Commission (TRC) was created. As written into the name of the founding act of the TRC, the overarching task of the Commission was 'the Promotion of National Unity and Reconciliation' (Truth and Reconciliation Commission 1998: 106).

After the divided past of the old South Africa, which was socially engineered into two intermingled but different countries, there was a most urgent need for justice, truth, national unity and reconciliation. But, precisely because of the effectively enforced separatedness of the preceding decades and centuries, clashing views about all these concepts could be expected. What was therefore needed, from each of the two sides, was a frank discussion, prejudice reduction and tolerant receptiveness, so that mutual understanding and sufficient consensus might be reached, or at least approached.

Four notions of *truth* were distinguished: 'factual or forensic truth; personal or narrative truth; social or "dialogue" truth ... and healing and restorative truth' (ibid.: 110).

With regard to *reconciliation*, it was acknowledged that 'religious' people who were involved in exploiting other groups had 'given a bad name to reconciliation' (Boraine 2004: 69).

Although *justice* was not included in the name of the TRC, it was very much present between the words 'truth' and 'reconciliation'. Justice, in the general sense of fairness to all parties involved, was obviously adhered to consistently by the TRC. With regard to the granting or withholding of amnesty, justice was indeed sought, but mostly as an *ubuntu*-friendly restorative justice which could contribute to the rehabilitation of perpetrators and their reintegration into the new society (Truth and Reconciliation Commission 1998: 125–31).

About *national unity* there were no illusions, in the TRC or among the public, that it was an easily attainable short-term goal. What was fairly generally realized, however, was that the revealing of truth about the gross human rights violations of the past – the entire system of apartheid being recognized as one of those atrocities – could contribute to the creation of a culture of convergence between the previously racially segregated sectors of the population.

A few years after the conclusion of the work of the TRC, a survey was made 'to assess how ordinary South Africans view the truth and reconciliation process' (Gibson and Macdonald 2001: 2). Overwhelming majorities of black, coloured, Asian and white respondents (94, 86, 89 and 73 per cent, respectively) agreed that apartheid was a crime against humanity. Large majorities of every group seem to accept the presence of the other groups, but 'find it difficult to understand people of the opposite race, and substantial minorities (sometimes majorities) subscribe to negative racial stereotypes' (ibid.: 17). About growing reconciliation no firm conclusion could be reached, but what could be said was that most South Africans 'seem committed to a multi-racial South Africa, and many hold attitudes compatible with a harmonious future for the country. Few would have predicted such findings a decade ago' (ibid.: 18).

In May 2000 the Institute for Justice and Reconciliation was launched. This institute has already done, and is continuing to do, remarkable work to promote justice and reconciliation as 'two inseparable and equally important challenges facing our nation' (Institute for Justice and Reconciliation 2002). It has also extended its work into six other countries in Africa and some beyond Africa.

Addressing transition as a comprehensive process

Post-genocide Rwanda and post-apartheid South Africa are two representative examples of situations in which justice was urgently needed, after more violent or less violent conflict. From such situations, important lessons and recommendations can be derived.

In any critical situation, however, there is always the temptation to focus on procedures that seem to deserve priority on account of pragmatic, political, ideological or emotional considerations. Other aspects are sometimes also acknowledged, but are too often postponed or ignored.

It is therefore important that we should not limit our studying, thinking and debating to popular or average thoughts about transition and transitional justice. We may of course use a typical, ad hoc approach as a starting point, but from there we should explore the entire paradigm shift and mindset change required in a transitional situation.

Generally, the obvious starting point is the political transitions 'that confront societies as they move from an authoritarian state to a form of democracy' (Boraine 2004: 67). With regard to the ruling system and the rulers, the change usually has to be from autocracy by a despot or dictator, or oligarchy by a dominating elite or clique, to democracy by elected rulers who represent the population. With regard to the legal system, overruling of the law and violation of human rights mostly have to be replaced by entrenching the rule of law and observing human rights without compromise or prejudice.

Almost always, however, the political change has to be combined with socio-economic change, so that the transformation can be described as a comprehensive transition from an 'old order' to a 'new order' (Heyns and Stefiszyn 2006: 363). Socio-economically, transformation may be needed from a divisive situation of discrimination, oppression and disadvantaging to a more harmonious situation of equality, tolerance and fair sharing.

In all these fields, a good deal of transition can be implemented through structural changes, but attitudinal changes are also necessary. Exclusive structures have to be transformed into inclusive structures. But what is also needed is that exclusively minded individuals should become inclusively minded fellow humans. We cannot expect all the people concerned to internalize such a change of mindset, but a significant part may respond to the transformation of systems and structures and to the emerging climate of understanding, caring and sharing. Enough people may change their orientation from dealing with an unjust past to promoting a just future. Through radiating their influence, not so much deliberately but especially spontaneously, they may indeed contribute to creating a new society.

In Africa most societies have the great advantage of consisting of inherently socially oriented people, but unfortunately Africa is not exempt from the problem of self-seeking politicians (see Habimana 2001: 390). In Africa, therefore, the deeply rooted inclination towards the *restorative* component of transitional justice very often has to be complemented with an urgently needed *retributive* component.

In the early stages of a transitional period, previously wronged parties usually demand prosecutions and reparations in order to punish the wrongdoers and rectify the wrongs of the preceding conflict. At the same time or later, however, some, or all, parties may begin working towards 'societal stability, economic growth, cultural adjustment and related forms of transformation' (Heyns and Stefiszyn 2006: 364).

Transition is indeed a process during which people can become liberated from an old situation and take part in developing a new situation. It is actually a dual process of addressing remaining issues from a conflictual past and preparing the way for a coexistent future. According to the particular background histories, prevailing circumstances and future scenarios, the various groups concerned may prioritize and emphasize different projects.

It is understandable that people who suffered (or suffered most) under violations (or perceived violations) of their human rights tend to put the major emphasis on appropriately dealing with the past. People who have been wronged in such ways have enough reason to be very insistent and vociferous about punishing the perpetrators. The media are usually ready to publicize such demands prominently and increase their impact on the general public.

There are also the situations, however, in which the people who had been opponents in a conflict give priority to the need to move forward into a new future. Such an approach may be prompted by the realization that both sides were guilty of gross human rights abuses (Graybill 2004: 391). Or it may fit into a process in which a negotiated settlement was reached and in which the prospect of coexisting with each other was taken seriously.

The purpose of changing a conflict-causing situation While it is the case that transitional justice usually comes into effect *after* a conflict, it should not be forgotten that an anti-injustice conflict usually forms the climax of a period of opposition against the injustice concerned. In both Rwanda and South Africa, as discussed above, the critical, recent period was indeed preceded by centuries of strife.

It is therefore necessary to extend our thinking about transition far enough into the past and far enough into the future. It may be helpful and meaningful to take two dynamic aspects of a conflict situation into account, and to take them seriously: *the need or desire for change*, and *the goal of the envisaged change*.

It is general knowledge that when an individual or a group experiences, or perceives, a situation as unbearable, such an individual or group will want it to be changed. At the same time, however, the people responsible for the situation causing concern will want it to continue without change.

Bearing in mind the phenomenal diversity of human beings, both as individuals and as belonging to groups, it is understandable that appeals for change and actions to bring about change are so widespread and numerous. At the same time, however, we have to bear in mind the selfishness and own-groupishness of human beings, as well as other divisive traits of 'human nature'. And then we realize that each call for change and each claim for preserving the status quo has to be assessed objectively and honestly. Among the underlying motives there may be valid grievances, but there may also be plain greed.

In literature on dealing with conflict, and especially in training manuals, proper attention is usually given to the *causes* of tensions and conflicts. Unfortunately, however, very little if anything is said about the *purposes* of the conflicts arising out of the causes. A possible explanation for this vacuum may be that authors and trainers regard it as unnecessary to emphasize what should be obvious. After all, if social *injustice* is the cause of a conflict, it should be self-evident that the purpose of such a conflict will be social *justice*.

This may indeed go without saying, but specifically saying it may make important differences. First, it can remind everyone that a conflict is not just a random reaction, but one with a definite purpose. Second, it emphasizes the intended constructiveness of a conflict by highlighting the objective, which usually is a positive rectification of a wrong – at least as perceived by the aggrieved party. Third, it focuses the attention on the perspective of the party that felt so wronged that it initiated a conflict. Fourth, the human element is brought into the picture of the conflict concerned. While causes may merely be regarded as less desirable *phenomena*, purposes have a way of forcefully communicating the *aspirations* of fellow human beings. And finally, it provides a clear indicator that the eventual resolution of the conflict will become a reality only when the purpose has been reached.

We should have no illusions, however, that by taking the dynamics of change-oriented purposes into account, conflicts become easier to resolve. There are the cases where there can be no doubt about the kind of change needed. In apartheid South Africa, for instance, the following drastic changes had to take place:

- Unjust discrimination and inequality had to be replaced with social justice and equality.
- Unfulfilled needs had to be satisfied by a fair sharing of resources.
- Hurtful stereotyping, prejudice and non-recognition had to be changed into attitudes of non-stereotyping, recognition and acceptance.

In Rwanda, however, it was the purpose of the one side against the purpose of the other side. Each side's version was obviously based on their own view of the causes and the history of the conflict, in which the wrongs of their opponents were condemned and their own wrongs were either omitted or rationalized. Where conflict was caused by different and unacceptable values, the objective should have been to understand and tolerate. And where group-centred or self-centred greed for power was the problem, the objective should have been to arrive at a fair sharing of power.

The conflict and its resolution When a conflict has been satisfactorily resolved, the conflict itself can become part of a deplorable but understandable background, and wounds can be allowed to heal. The level of satisfaction of each party will depend, however, on the extent to which they have reached their purpose – either their original purpose or an adapted purpose they accepted during negotiations.

When parties are genuinely satisfied, psychologically, procedurally and substantially, with the talks and their outcome, the resolving of the conflict can indeed be regarded as an important part of the overall process of transition. If, however, one of the parties feels dissatisfied, the transitional task will be much more difficult, if not impossible.

After all, if an agreement is merely a superficial show and the conflict is just temporarily suppressed, it will be a futile attempt to embark on a 'post-conflict' transitional process.

The transformation of the entire situation When a situation has eventually been reached which can truly be called a *post*-conflict situation, it is understandable that most attention will be focused on the short-term past – the climactic part of the *conflict* with all its physical and structural violence – and that most demands will be for a rapid process of retributive justice. In such a situation, it is also understandable that those who suffered most will not be impressed by lectures on a comprehensive transition. They may fear that an idealistic long-term programme will place less emphasis on summary punishment of those who inflicted all the injustice upon them.

It may therefore be advisable to take immediate priorities seriously, but at the same time to promote ongoing commitments *and* to stress the importance of wider thinking wherever possible. Narrow-minded thinking should be avoided also when specifically focusing on dealing with the wrongs of an old order. Two examples may indicate the value of such open-mindedness.

In South Africa it was found inadequate simply to identify and punish direct perpetrators. Beneficiaries also had to be brought into the process. And when it came to pardoning perpetrators, it was accepted that beneficiaries should also be pardoned – individually and collectively.

In Rwanda, and other African countries, it became clear – at least to some open-minded thinkers – that there have been two kinds of old order in Africa. One was the domination by colonial powers, and the other the domination by military or tyrannical dictatorships, or by other types of authoritarian leadership.

When the risk is taken of thinking wider and further, ad hoc projects such as retributive justice are transcended and plans for forging a new future are explored. These may include a parting of ways – where this can indeed be an option – or a reasonable coexistence – especially where staying together is inevitable – and/or a definite orientation towards reconciliation.

One of the most essential components of such thinking is that transition is comprehensively envisaged as structural *and* attitudinal. What has to be left behind is not only authoritarian power-wielding and discriminatory practices but also divisive attitudes. And what has to be moved towards is not only democratic governance and observance of human rights, but also attitudes promoting coexistence.

This dual perspective is necessary because both ideologies – authoritarianism and democratism – are not only established in structures; they are implemented by individuals. And individuals function in accordance with their mindsets, which can range from unashamed self-aggrandizement to genuine caring for fellow humans.

It can therefore be said that when structures for the upholding of human rights, the rule of law and good governance are in place, transition has advanced to an important halfway mark. But then the other half of the transitional task still needs to be fulfilled as far as humanly possible. A supportive and empowering climate has to be created by propagating and promoting mindsets and attitudes of justice, fairness and cooperation.

Putting the possibilities of transitional justice into practice

Everything mentioned in the previous section may of course not apply to each situation where transition is needed. Nevertheless, it may be a valid generalization to say that when a transitional process is needed, it will almost always be a comprehensive one. It is, after all, usually a matter of moving from an old, exclusive politico-socio-economic monopoly of power-greedy politicians to a new, inclusive dispensation in which accountable leaders share the political, social and economic running of the country with the people.

For effective planning, it is essential to continually bear the enormity of the task in mind. If that is done, it should be recognized that transitional justice is an important item on the agenda, but that it happens to be *one* of several important items.

What also has to be borne in mind is that neither justice in general nor transitional justice in particular is a field that can be rushed into. There are questions that have to be asked and various replies that have to be interpreted and assessed before appropriate processes can be planned and undertaken.

When 'justice' in the sense of conformity to law has to be applied, questions about the origin of the law or laws concerned become relevant and can become problematic. Why, how, when and where was the law made? Who made it and who is bound by it? What should be done when parties from cultures with different legal systems are involved? Serious questions also arise with regard to the application of the law(s) concerned. How can the uniqueness of a similar but different 'case' be honoured? How can just, unprejudiced decisions be made?

When transitional justice has to be embarked on, a choice has to be made between various options. Crocker (1998: 10) correctly suggests that 'two extreme and opposite goals' seem to be 'morally defective and should be ruled out: revenge and "forgetting and moving on"'. Both of these options can hardly be regarded as versions of *justice*. Revenge may be seen as an attempt to take justice into one's own hands, and oblivion as an attempt to bypass justice. Two interesting examples of experiments with forgetting may be noted, however.

The first is the futile exercise of most South African whites, especially on the Afrikaans-speaking side, who showed disappointingly little interest in the TRC hearings (see Borris 2002: 174) and came up with the excuse that forgetting and carrying on would be better than reopening old wounds.

The second is the apparently successful experiment of neighbouring Mozambique – after almost three decades of war and violence. Sixteen years of civil war had left a million dead and thousands tortured, and included 'horrendous acts of barbarism' (Graybill 2004: 391). What happened, however, just ten days after the signing of the peace accord, was that the Frelimo government declared a general amnesty for acts committed by both sides during the war. Both sides knew very well how much they were accountable for and guilty of. Both sides had also learned how revenge can lead to counter-revenge and to a spiral of escalating retaliation. There were therefore 'no calls for justice, punishment or account-ability ... Rather, Mozambicans have decided to deal with the past through traditional African ceremonies of healing at the local level' (ibid.: 391).

It is between the extremes of revengefulness and forgetfulness that we then find the two best-known and most often used approaches of retribution and restoration. We should have no illusions, however, that when the extremes have been rejected, we are left with a simple choice between two options. After all, each of these options has inherent limitations that have to be tolerated.

Truth has to be searched for, but almost always it will be impossible to pen-etrate to all aspects of the truth and all perspectives on the truth (Borris 2002: 176; Boraine 2004: 68). Offenders have to be charged and tried, but in most cases of countrywide transition it will be impossible to prosecute all offenders (Boraine 2004: 67). Ideal plans for the process of transitional justice may be drafted, but too often the implementation may have to be slanted towards realpolitik, while ethical or other shortcomings will have to be connived at (Heyns and Stefiszyn 2006: 364; Mamdani 1998: 382).

Moving towards a conclusion, we may now summarize meaningful thoughts emerging from our examples and discussion of retributive and restorative transitional justice in Africa.

Possible procedures and possible outcomes of retributive justice In the field of applying criminal law, there are the options of international war crimes tribu-nals, foreign criminal trials and domestic criminal trials. For less than criminal offences, domestic civil suits may be considered (Crocker 1998: 5).

If more than one legal system is used in the same situation, the Rwandan ex-ample can be followed of categorizing levels of criminality and allocating particular levels to each of the systems. This will obviously require matching the criminality levels with the punishment levels mandated to each tribunal or court.

Investigatory procedures may be necessary, either in conjunction with some legal mechanism or, in less serious cases, on their own. Access may have to be gained or enforced to police, military or government records (ibid.: 5).

As in the case of Rwanda, it may be unavoidable to supplement formal litiga-tion with traditional ways of dealing with conflict and crime. When this happens, especially in an African context, it will usually have the effect of transcending the ordinary limits of retributive justice and moving into the dimension of restorative justice.

When only or mainly retributive justice is practised, outcomes such as the following may be reached:

- After thorough investigation and verification, and after fair trials, the per-petrators of gross human rights violations can be sentenced to appropriate punishment, which can include life imprisonment as a maximum sentence

(International Criminal Tribunal for Rwanda 2007). In the Rwandan case, the possibility of lighter punishment after confession of guilt was granted (Gasana et al. 1999: 166–7).

- In cases of damage to property (arson, killing of livestock, theft) suitable payment of reparation and/or compensation to victims or their families can be enforced (Crocker 1998: 5).
- Perpetrators, even if they were granted amnesty, can be banned from public office.
- Guilty institutions and structures can be identified and dismantled, and this can help to prevent the recurrence of similar human rights violations (Goldstone 1996: 371–2).
- Victims may not experience a process of healing, but may at least acquire due acknowledgement and possibly also a fair amount of satisfaction with the punishment of the perpetrators and the reparation they have received themselves.
- When through the revealing of truth during court cases the guilt is focused on individuals, the larger groups to which they belong, of which the majority may be innocent, are exonerated from collective guilt (ibid.: 370).
- As a by-product that can be of great importance in the new dispensation, the entrenching of the rule of law can be achieved.
- Due respect for the law can contribute to a curbing of criminal conduct.
- At any rate, a process of retributive justice may help to establish at least negative peace and at least a partial sense of closure.

Possible procedures and possible outcomes of restorative justice When a process of transitional justice is oriented towards restoration, the above-mentioned procedures and outcomes are not excluded. The difference will be, however, that the same things are done in ways that can contribute to a climate of reconciliation.

A mechanism for granting either general or individual amnesty can be put in place for both perpetrators and victims.

If individual amnesty is decided upon, a subcommittee of a truth and reconciliation commission, as in South Africa, or a separate amnesty commission can be mandated to assess applications and to grant amnesty where justified.

The most typical method of addressing the need for restorative justice is to entrust the task to a truth and reconciliation commission. On the one hand such a commission will do its best to let justice prevail, by granting pardon or ensuring that punishment is inflicted. On the other hand, such a commission will promote reconciliation and social harmony as far as possible.

While retributive justice is focused on perpetrators, restorative justice is focused on both perpetrators and victims, and particular attention is devoted to victims. Their needs are taken seriously. Their dignity is restored. Their reintegration in society is promoted.

When restorative justice is practised, outcomes such as the following may be expected:

- Truth is revealed about what actually happened and why it happened.
- Restoration, which mainly tends to be victim-friendly, is promoted in more than one way. Victims may feel satisfied and empowered by having their dignity restored and their identity, culture and gender rights recognized. Victims may also experience that more is done about their needs than just providing reparation or compensation.
- Important social processes can be initiated or promoted. Such processes are the transformation towards a new society, the restoring of social harmony and the promotion of at least political reconciliation but possibly also reconciliation at community level and reconciliation between perpetrators and victims (Truth and Reconciliation Commission 1998: 106–8).
- In addition to negative peace, as much positive peace as possible can also be established.

Promoting transformational transitional justice

In the first section of this chapter, retributive justice and restorative justice were called core options of transitional justice, but it was also emphasized that they are interrelated. The examples of Rwanda and South Africa showed that whichever of the two is given priority, the other also has to be taken into account. It is not a matter of an either/or choice; it is rather a both/and package.

We may therefore regard them as core *components* of transitional justice and even include them in our description of transitional justice. And to be in tune with the philosophy of Africa, in which human beings are put first and community-oriented action gets priority (see Biko 1984: 29), we may invert the order and put restorative justice first.

Transitional justice may then be described as the interrelated processes of restorative and retributive justice that usually play a crucial part in the period of politico-socio-economic transition between the resolving of a conflict that managed to oust an unjust authoritarian regime and the effective establishment of a new and just democratic dispensation.

If gross violations of human rights and/or war crimes were committed during the situation that caused the conflict and/or during the conflict itself, retributive justice of a criminal justice type will have to be applied. In all cases, however, much more is usually needed than the mere punishment of the wrongs of the past. Restorative structural and attitudinal transformation can lead to the best possible levels of coexistence and cooperation. Then transitional justice can more appropriately be called 'transformative' justice. '"Transition" refers to top-down processes ... Transformation on the other hand, calls upon a society to "reinvent itself"' (Wierzynska 2004: 389).

9 | Democracy and democratization in Africa

BELACHEW GEBREWOLD

Twelve of the twenty critical states in the world, according to the *Foreign Policy* Failed States Index of 2007, are in Africa and result from various factors: corruption and militarized politics and resource-based conflicts in Nigeria; concentration of power in the presidency and corruption in Angola; devastated democratic institutions and international isolation of Zimbabwe and Eritrea; political division and poor economic performance in Côte d'Ivoire; political and economic devastation in DR Congo; in Sudan conflicts based on Arabization and Islamization; post-1998 undemocratic Eritrea and Ethiopia; authoritarianism in Togo, Cameroon, Guinea, etc. – these are just some of the cases where conflicts, bad governance and undemocratic institutions are interacting. Most of the African states are characterized by state *dirigisme*; administrative ineptitude; overspending, wasteful practices, extravagance with public funds; many failed political and economic grand initiatives (Ayittey 2005: 307–16). Similarly, the Failed States Index enumerates some reasons for state failure: according to the magazine, 'the problems that plague failing states are generally all too similar: rampant corruption, predatory elites who have long monopolized power, an absence of the rule of law, and severe ethnic or religious divisions'. Strangely enough the magazine (deliberately or otherwise) presents these examples as if all the causes were internal. The role of global competition for resources such as oil, arms transfers, alliances with non-democratic governments, etc., are not given due consideration in the analysis as causes of the state failure.

According to Jean-François Bayart (Bayart et al. 1999), there are five symptoms that characterize current African political and economic situations: first, the relegation of sub-Saharan Africa in diplomacy, economics and finance (i.e. loss of diplomatic importance with an economic and financial crisis, caused by the devaluation of Africa in the estimation of great powers); second, the failure of democratic transition; third, the continuation and spread of armed conflicts in most parts of Africa; fourth, the recomposition of the subcontinent around new foreign influences and powers such as China and India; and fifth, the growing implication of African, Western and Eastern economic and political entrepreneurs based in Africa in activities which may be considered illegal or criminal, according to Western criteria (ibid.: 2–9). Ayittey suggests that the basic problem of Africa lies in the fact that there are three Africas that are constantly clashing.

The first is traditional or indigenous Africa that historically has been castigated as backward and primitive. Yet it works – albeit at a low level of efficiency. Otherwise, it would not have been able to sustain its people throughout the centuries. Today it is struggling to survive. The second Africa is the modern one, which is lost. The third is the informal sector, a transitional sector between traditional and modern. Most of Africa's problems emanate from its modern sector. They spill over onto the traditional, causing disruptions and dislocations and claiming innocent victims. Most Westerners generally have difficulty dealing with and reconciling these two Africas. (Ayittey 2005: 19–20)

In this chapter I attempt to address 'why Africa gets a hard time on its way towards democratization'. I argue that undemocratic institutions emerged in Africa because of metaphysical understandings of democracy and state. It is worth discussing the metaphysical aspect of democracy and ideology as something counterproductive to the 'idea of the state' (Clapham 1996). First I briefly discuss the concept of democracy and present the Deweyian and Rortian pragmatic concept of democracy as an alternative to the metaphysical concept of democracy. Following this the quality of governance and of democracy are discussed. Various challenges to, as well as the successes and failures of, the African democratization process are dealt with. It is not easy to cover this huge continent in one chapter, but I have attempted to discuss the most important cases.

Discussing democracy

Democracy is more than mere rituals of voting and elections (Kabongo 1986: 35). It is the plurality of opinions, freedom of expression, multi-party political system, political competition, free and universal multi-party elections (Chabal 1998: 295), fundamental and human rights, rule of law and accountability of the rulers which constitute democracy. This is more than mere majority rule, because even a majority can be a dictator (Tocqueville 1956: 112–27) over the ideational, ideological, racial, ethnic, lingual and religious minority. Thomson has summarized the constituent elements that are considered to be the most important for democratization. According to him, democratic consolidation needs a credible opposition; a strong civil society; strong economies; separation of state and ruling party; regime change through democratic elections; addressing the challenges of ethnic mobilization; dealing with the threat of the military; establishing political culture: shared political ideas, attitudes and belief that underlie a society (Thomson 2007: 236–44).

The quality and extent of democracy can be judged on the possibility of freedom and equality; the possibility of associating and communicating in public spheres, 'informed by liberal presuppositions, and governed politically by representative institutions based on wide suffrage and contested elections' (Mackie 2003: 1). Habermas suggests approaching democracy as a communicatively generated power and as deliberative politics (Habermas 1996: 27–8).

This is about public deliberation of matters of mutual concern to all (Benhabib 1996: 87). Since democracy is a public deliberation about common concerns, it is a symbol of freedom. But it also, at the same time, points to anxiety and agony (Parry and Moran 1994: 283). Pointing to this problem of democracy, Birch (1993: 47–8) argues that if we define democracy as the 'rule of the people', we will have problems because we have to define 'people' and 'rule'. Similarly, Robert Dahl (1989) argues that it has become self-evident that democracy means 'rule by the people', but who ought to comprise 'the people' and what does it mean 'to rule'? (ibid.: 3). This means that we have to define as well as agree on the definition. Who is entitled to define and how universally applicable is the definition? According to Benjamin Barber, 'democracy is the regime within which the struggle for democracy finds legitimacy – legitimates itself' (Barber 1996: 357). Birch concludes that 'we cannot arrive at an objective and precise definition of democracy' (Birch 1993: 48). Chantal Mouffe underlines the shortcomings of belief in objectivity or universalism and discusses a radical democratic politics for the sake of the multiplicity of the democratic demands (Mouffe 1996: 245).

In the meantime it seems to be widely accepted and self-evident that there is no alternative to democracy (Dahl 1989). The logical consequence is that democracy has to be spread everywhere. This presupposes two things: first, democratization is a deliberate action; second, there are areas that are not part of the idea of democracy. African state weakness or failure is usually attributed to the lack of democracy. But others argue that Africa has democracy albeit in a different form. Various African leaders tried to substantiate through various Africanist ideologies that there is already democracy in Africa. The *Pan-Africanism* of Nkrumah, *African Socialism* of Nyerere, *African Humanism* of Kaunda, *Négritude* of Senghor, *Authenticity* of Mobutu, etc., tried to demonstrate that there is already democracy in Africa, and argued that state-building as well as national political culture in the African states has to be based on African conceptions of democracy. But which are African democratic concepts? The 'village democracy' in which elderly *male* members of the village come together and conduct a long parley until they agree or solve a problem?

But there are at least three fundamental problems here: first, this palaver democracy mainly consists of men; second, the political system during the palaver democratic system is different from the 'modern' state-based political system; third, those who try to sell palaver democracy as the African way of democracy intend to prove to the Western world the 'African democratic civilization' and to disprove the Western superiority complex. This tedious attempt is itself the outcome of the inferiority complex of African intellectuals and political elites inculcated by the missionaries, colonizers and neocolonizers.

Various researchers have shown that democracy was already there in Africa when the colonizers came (Ayoade 1986; Molutsi 2004; Kabongo 1986; Mazula

2004; Magang 1986). Many African statesmen and intellectuals on the one hand advocated palaver democracy as an identity card of the African democratic culture, but on the other hand they adopted the Western state system created by the colonizers. This is a paradox with serious political consequences for Africa today. For example Nyerere (1971) (*ujaamaa*) as well as Nkrumah (1970: 69, 73–4) (communalism) thought that African communalism would be the best way to actualize socialism in Africa. They tried to integrate both the African (palaver democracy) and the Western (state system). The project failed. I argue that it failed because of the 'simultaneity of the unsimultaneous': the palaver democracy understanding does not fit into the Western state system. The option is: either we accept the Western state system and drop the palaver democracy, or we pursue palaver democracy as a political system but drop the Western state system. Who decides that? If African intellectuals or political elites are deciding which way to go, is that really democracy?

Kabongo argues that democratic systems functioned in Africa in the past and are functioning in the present, therefore democracy is not *intrinsically* alien to African people (Kabongo 1986: 35). Africa in the past refers here to the pre-colonial period in which the political system was different from the one introduced by the colonizers or 'civilizers'. A different political system presupposes a different democratic system or understanding. A local basic democracy was replaced by representative democracy. It was ironically a period of undemocratic political transformation. The relationship between the representatives and the represented was alienated geographically as well as emotionally because of the new political situation in a new and huge political community. This different political culture introduced by the colonizers superseded the existing democratic understanding, which was indeed deficient but at least applicable to the local system. Here my intention is not to idealize the former 'parochial' democracy, which was widely patriarchal, but the colonial democratic understanding did not perform better. Men and women were uprooted from their culture by the colonizers; patrimonialism increased; Africans were treated as subhumans without culture; inferiority complexes were inculcated; through the new political system the colonizers clothed as civilizers prevented local attempts to develop an indigenous democratic process.

Kabongo suggests that, 'A more pertinent question at this juncture to ask oneself is why the Western type of democracy has been so difficult to implement in the African context over the years, and what kind of democratic mechanisms are more suitable ...' (ibid.: 35). Kabongo attributes the failure of the Western democratic system in Africa to the 'artificiality' and 'sophisticatedness' of the former (ibid.: 36). But in my view the cause of the failure is that from the very beginning the project was misconceived and hampered by the cultural superiority complex of the West and the inferiority complex of the African political elites, as well as by the simultaneity of the unsimultaneous. This simultaneity of the unsimultaneous happens when the concept of democracy becomes something metaphysical and decontextualized.

The democracy concepts of John Dewey and Richard Rorty will help us to address this problem. Basically and helpfully, for Dewey and Rorty democracy is a non-metaphysical, pragmatic or contextual concept. According to Dewey, two elements of a democratically constituted society are: democracy as recognition of mutual interests; continuous readjustment through meeting the new situations produced by varied intercourse (Dewey 1955: 100). Dewey has suggested that 'a democratic society repudiates the principle of external authority, it must find a substitute in voluntary disposition and interest ... A democracy is more than a form of government; it is primarily a mode of associated living, of conjoint communicated experience' (ibid.: 101).

Dewey distinguishes between democracy as a social idea and political democracy as a system of government, although the two are of course interconnected. The former is a wider and fuller idea than can be exemplified in the state even at its best (Hickman and Alexander 2004: 293). Dewey contends that universal suffrage, frequent elections, majority rule and congressional and cabinet government are just devices to serve the purpose of meeting existing needs that are too intense to be ignored, rather than that of forwarding the democratic idea, which is metaphysical (ibid.: 294). These devices are adopted to help in justifying some particular practical polity struggling for recognition, even though they are asserted to be absolute truths of human nature or morals, final truths or dogmas (ibid.: 295). This metaphysical approach is the challenge for democracy. Democracy in Dewey's view is a consequence of a combined action of 'we', and this action is an object of desire and effort, not something metaphysical (ibid.: 296).

Dewey argues that 'two essential constituents in the older democracy theory were the notions that each individual is of himself equipped with the intelligence needed, under the operation of self-interest, to engage in political affairs; and that general suffrage, frequent elections of officials and majority rule are sufficient to ensure the responsibility of elected rulers to the desires and interests of the public' (ibid.: 298). For Dewey, absence of legal restrictions is not equal to democracy. Democracy becomes metaphysical and against freedom itself when the power-holders disguise their private advantages by all kinds of rationalizations. The power-holders can raise democracy to the level of religious idealization, reverence for established institutions, the constitution, the Supreme Court, private property, and so on. They do this usually by inducing in citizens fear that without these institutions life is threatened. What emerges is a religious aura that protects the institutions.

> The words 'sacred' and 'sanctity' come readily to our lips when such things come under discussion. If 'holy' means that which is not to be approached nor

touched, save with ceremonial precautions and by specially anointed officials, then such things are holy in contemporary political life ... The actuality of religious taboos has more and more gathered about secular institutions, especially those connected with the nationalistic state ... There is a social pathology which works powerfully against effective inquiry into social institutions and conditions ... which manifests itself ... in riotous glorification of 'things as they are', in intimidation of all dissenters. (ibid.: 302)

Dewey underlines the fact that democracy is a name for a life of free and enriching communion and communication which allows security for individuals and opportunity for their development as personalities (ibid.: 307). The fundamental principle of democracy is that the ends of freedom and individuality for all can be attained only by means that accord with those ends, since if democracy as an end limits the freedom of the citizens it is a paradox and self-negation of the democracy itself. Most of the African democratization processes failed because of these paradoxes. Right after independence, many African officials and intellectuals were led by a kind of intellectual hypocrisy and moral contradiction in their policy of at least 'temporary dictatorship' (ibid.: 338). A dictatorship that claims to operate on behalf of the oppressed masses while actually operating to wield power against the masses is a paradox. This is why, for Dewey, the 'end of democracy is a radical end. For it is an end that has not been adequately rationalised in any country at any time. It is radical because it requires great change in existing social institutions, economic, legal and cultural' (ibid.: 338-9). Dewey's democratic understanding is radical because it rejects any metaphysical foundations of democracy.

> For to get rid of the habit of thinking of democracy as something institutional and external and to acquire the habit of treating it as a way of personal life is to realise that democracy is a moral ideal and so far as it becomes a fact is a moral fact. It is to realise that democracy is a reality only as it is indeed a commonplace of living ... Democracy as compared with other ways of life is the sole way of living which believes wholeheartedly in the process of experience as end and as means ... The task of democracy is that of creation of freer and more humane experience in which all share and to which all contribute. (ibid.: 342-3)

Richard Rorty is another US philosopher who strongly rejects a metaphysical democracy concept. Rorty understands and frames democracy in the context of pragmatism and polytheism. His political-philosophical polytheism maintains that there is no actual or possible object of knowledge that would permit us to rank all our human needs. Our responsibility to others consists of permitting them as much space as possible to pursue their private concerns and to worship their own gods (Rorty 2007: 30). Rorty suggests democratic antifoundationalism. This means that democracy is not be conceived as something that exists independently of concrete and situational practices. Democracy cannot be studied without reference to special cases and times (Rorty 1996: 333). For Rorty, democratic politics as free consensus means to turn away from metaphysicians and physicists as monotheistic priest-substitutes, from anyone who pretends to tell how things *really* are (Rorty 2007: 30–31). He urges that democracy as pragmatism is 'inter-subjective agreement' (ibid.: 35). 'In a democratic society, everybody gets to worship his or her personal symbol of ultimate concern, unless worship of that symbol interferes with the pursuit of happiness by his or her fellow citizens' (ibid.: 40).

Quality of governance as a benchmark for the quality of democracy

Governance as the art and process of decision-making is the most important parameter for judging the quality of democratization. Recently (July 2007) the World Bank has published a study on worldwide governance indicators. The study measured six dimensions of governance:

1 *Voice and accountability:* the extent to which a country's citizens are able to participate in selecting their government, as well as freedom of expression, freedom of association, and free media;
2 *Political stability and absence of violence:* perceptions of the likelihood that the government will be destabilized or overthrown by unconstitutional or violent means, including domestic violence and terrorism;
3 *Government effectiveness:* the quality of public services, the quality of the civil service and the degree of its independence from political pressures, the quality of policy formulation and implementation, and the credibility of the government's commitment to such policies;
4 *Regulatory quality:* the ability of the government to formulate and implement sound policies and regulations that permit and promote private sector development;
5 *Rule of law:* the extent to which agents have confidence in and abide by the rules of society, and in particular the quality of contract enforcement, the police and the courts, as well as the likelihood of crime and violence;
6 *Control of corruption:* the extent to which public power is exercised for private gain, including both petty and grand forms of corruption, as well as 'capture' of the state by elites and private interests (Kaufmann et al. 2007).

Positive effects of these six criteria seem to be self-evident. But if we look at them carefully, government effectiveness does not necessarily mean that everyone profits from the economic performance and efficiency of government policy. Many people can live in poverty in spite of the effectiveness of the government and its economic policies. Similarly, there are various mechanisms to make a state look stable. A state can be without obvious violation of human rights or inter-ethnic or similar conflicts, and it can be stable; but this does not mean that a state is peaceful. Even where we cannot observe physical or direct violence in which civilians are killed, women are raped or children abused, as in DR Congo or Sudan, there are cases in which structural violence takes place, as in post-civil-war Angola, corrupt Nigeria or Gabon, where 15,000 (out of 1.5 million) people hold 80 per cent of the nation's wealth. Here, there is no physical violence but an appalling structural violence. Good governance study should include this phenomenon.

At the same time it is obvious that these indicators of good governance have impacts on political as well as economic development. It is not easy, however, to draw conclusions as to whether there is a positive correlation between democracy and economic growth. Of course, in the case of Botswana one could argue that successive democratic governments played a positive role in the country's economic performance (Molutsi 2004; Rotberg 2004). Mauritius, with its $13,700 GDP per capita, shows that there is a correlation between democracy and economic growth. Diamond suggests that Africa lags behind economically because it lags behind in governance (Diamond 2004: 267). But if we consider the economic growth in China, there is no necessary correlation between economic growth and democracy. This is a contentious issue which I cannot discuss in detail here.

Though donor agencies know that corruption is the bane of development and democracy in Africa, they are not willing to act accordingly. Various corrupt and undemocratic rulers in Africa – Biya of Cameroon, Eyadema of Togo, Mobutu of Zaire/Congo, Arap Moi of Kenya, etc. – have been supported by the West. Diamond maintains that:

> highly authoritarian and corrupt governments, in countries such as Cameroon, Angola, Eritrea, Guinea, and Mauritania, received levels of aid equalling or even well exceeding the African average of US$20 per capita. Almost all the authoritarian regimes, including those under international pressure for bad governance (such as Kenya and Zimbabwe), received aid well above the global average (US$11 per capita) in 2000 for low- and middle-income countries ... Africa needs a truly new bargain: debt relief for democracy and development for good governance. (ibid.: 272, 278)

Because of bad governance in Africa, African states and governments attract varieties of designations – 'vampire state' (Ayittey 1999: 157–8; 2005: 239); 'criminalised states' (Bayart et al. 1999); 'shadow state' (Reno 1995) – which imply the non-existence or weaknesses of states and governments.

The discussion about governance and quality of democracy leads us to some fundamental questions. What is government? What are its benchmarks? How can we gauge its quality? Answers to these questions depend on the definition of government one uses. Karl Deutsch defines government as the direction and self-direction of large communities of people. This self-controlling or self-steering of the community (city, state or nation) requires mastery of knowledge or techniques. According to Deutsch, there are four elements that constitute government, reflecting the type of governance: first, the manner of staying in control or in power; second, the basic nature and state of the country or organization being controlled; third, the limits and opportunities to cope with; and fourth, the intended results. Deutsch maintains that the art of government lies in combining these four kinds of knowledge and acting upon them (Deutsch 1974: 8–9). Most of the governments in Africa do not seem to be able to combine the four kinds of knowledge and implement them.

Gyimah-Boadi concludes that the general tendency in Africa to appoint incompetent persons to key bureaucratic and technocratic positions reflects the immaturity of African democratic systems and processes (Gyimah-Boadi 2004: 7–12). But Chabal suggests that some internal factors have caused the democratization process: 'the erosion of the legitimacy of the one-party state; the decline in all aspects of state capacity; the failure of development; the depth of economic crisis; and the strength of political protest and/or pro-democracy movements' (Chabal 1998: 291). According to Alex Thomson the democratization process in Africa in the early 1990s happened because of the state's loss of authority, i.e. its coercive power diminished, its co-option abilities were starved by lack of resources; a new international political environment emerged which reduced aid from international financial institutions and foreign governments; rejuvenation of civil society (churches, trade unions, ethnic associations, women's organizations, professional bodies, etc.) began to play a role. These developments were furthered by the wave of democratization on the global level, such as in eastern Europe since 1989 (Thomson 2007: 232–6). Similarly, according to Chabal, there were external factors that have been at least as important as the internal factors for the democratization process: first, emergence of a more conservative outlook on North–South relations in the West (especially by the Thatcher and Reagan administrations) and aid to Africa, which was accorded a lower priority, and support for one-party states; second, the widespread imposition of structural adjustment programmes; third, the collapse of communism and the end of the cold war (Chabal 1998: 293).

These developments towards democratization lead us to question what democracy or a democratic government is. Karl Deutsch has suggested that under a democratic government we understand that on the one hand the majority (directly or indirectly) makes or confirms laws and elects or confirms the government, its officials and its policies. But on the other hand the minority that disagrees today with these policies and laws should have the possibility of becoming a majority tomorrow. A political system can be designated as democratic only if a minority can remain free to express its views, to agitate for them, to organize and try to win converts to its side. According to this democratic concept, the minority must have this freedom not only in its own interest but also in the interest of every member of the majority. The benefit of the rights of the minority for the majority is that if minority views are silenced, the majority cannot compare its ideas, cannot learn new ones and cannot change its action. Democracy also means the possibility of the majority switching back and forth between majority and minority roles or situations (Deutsch 1974: 20).

> If so, they may find themselves in a minority on one specific issue but will get their way as a majority on some other, or they are now in a minority whose view may win majority support later. When the members of a minority group find themselves outvoted permanently and on most or all issues about which they care, then they may no longer see the prospect for political give-and-take – of reciprocity and change of roles – as realistic. When this happens, the minority status of the group has become diffuse oriented to many issues [or almost all issues] and permanent; their identification with the larger democratic community will be weakened, and their feelings of legitimacy and loyalty toward it may become severely strained. The outcome of such a development may be an effort on the part of the minority at secession, revolution, or rebellion ... (ibid.: 20–21)

From the background of the flexibility of the border between minority and majority, a legitimate and stable democracy in the eyes of the entire population is gauged by the performance of the political system, which consists of effectiveness (making an unlikely outcome more likely to happen) and efficiency (how the benefits outweigh the costs) (ibid.: 230). The flexibility between the state of minority and majority leads us to the fundamental quality of democracy. Democracy is a process, not an end state. Democracy is not an apocalyptic promise fulfilled after evil is defeated. Democracy is a point of departure, the way as well as the goal. Mansfield and Snyder (1995: 50) suggest that democratization is a rocky transitional period during which there will be reversals. Further, they conclude that violence is concomitant to the democratization process or democratic transition (ibid.: 12–15).

Various African and non-African politicians and researchers have argued that Africa is not ripe for democracy. This assertion is against the concept of democracy. To suggest that Africa is not ripe for democracy is to legitimize or justify violence that takes place in the 'course of democratization'. There is no goal or ideal that would justify violence against the poor or rich. The quality of democracy depends on the state of cultural, structural or physical violence against the poor and marginalized. Ethiopia and Kenya are two of the best recent examples of democratization and violence. After the 15 May 2005 elections the Ethiopian government perpetuated the border between majority and minority by not accepting the huge move of the votes from the EPRDF majority to the opposition minority. The ruling majority remains always the same majority, and the opposing minority remains always the same opposing minority. After the 27 December 2007 elections, Kenya followed the same example. In the post-election period hundreds of civilians were killed by the police as well as by the inter-ethnic violence, and thousands more were chased out of their homes by mobs made up of former neighbours.

Challenges to democratization in Africa

Factors that exacerbate poverty and inequality and challenge the establishment and consolidation of democracy in Africa include: centralized governments, personalized powers, ethnicized politics and lack of transparency and accountability. This lack of accountability consists of lack of answerability (public officials informing and explaining to the public what they are doing) and enforcement (accounting agencies imposing sanctions against the violators) (Kpundeh 2004: 121–3).

Ethnicity The one-party state in Africa did not allow the articulation and functioning of the majority–minority relations that Deutsch has analysed. According to Alex Thomson (2007), the causes of, or arguments for, one-party state (centralization) in Africa were: a multi-party system would be socially divisive (K. Nkrumah); no opposition actually existed in Côte d'Ivoire (Houphouet-Boigny); socialist ideology needed a one-party system (Sekou Touré); a one-party system was most appropriate for democracy in Africa (J. Nyerere). Many Africans and non-African intellectuals argued that there is no reason why Africa should imitate the Western political culture (multi-party system).

It is one of the common arguments that bad governance in Africa is at least partially caused by ethnicized political culture. This type of political culture based on ethnic alliances is usually criticized and rejected as irrational. But Berman (2004: 51) suggests that 'ethnic patron–client politics is not quite the same thing as corruption, although both involve appropriation of public resources for private purposes'. Clientelism is based on structural inequality within an ethnic group or between ethnic groups and on reciprocal differentiation of authority and loyalty; but it also implies shared identity. This shared ethnic identity implies mutual expectations and affective trust politically, economically and morally (ibid.: 51).

Berman et al. not only suggest that an ethnicized political clientelism is not necessarily a synonym for corruption, but also maintain that ethnic pluralism is and will remain a fundamental characteristic of African modernity which must be recognized and incorporated within any project of democratic-nation-building (Berman et al. 2004: 3). 'There is little doubt that the wave of "democratisation" in Africa since the 1990s has seen an increase rather than decrease in the visibility of ethnic politics and conflict' (ibid.: 9). Further, a rigid focus on ethnicity as the main cause of corruption and clientelism is not necessarily appropriate because even within a single ethnic group there are subcategories based on kinship or membership of an extended family. Berman et al. suggest that competition for power between elites of the same ethnic communities plays a decisive role in the process of governance and democratization. Elites of ethnic communities are never homogenous. There are symbols, grievances and expectations that are marshalled by elites to foster political consciousness of some of the members of the ethnic group while excluding some members and elites in the same community (ibid.: 10).

Berman et al. suggest that ethnicity is a decisive reality in African culture and politics. Ethnicized politics constructs a kind of iron curtain between the ethnic groups by primordializing ethnicity and ethnic differences. If ethnic differences are primordialized the differences between minority and majority are also primordialized. Ethnic differences in Ethiopia, Sudan, Nigeria, Rwanda, Burundi, etc., are primordialized by perpetuating the majority–minority relations. This is not only a decisive cause of conflict, but also a major hindrance for democratization, as Karl Deutsch has suggested.

Since ethnically divided societies in all African countries were perceived as a danger to state integrity, strong leadership has been demanded as indispensable for economic development and political stability (Thomson 2007: 110–11). But single-party structure encouraged corruption and an exploitative bureaucratic bourgeoisie and subordinated 'peripheral' state institutions (parliaments) to the core executive (government) (ibid.: 112–13). 'In a political environment where executives were so powerful, laws became arbitrary. Politicians and bureaucrats felt disinclined to obey the constitution if their private interests were threatened. Laws became less binding on those who ran the state, while those in civil society were still expected to conform' (ibid.: 114).

Friedman points out that threats to democracy in South Africa still exist, such as re-racialization of politics in the 1999 election campaign; the unassailable electoral majority of the ANC; race as the key determinant of party affiliation and electoral choice. Political debates are being increasingly polarized: whites search for faults in the black government, whereas government officials dismiss whites' criticisms as racism (Friedman 2004: 236). Cheryl Hendricks argues that even if ethnic identities are socially constructed, they become real for their bearers and have consequences. In the South African case they have become an 'institutionalised difference' (Hendricks 2004: 113, 126). Because of the unassailable majority of the ANC, democracy in South Africa is seen as threatened. In spite of these dangers, the black-dominated South African government has demonstrated that the myth that African governments are incapable of managerial efficiency is baseless (Friedman 2004: 236–7).

A stable democratic society, rule of law and economic development can happen in Africa only if there is a strong civil society, a private sector and a political society. Civil society means more or less autonomous associations, not state controlled, 'that capture the private concerns of social forces and condense and transmit them to the public sphere of politics' (Mazula 2004: 183). A political society exists if state and political parties adjust to the social and economic norms, in conditions of market economy and civil society, multi-party parliament, independent media and a proliferation of NGOs. In his studies on civil society Mazula shows us that there were 427 NGOs in Mozambique in 2000. According to Mazula, the stability of Mozambique since the Peace Accord of 1992 results from the combination of these factors (ibid.: 195–6). The contributions of civil society are: to help pry open authoritarian systems; limiting the power of the state and challenging abuses of authority, monitoring elections and enhancing the credibility of the democratic process; educating citizens and building a culture of tolerance and civic engagement, incorporating marginal groups and enhancing responsiveness; providing alternative means for material development; opening and pluralizing the flow of information; building a constituency for economic and political reforms. African civil societies are severely constrained by extremely weak material bases, and rely on the state and international donors. Because of the state dependence the civil societies compromise their autonomy and are co-opted by undemocratic regimes, which further distorts their accountability (Gyimah-Boadi 2004: 100–08).

Corruption Economists suggest that even if Africa's economic prospects are very promising for the first time since the 1970s, with 5.5 per cent GDP growth in 2006, projected to hit 6.2 per cent in 2007, Africa's image is shattered by corruption, poor economic performance and weak competitiveness. Economic data suggest that just 3 per cent of global foreign direct investment flowed to sub-Saharan African in 2005, whereas most of the money has gone to only a handful of resource-rich countries like South Africa, Nigeria and Angola. Only 22 per cent of African households benefit from a power supply. The number of mobile phone subscribers in Africa, which soared by over 50 per cent in a year, is, however, expected to boost the African economy (Green 2007: 48).

Corruption in Africa increases the costs of goods by up to 20 per cent, deters investment and impedes growth by 0.5 per cent (Lockwood 2006: 66). Corruption and undemocratic institutions in most African states have increased the continent's current indebtedness by $300 billion. Nigeria's $400 billion in oil revenue since the early 1970s, crude oil output of 2.1 million barrels per day and about 184 trillion cubic feet of natural gas reserves should have made Nigeria one of the most stable and richest countries in Africa. Their failure to do so is caused by such factors as $35 billion of foreign debts, 60 per cent of its population living below the poverty line, and a life expectancy of forty-seven years. Nigerian rulers between 1960 and 1999 stole $400 billion in oil revenues. This economic exploitation and corruption in Nigeria was accompanied by a civil war that killed a million people, thirty years of military rule and six coups (Perry 2007: 26; Smith, D. J. 2006). This structural injustice and exploitation have left two-thirds of the country's 135 million people in poverty, a third in illiteracy and

40 per cent without a safe water supply, together with environmental damage caused by spillover of more than 1.5 million tons of oil over fifty years in the Niger Delta, which is one of the most polluted places on earth. It is estimated that corruption costs Africa $148 billion per year.

Gabon's Libreville ranks among the top ten most expensive cities in the world; 15,000 people in Gabon hold 80 per cent of the nation's wealth; four-fifths of the country consists of rainforest and it has coastal waters full of fish, but nearly all of the country's food is imported from Europe (Perry 2007: 28). States such as Kenya, Angola and Chad are also affected by the high level of corruption in Africa. Angola's economy is expected to grow by 27 per cent this year. Nigeria in 2006 was the twelfth-largest oil producer. Gabon's wells are slowly drying up but it is one of the major oil producers. Angola is the second-largest oil producer in sub-Saharan Africa, and production is growing by 25 per cent a year, mainly because of China (ibid.: 25). China is always ready to offer money to corrupt countries such as Angola if its oil interests are at stake – it offered $2 billion credit in 2004 without particular requirements of democracy and good governance, and announced in 2005 and 2006 an additional $3 billion in loans. 'Well-connected businessmen and unscrupulous government officials grow impossibly rich, and the ruling elite uses its wealth and largesse to consolidate its own power.' In spite of the $10 billion in oil revenues in 2005 alone, 70 per cent of Angolans still live below the poverty line (ibid.: 25–6).

I have discussed the challenges to democracy in Africa. These include patronage politics, corruption, neopatrimonialism, ethnicization of political alliances, elections marred by violence, rigged elections or a pseudo-multi-party system, manipulations of the constitution and frequent postponement of elections. Such political cultures hinder the emergence of any viable democratic institutions and culture. At the same time it has to be stressed that the emergence of viable democratic institutions and culture by getting rid of these challenges depends not only on the goodwill of the national political actors but also on a genuine will of the international actors or international system in Africa. Unfortunately, the international system has been contributing to anti-democratic systems on the continent.

Anti-democratic international system While discussing problems of democracy in Africa it is important to take into account the global systemic problems of democracy and governance. On the global level there are very often policies that are selective and at times selfish and contradictory. Selectivity refers to the concentration of criticism on some fraudulent elections in Africa (such as in Zimbabwe in 2002) while virtually ignoring others, such as in Zambia (November 2002) and Madagascar (December 2001). In the 'fight against global terror' external powers like the USA are guided by selfish interests rather than a desire for engagement in global democracy or good governance. Since the US bombings in Nairobi and Tanzania in 1998 Kenya has become one of the key US allies in Africa. In the context of the US-led 'war on terrorism' and the search for Islamic militants in eastern Africa, the USA as well as the UK ignored then president Daniel Arap Moi's poor human rights record in favour of renewing a military cooperation agreement that allowed British troops to use bases in Kenya. In the Great Lakes region, there have been cases of pushing for peace in the DRC but without openly criticizing leaders in friendly states, such as Yoweri Museveni of Uganda and Paul Kagame of Rwanda, for their involvement in the war (Paul Williams 2004: 48–9). Between 1965 and 1997 Mobutu was supported by various international actors in spite of the fact that he economically depleted and undermined all democratization moves.

Oil-producer regions of Africa belong to the 'strategic national interest' of the USA. Warships patrol off West Africa, and there are demands for a permanent military base in the region, such as a separate US African Command. Whereas Nigeria supplies 10–12 per cent of US oil imports, the Gulf of Guinea will supply 20–25 per cent of total US oil by 2010 (Perry 2007: 24). Angola supplies 47 per cent of Africa's oil exports to China, followed by Sudan (25 per cent), the DRC (13 per cent), Equatorial Guinea (9 per cent) and Nigeria 3 per cent (Broadman 2007: 81). Russia, Japan and India are increasingly interested in the oil of Equatorial Guinea, Cameroon, Chad and the DRC. The Gulf of Guinea will earn $1 trillion from oil by 2020 (ibid.: 24). These countries are neither politically stable and democratic nor institutionally strong.

Successes and failures in the African democratization process

Chabal suggests that in the years 1989–94 most African countries began to move towards multi-party democracy and away from single-party political systems (Chabal 1998: 290). Political developments such as democratization since the beginning of the 1990s have been dubbed as a 'second liberation' caused by the end of some single-party political systems and military dictatorships, such as in Ethiopia and Eritrea, starting in 1991 (Gyimah-Boadi 2004: 6). Even Mobutu claimed to be moving towards the democratization process in 1992. Apartheid came to an end in 1994. Liberal democratic constitutions in countries such as Benin (1990), Mali (1992), South Africa (1994), Ghana (1993), Malawi (1994), Nigeria (Third Republic in 1993, Fourth Republic in 1999), Ethiopia (1995) and Eritrea (1997) began to change the democratic face of Africa. Civil society and parliaments began to perform in political arenas (ibid.: 6–7). Gyimah-Boadi argues that some basic conditions for the establishment of rule-based governments and states are increasingly introduced; official arbitrariness is being reduced; human rights are increasingly enjoyed; corruption is more and more addressed; constitutional documents are becoming the normative point of reference for African politicians; mass media are expanding, though confined to urban areas.

There are some democratically *well-performing* countries in Africa. Though the ethnic violence between Inkatha/Zulu and ANC supporters marred the first democratic elections campaign of 1994 in South Africa, the elections in 1999 happened peacefully. According to Marks, some of the positive factors that contribute to the peace between the ANC and Inkatha are that the apartheid 'divide and rule' strategy came to an end; even the formerly hostile anti-Inkatha youths began to approach the traditional Zulu leaders; there was good diplomatic progress between the ANC leaders and the Inkatha, a lack of external support for Inkatha, international recognition of the new South Africa and high sympathy for Mandela in particular on the international level (Marks 2004: 194–9).

An active free press, an independent judiciary, respect for human rights on the part of the authorities and lack of corruption render Botswana and Mauritius exemplary democracies in Africa. Botswana is usually considered as one of the few African success stories, politically as well as economically. Some factors that contributed to democracy and development in Botswana are: historically, the protectorate established in 1891 was negotiated between the British government and individual chiefs; ethnocultural homogeneity; 'getting the politics right', i.e. continuous, overlapping policies with successors following in the footsteps of their predecessors with a stable party and leadership (the Seretse Khama period, 1965–80; Ketumile Masire, 1980–98; Festus Mogae since 1998) (Molutsi 2004: 160–70). Namibia is a democratic and human-rights-respecting state, even if SWAPO has dominated politics since independence in 1990.

There are a good number of democratically *promising* countries. When Ghana's President Rawlings stepped down in 2000, the current government of President Kufuor, of the opposition NPP (New Patriotic Party), was elected, first in December 2000 (with 57 per cent of second-round votes) and again in December 2004 (with 53 per cent of second-round votes). Not only on the governmental but also on the legislative level the NPP dominates Ghanaian politics. As well as politics, the human rights record in Ghana also seems to be good. Similarly, presidential elections, which took place on 5 March 2006, and parliamentary elections held in March 2007 witnessed promising democratization progress in Benin. Proliferation of political parties, a vibrant independent press, powerful trades unions, civil society, some five thousand local NGOs, including human rights groups operating freely without government interference, characterize politics in Benin. In Zambia, by regional standards, neither the democratization process nor the human rights record are particularly bad. In the 2006 elections, a serious but democratic challenge from Michael Sata's Patriotic Front confronted Levy Mwanawasa's Movement for Multi-party Democracy (MMD), but in the end Mwanawasa secured 43 per cent of the popular vote against Sata's 29 per cent. On 1 October 2007, however, Mwanwasa threatened those who oppose plans for a new constitution with treason charges, which is an undemocratic democratization.

Senegal used to be one of the stable countries in Africa; the tumultuous elections of February 2007 have shown, however, that this can change. The tradition of democracy in Senegal has been a rare model but fights between supporters of President Abdoulaye Wade and those of his former prime-minister-turned-rival, Idrissa Seck, before the elections on 25 February 2007, overshadowed the Senegalese democratic record of remaining stable despite its religious and ethnic heterogeneities. In the weeks before polling for the February elections, police used teargas to disperse protesting oppositions, critics of Wade received death threats, and votes were rigged.

Uganda's political system since 1986 has been known as the 'no party' political system, or Movement System. Uganda's 1995 constitution provided, however, for political participation. The Movement System was endorsed by 91 per cent of voters in the referendum of 2000. But since the turnout was low and the pro-multi-party side had limited opportunities to present their case it cannot be designated as entirely democratic. The 2001 elections were marred in some places by violence and intimidation, which sent Dr Kizza Besigye into exile for four years in South Africa. Museveni orchestrated a parliamentary move in August 2005 to lift the constitutional two-term limit. Consequently, in the February 2006 elections, which the EU Observation Mission and the Commonwealth Observer Group concluded were free and fair, despite identifying significant flaws in the campaign process, Museveni won 59 per cent of the vote, whereas Dr Kizza Besigye of the main opposition group, Forum for Democratic Change (FDC), gained 37 per cent, and now controls 37 out of 215 parliamentary seats. Uganda still has reasonably free media, however, and the human rights record has improved enormously since Museveni came to power in 1986.

Though a large number of different ethnic groups comprise the population, and despite the Chama Cha Mapinduzi (CCM – 'Movement for the Revolution') remaining the overwhelmingly dominant force, Tanzania is one of the more peaceful, stable and relatively democratic countries in Africa. Sometimes, however, violent conflicts between the CCM and the Civic United Front (CUF) (with a strong power base on Zanzibar – most notably the island of Pemba) have affected not only political stability but also the democratization process. Violence, intimidation and serious allegations of vote rigging overshadowed the 1995 and 2000 elections. The rest of the opposition seems to be weak and divided. In May 2005 CCM's Kikwete comfortably won the election, securing 80 per cent of the vote.

Madagascar seems to have recovered from the presidential elections of December 2001 that pitched the country into crisis when the supporters of Ratsiraka and Ravalomanana became embroiled in a period of civil unrest that lasted for several months. But Madagascar's High Constitutional Court carried out a recount of the first-round votes and declared Ravalomanana the winner in April 2002. Neither the December 2006 presidential elections (which granted President Ravalomanana a second five-year term) nor the legislative elections of 15 December 2002 (which enabled President Ravalomanana's TIM to control 102 out of 160 seats) led to similar crises.

Sierra Leone's presidential and parliamentary polls of 11 August 2007 were designated as free, fair and credible – at least partly thanks to the great job done by Christiana Thorpe, chief electoral commissioner – as a continuation of the democratization process that started in 2002 when a ten-year civil war that began in 1991 and killed 50,000 people came to an end. Whereas Rwandan politics is still strongly ethnicized, the 'power-sharing politics' of Burundi is trying to overcome the Hutu–Tutsi hatred (Lemarchand 2007: 1–20), and large numbers of Tutsi have been joining previously Hutu parties.

There are *crippled democracies* in Africa, mainly resulting from corruption. Angola is one of the most highly corrupt states in Africa. New election laws were passed in April 2005 which gave the Angolans the hope that elections would take place no later than September 2006. On the contrary, voter registration started only in November 2006, and the legislative elections are expected to take place in 2008, with presidential elections in 2009 (Transparency International 2007). Angola and Nigeria have some similarities: dominant oil economies and corruption. According to Abgaje, even the 1999 Constitution of the Fourth Republic of Nigeria is fundamentally flawed and fraudulent, 'given the fact that the final version of the document was authored by a few military officers in the countdown to the Fourth Republic' (Abgaje 2004: 209). Moreover, the constitution has bestowed upon the president legislative powers; it is centralistic, favouring federal government over states and local governments (ibid.: 209–12). Abgaje concludes that 'an enduring legacy of the many years of undemocratic rule (colonial, military, and civil) to which Nigeria and Nigerians have been exposed is a deep-rooted militarization of the socio-cultural landscape' (ibid.: 220).

Abgaje suggests that key challenges for Nigeria are: managing ethnic conflicts, regional and religious tension; managing Nigeria's size, resource endowment and economic development; addressing corruption and rent-seeking practices (ibid.: 205). Mustapha underlines the important aspect that inter-ethnic as well as intra-ethnic sectarian processes threaten democracy and Nigerian unity (Mustapha 2004: 257). Even the April 2007 presidential elections in Nigeria are widely considered as undemocratic. Olusegun Obasanjo paved the way for the victory of his favoured candidate, Umaru Yar'Adua, in the 21 April 2007 elections (Perry 2007: 26).

Egypt, Libya, Morocco and Ethiopia have been *bypassed by the democratization* process. Egypt's undemocratic politics can be traced to the fear of terrorism. It is not just Islamist parties such as the Muslim Brotherhood which are banned, however; all religious parties are prohibited under the constitution, and even secular parties are subject to restrictions. By taking advantage of the fear of terrorism, President Mubarak has held on to power since 1981. Libya is an authoritarian state led by Colonel Muammar Abu Minyar al-Qadhafi. Morocco is a constitutional monarchy with an undemocratic record, but the political system is evolving from a strongly centralized monarchy to a parliamentary system. The election of 7 September 2007 was considered transparent, and the entire election campaign was professionally organized; the voter turnout of about 37 per cent was, however, a historic low. Ethiopia was for years one of the African darlings of the West. During the general elections of 15 May 2005 the public support for opposition parties became very clear. This support resulted in deterioration of the political atmosphere and the arrest of a number of opposition leaders, civil society representatives and journalists for alleged roles in stimulating violent protests in November 2005. The unrest triggered after the election of 27 December 2007 has not only killed hundreds, displaced thousands and ignited inter-ethnic conflict but has also substantially damaged the democratization process in Kenya and its image on the international stage.

Countries such as Burkina Faso, Cameroon, Côte d'Ivoire, Togo and Guinea have gone *astray from democracy*. Burkina Faso's Compaore believes he alone guarantees political stability and economic progress, and he stood for a third term in the presidential elections of 13 November 2005, which he won with 80.3 per cent of the vote against eleven other candidates. In the name of this stability opposition parties are often harassed. After the 22 July 2007 elections in Cameroon, a country in which opposition to Paul Biya is limited, Biya's Democratic Rally of the Cameroonian People party holds 149 of the 180 seats in parliament. The leader of the opposition SDF party, John Fru Ndi, called the polls 'a sham' marred by fraud, and fears that the ruling party might try to use its two-thirds majority in the assembly to amend the constitution to allow Biya, already head of state for twenty-five years, to seek a new term in 2011. Moreover, in the municipal polls, the governing party won 303 out of 363 communes. Togo has been known as one of the dictatorial states in Africa, especially until President Eyadema Gnassingbe died on 4 February 2005. His son, Faure Gnassingbe, won the presidential election of April 2005, which the opposition condemned as rigged, but the African Union and ECOWAS accepted this result and urged Gnassingbe to include members of the opposition in the new government. Togo had an appalling human rights record under Eyadema.

The Central African Republic (CAR) and Chad are two examples of uncontrolled states and non-existent democracies. CAR is politically unstable, affected by the conflicts in Sudan and Chad, and government authority barely extends outside the capital. It is dependent on French army support, not on the democratic sanction of the population; human rights are abused by the security forces, which are rarely under the full control of state authorities. In Chad, Idriss Deby stood for a third term as president in elections on 3 May 2006 after having successfully orchestrated the removal of presidential term limits through a referendum in June 2005, and won a new mandate with 64.67 per cent of the vote, which was boycotted by the main opposition parties.

The incursions by rebels in Guinea's border regions with Liberia and Sierra Leone since September 2000 have claimed more than a thousand lives and caused the displacement of thousands of the population. In late 2001 President Conte proposed to extend his presidential term, which contributed to further escalation of the conflict. Even though the agreement in March 2002 between Guinea, Sierra Leone and Liberia, on measures to secure mutual borders and to tackle insurgency, eased the relations between these neighbouring countries, the detainment and suppression of opposition within Guinea has remained an unresolved internal problem. Elections boycotted by the opposition parties in 2003, assassination attempts against the president in 2005, crippling general strikes since 2006 and the declaration of a state of emergency on 13 February 2007 have made Guinea one of the most out-of-control states in Africa.

In Côte d'Ivoire, after the conflict divided the country into north and south, a buffer zone between the two sides was created. On 27 March 2007 the two sides agreed to appoint the prominent rebel leader Guillaume Soro to the position of prime minister. On 30 July 2007, when President Laurent Gbagbo set foot in the north for the first time since rebels occupied it in 2002, he declared, 'The war is over!' For Soro, Gbagbo's presence in Bouake, the former rebel stronghold, sealed the reunification of the country. We have to wait and see whether the peace process will lead to a sound democratization process.

Somalia is a political *vacuum*. Somalia collapsed in 1991. In 2000 the Transitional Government of Somalia, and towards the end of 2004 the Transitional Federal Government of Somalia were created, but were not successful, mainly because of the influx of arms as regional states such as Ethiopia, Eritrea, Yemen, Syria, Saudi Arabia and Iran, and many other Middle East countries, support various factions not only financially but also with weapons (Menkhaus 2006/7: 74–106). There is no functioning democracy and the human rights situation is appalling.

Zimbabwe and Eritrea have taken a path from democracy to *dictatorship*. With unemployment at 80 per cent, by November 2007 Zimbabwe's inflation had reached 85,000 per cent. More than 80 per cent of the population are living below the poverty line, and with a life expectancy of thirty-five years, Zimbabwe is probably the worst-performing country in the world. Hundreds of thousands of Zimbabweans were made homeless in the government's Operation Murambatsvina or 'urban clean-up' campaign of 17 May 2005, designed to destroy slums in the cities where both opposition to the government and informal economies flourish; in addition, economic mismanagement, official corruption, ethnic favouritism and political intimidation thrive. The 'clean-up operation' could bring forth very short-term solutions but the fundamental problem of lack of democracy and devastating economic mismanagement are still there, and the 'clean-up' operation was opposed by about 70 per cent of Zimbabweans (Bratton and Masunungure 2007: 43–4). Draconian media laws curtail the media, reduce access to information and restrict protection of privacy, because the media, like foreign interventions, are seen as a threat to national security (Ronning 2003: 196–221). Mugabe has support from the Eastern world (in particular China) and fellow Africans. Even though the current chair of the African Union and Ghanaian president John Kufour has described the situation in Zimbabwe as 'embarrassing', African leaders are mixed in their condemnation of Mugabe, and neither the 'big player', South Africa, nor the SADC are willing to put pressure on Mugabe, the former anti-apartheid hero. In the meantime Zimbabwe has become the symbol of authoritarian state ideology and the democratic agenda of a multifaceted civil society (Ronning 2003: 221). In March 2002 Mugabe stole the elections; he and his media denigrated Tsvangirai as 'tea boy'; opposition supporters were hunted down; 'party cards' determined the safety of most Zimbabweans; criticizing the president was forbidden; the commander of the defence force, General Zvinavashe, declared that the army would not give support if anyone other than Mugabe won (Meredith 2003: 225–36). Critics of Mugabe in Zimbabwe and from outside hoped for a lot from the SADC summit of 30 March and 17 August 2007, but the issue of Zimbabwe did not play any significant role during the meeting.

Eritreans hoped that after independence in 1993 their country would become one of the most democratic and prosperous in Africa. Eritrean politics are completely militarized, however; the constitution ratified in 1997 has not been implemented on the grounds that Eritrea's priority is the war with Ethiopia, not democratization (Mengisteab and Yohannes 2005: 131–60); the economy has been destroyed and the country is becoming increasingly isolated both regionally and internationally. It is estimated that every month between four hundred and six hundred Eritreans flee poverty and conscription through the dangerous Sudanese deserts, mainly towards Europe.

DR Congo and Sudan are failed states as well as *failed democracies*. In DR Congo, the transitional government was sworn in on 30 June 2003 and was supported by the troops of the European Union and peacekeepers of the United Nations. One of the key objectives of the transitional government was to prepare elections for 2005, but belligerent leaders, corruption and mismanagement had been threatening the population throughout the transition period. Ongoing conflicts and institutional weaknesses caused the postponement of national elections from June 2005 until March 2006. Moreover, the election preparations faced huge challenges because there were 33 presidential candidates, 8,650 parliamentary candidates for 500 parliamentary seats, and 267 registered political parties. In October 2006 Joseph Kabila was elected president with 58.05 per cent of the vote in the second round and was inaugurated on 6 December 2006 for a five-year term. Now Kabila's PPRD controls 114 of 500 seats, the largest number of any political party, and a further 200 through its political allies. Similarly, the Senate (108 seats), elected on 19 January 2007, is controlled by the PPRD, which has the largest share of seats (22), with the MLC (the party of Jean-Pierre Bemba) obtaining 14 parliamentarians for a five-year mandate. President Kabila and PM Gizenga announced a government of sixty ministers on 5 February 2007. This high number of ministries shows that in Congolese politics it is power-sharing, not political efficiency, which matters. The democratic future of the Congo will depend not only on internal developments, but also on the impacts of politics in the region, as well as global competition for natural resources.

Since early 2003 the Arabization campaign of the Khartoum government in Darfur has killed more than 230,000 black Africans, displaced more than 2.3 million and sent more than 200,000 as refugees into Chad. The mutual destabilization between Sudan and Chad has displaced at least 140,000 Chadians and 235,000 Sudanese refugees and exposed them to the deserts in eastern Chad. National elections are planned for the 2008–09 time frame, but because of the marginalization and brutality of the Khartoum regime against the Darfurians this democratization process will not materialize. Moreover, because of the very slow implementation, and deliberate hampering, of the Comprehensive Peace Agreement of January 2005, in the first half of October 2007 the SPLM/A threatened to leave the transitional government. Because of the continuous political threat of Arabization and Islamization, Sudan is in my view the leading undemocratic state in Africa.

Conclusion

In this chapter I have discussed the concept of democracy, challenges to democratization and African success stories and failures in the democratization process. Ethiopia's and Eritrea's bright democratic futures in the first half of the 1990s, as a symbol of a new African leadership, were nipped in the bud after the outbreak of the border war in 1998. Eritrea continues its anti-democratic policy and Ethiopia disappointed many after the elections of May 2005. Kibaki's Kenya has become a further disappointment, as the violence after the elections of December 2007 demonstrates. There are, however, different variables which determine successes as well as failures on the *intra-state*, *regional* and *global* levels. On the intra-state level, for example, the political elites in Botswana and post-apartheid South Africa determined the democratic success story, whereas in Togo, Cameroon, DR Congo, etc., political elites hampered the democratization processes. On the regional level, the war between Eritrea and Ethiopia is unfortunately contributing to undemocratic policies in both countries, where the governments' policies seem to be geared towards war rather than democratic reform. On the global level (facilitated by the internal corrupt elites), the intrusion of global interests (fighting terrorism, and resources, especially oil) undermined the democratization process in countries such as Nigeria, Angola and Sudan. Democratization and stable governments cannot come about through incessant exhortations, appeals, threats and orders, nor by making the state omnipotent, but rather by addressing the variables on the above three levels. But at the same time it is important to note that global pressure on states such as Zimbabwe or Eritrea, paradoxically, can exacerbate undemocratic policies in those countries.

The problems of democracy in Africa lie in its *metaphysical* approach: the metaphysical belief in territorial integrity and in a centralized state as a principle for stability and development has led to the emergence of undemocratic intuitions. There are clashes between two Africas (traditional and modern), caused by the metaphysical concept of the state. This African political metaphysics arose because in their political behaviours many African politicians do not always act to solve African problems, but rather to impress the rest of the world or to prove to the outside world that they are following the same 'civilized' or 'rational' principles. When those African leaders realized that they were not successful in their political projects based on Western principles, they began to underline the 'otherness', the 'peculiarity', of the African. Criticisms from outside are usually rejected as neocolonialism. This leads to isolationism and antagonism. Africa needs *pragmatic* principles: to look for concrete solutions for concrete problems without making the West a benchmark. African democracies failed or fail because they transform democracy from pragmatic and practical to the metaphysical entity that has resulted in idolatry of the state from the colonial period or culture. Neither a radical backlash against the Western political culture nor using this culture as a benchmark can solve African democratization problems. What Africa needs is contextuality and pragmatism based on local political and cultural understanding.

10 | Poverty and human security in Africa: the liberal peace debate

M. A. MOHAMED SALIH

The relationship between human insecurity and poverty is obvious, as the former complicates the latter's consequences for individuals and groups, often exemplified by basic needs deficits, abuse of human rights and, in some extreme cases, physical and psychological abuse, including the denial of the right to live. Broadly understood, human security is about protecting and empowering citizens to obtain vital freedoms from want, fear and hunger, as well as freedom to take action on one's own behalf, including, among other things, creating the building blocks for human flourishing, peace with dignity and a secure livelihood.

Poverty is one of the complicating factors affecting the possibility of attaining the noble attributes of human security. In the sense that human security can coexist with poverty, poverty in itself is not always associated with the negation of peace (i.e. conflict) and abuse of human rights. In other words, many poor societies enjoy peace, as much as poverty may undermine peace by creating situations that contribute to the abuse of human rights as a result of horizontal (such as ethnic, religious, regional, etc.) or vertical (such as class and elite) inequality and inequitable distribution of resources.

Currently, liberal peace is the dominant paradigm informing the debate on peace and security, including conflict management and poverty reduction. I argue that liberal peace alone is an insufficient condition for poverty reduction and attainment of human security. In particular, I have interrogated poverty in Africa with reference to three human security attributes (secure/insecure livelihood, peace/conflict and inclusion/exclusion).

The implications of poverty and conflict for human insecurity in Africa are telling. Realizing that poverty and inequality result in exclusion, which exacerbates grievance with its conspicuous role in conflict perpetuation, Ramcharan (2002: 9) reminds us that 'human rights norms define the meaning of human security whereby the Universal Declaration on Human Rights, the International Covenant on Civil and Political Rights ... are all meant to make human beings secure in freedom, in dignity, with equality and protection of human rights'. Although I will not dwell on jurisdiction issues relating to the relevance of this seminal statement to poverty and human security in Africa, human rights as human security are a major concern in the African context and will therefore attract some of my attention.

Evidently, there is a strong association between peaceful management and just resolution of conflicts and respect for human rights, and by extension the creation of a situation susceptible to better human security provision. In Africa and elsewhere, severe governance deficit, an apparent condition of human rights abuse, often occurs in countries where core values of rights embedded in the variety of human, civil, social, cultural and political rights are violated.

In particular, I attempt to broaden the definition of human security based on Krause and Williams's (1997: 44) contention that 'security is synonymous with citizenship, whereby security is a condition individuals (and groups) enjoy'. Citizenship refers not only to individual duties/responsibility and consequences (reward or punishment), but also to the citizen's fundamental rights (human, civil, political and economic) with practicable provisions to redress violations of rights. What citizens should enjoy as human security, Thomas (Thomas and Wilkin 1999: 3) comments, 'has both qualitative and quantitative aspects. At one level it is about the fulfillment of basic material needs, and at another it is about the achievement of human dignity, which incorporates personal autonomy, control over one's life, and unhindered participation in the life of the community.' This conception of human security has direct relevance to poverty and conflict as both undermine 'safety from chronic threats such as hunger, disease, and repression and protection from sudden disruption in the pattern of daily life' (UNDP 1994: 23).

More recently, a number of practical linkages to human security have been made: food aid and human security (Clay and Stokk 2002), violence, underdevelopment, human rights and human security (Ramcharan 2002), concepts and implications for state and domestic responsibilities, intervention and responsibilities of the international community (Tadjbakhsh and Chenoy 2007), among others. Although these new, more practical approaches have not yet been fully synthesized, they inform the current debate on human security in ways that traverse earlier ideologically ridden contentions, conceptions and paradigmatic convictions.

In sum, human security debates are relevant in that poverty alleviation, human security and the very concept of rights hinge on articulating a more humanistic practical approach to human security-cum-development and its implications for peace, security, well-being and social justice. Essentially, three elements pertaining to poverty, human security and conflict in Africa provide an analytical framework for this chapter. In particular, I interrogate poverty in Africa with reference to three human security attributes: 1) the poverty–human insecurity nexus; 2) human insecurity consequences for/of conflict; and 3) the liberal peace connection and debate.

A synopsis of African poverty and human insecurity indicators

Despite its natural beauty and huge strategic mineral deposits, oil reserves and other natural resources, Africa features as one of the poorest continents. According to the United Nations Conference on Trade and Development (UNCTAD

TABLE 10.1 Human Poverty Index in fragile states or states with severe social conflicts, politically unstable or experiencing violent conflicts

No.	Country	Human Development Index rank	Human Poverty Index rank	Value (%)
1	Comoros	134	61	31.3
2	Ghana (northern Ghana)	135	65	32.2
3	Mauritania	137	87	39.2
4	Congo	139	57	26.2
5	Swaziland	141	73	35.4
6	Sudan	147	69	34.4
7	Kenya	148	60	30.8
8	Djibouti	149	59	28.6
9	Zimbabwe	151	91	40.3
10	Uganda (northern region)	154	72	34.7
11	Eritrea	157	76	36.0
12	Nigeria	158	80	37.3
13	Guinea Conakry	160	103	52.3
14	Côte d'Ivoire	166	92	40.3
15	Burundi	167	81	37.6
16	DR Congo	168	88	39.3
17	Ethiopia (Somali region)	169	105	33.3
18	Chad	170	108	56.9
19	Central African Republic	171	98	43.6
20	Guinea Bissau	176	99	44.8
21	Sierra Leone	177	102	51.7

Source: UNDP (2007: 238–40)

2005), thirty-four (68 per cent) of the fifty least-developed countries (LDCs) in the world are African. Income poverty has fallen in all regions of the world since 1990, except in sub-Saharan Africa, which is the only region that has witnessed an increase both in the incidence of poverty and in the absolute number of poor. Some 300 million people – almost half of the region's population – live on less than $1 a day.

Among Africa's thirty-four LDCs, fifteen are currently experiencing conflict, with active insurgency, post-conflict or political instability. Sadly, in twenty-five of Africa's LCDs the gross domestic income (GDI) per capita is less than US$500. In some countries, such as Burundi (US$90), Liberia (US$110), DRC (US$120), Eritrea (US$180) and Chad (US$260), GDI is far below US$200 per capita.

Poverty, and the relatively high incidence of social and violent conflicts, is compounded by inequality. According to the UN *Report on the World Social Situation* (UN 2005), between- and within-country inequality in sub-Saharan Africa is pervasive, whether assessed in terms of poverty, income, health, education or access to power. While a small segment of the population of most countries lives under conditions that are comparable to those in more developed regions, a large share of the population in most African countries is poor. The number of poor people in the region has increased by almost ninety million in a little more than a decade (1990–2001). Seventy-seven per cent of the population subsists on less than two dollars a day, and this percentage has hardly changed over twenty years (1981–2001).

Table 10.1 shows the Human Poverty Index (HPI) ranking and percentage of people living under poverty in twenty-one African states. Some of these states can be described as fragile states, while others are states with severe social conflicts, politically unstable or experiencing violent conflicts.

Three major conclusions can be drawn from the 2007/2008 Human Development Index (HDI) and HPI rankings for twenty-one African countries:

1 The relatively better off in HDI terms and those with less human poverty than others also score better in terms of peaceful coexistence, an important element of human security. The best-performing African countries in HDI terms are Mauritius, Seychelles, Gabon, Botswana, Namibia and South Africa. South Africa is an anomaly, however, owing to its high level of inequality and high level of crime, which endanger the physical and psychological security of a large number of its citizens.

2 African countries with the lowest HDI can, in the majority, be described as fragile states, in particular Sudan, Kenya, Uganda (northern part), Zimbabwe and Chad as well as countries that have no statistical information to inform HDI because of prolonged civil strife, such as Somalia, Liberia and Sierra Leone.

3 In all African countries with high HDI income poverty has coincided with one or another incidence of conflict – either severe social conflict, political instability and tensions (Djibouti, Mauritania, Zimbabwe, Swaziland, Guinea Conakry, Central African Republic, Burundi, Guinea Bissau, Niger and Comoros, among others) or outright violent conflicts (Kenya, Sudan, Côte d'Ivoire, Chad, Eritrea and DRC). There is no information on Liberia and Somalia owing to their protracted conflicts and the lack of the skilled human resources needed to produce data for HDI.

Table 10.1 makes grim reading, not only in terms of Human Poverty Index rankings, but also in terms of people living under acute poverty, ranging from 26.2 per cent in the case of Congo to 52.3 per cent in the case of Guinea Conakry and 56.9 per cent in the case of Chad. Examining African poverty indicators assists in articulating Africa's special needs, contextualizing their linkages to human insecurity and the corresponding global as well as Africa-specific discourses and policy responses. The following section of the chapter is an attempt to explore these issues more systematically.

Poverty–human insecurity nexus

The introduction to this chapter provided several entry points into the poverty–human security nexus relevant to the current debate on poverty reduction in Africa and the pan-African and external response to it: the New Partnership for African Economic Development (NEPAD) and the Millennium Development Goals (MDG). Since the content of both initiatives is common knowledge, I will introduce only their salient features, with specific reference to their relevance to human security, and their emphasis on building an African security architecture.

The NEPAD strategic framework document was formally adopted at the 37th Summit of the OAU (now African Union or AU, inaugurated at the Durban Summit of 14 March 2002) in July 2001, which formally adopted the strategic framework document, and is designed to eradicate poverty in Africa and to place African countries, both individually and collectively, on a path of sustainable growth and development and thus halt the marginalization of Africa in the globalization process; and to promote the role of women in all activities. The aim is to achieve and sustain an average gross domestic product (GDP) growth rate of over 7 per cent per annum for the next fifteen years, and to ensure that the continent achieves the agreed International Development Goals (IDGs), which are:

- to reduce the proportion of people living in extreme poverty by half between 1990 and 2015;
- to enrol all children of school age in primary schools by 2015;
- to make progress towards gender equality and empowering women by eliminating gender disparities in the enrolment in primary and secondary education by 2015;
- to reduce infant and child mortality ratios by two-thirds between 1990 and 2015;
- to reduce maternal mortality ratios by three-quarters between 1990 and 2015;
- to provide access for all who need reproductive health services by 2015;
- to implement national strategies for sustainable development by 2005, so as to reverse the loss of environmental resources by 2015.

The African peoples have learned from their own experiences that peace, security, democracy, good governance, human rights and sound economic management are prerequisites for sustainable development. Little wonder, therefore, that the African leaders have commenced an auspicious Peace and Security Initiative as part of the overall NEPAD process.

The African Peace and Security Initiative consist of three elements: promoting long-term conditions for development and security; building the capacity of African institutions for early warning, as well as enhancing their capacity to prevent, manage and resolve conflicts; institutionalizing commitment to the core values of NEPAD. It has been emphasized that long-term conditions for ensuring peace and security in Africa require policy measures for addressing the political and social vulnerabilities on which conflict is premised.

Likewise, Article VII of the Millennium Declaration (2000) is about the consolidation of democracy in Africa and assisting Africans in their struggle for lasting peace, poverty eradication and sustainable development, thereby bringing Africa into the mainstream of the world economies. The UN, therefore, resolved to meet the special needs of Africa and:

- To give full support to the political and institutional structures of emerging democracies in Africa.
- To encourage and sustain regional and subregional mechanisms for preventing conflict and promoting political stability, and to ensure a reliable flow of resources for peacekeeping operations on the continent.
- To take special measures to address the challenges of poverty eradication and sustainable development in Africa, including debt cancellation, improved market access, enhanced Official Development Assistance and increased flows of foreign direct investment, as well as transfers of technology.
- To help Africa build up its capacity to tackle the spread of the HIV/AIDS pandemic and other infectious diseases.

By and large, NEPAD objectives coincide with those of the MDGs (eradicate extreme poverty and hunger; achieve universal primary education; promote gender equality and empower women; improve maternal health; combat HIV/AIDS, malaria and other diseases; and develop a global partnership for development). NEPAD and the MDGs also operate within the same time frame, with the expectation that their common goals should be achieved by 2015.

From a human security perspective both NEPAD and MDGs share certain parameters designed to impact upon poverty, peace/conflict and security. For example, Chapter 5 of the NEPAD main document (AU 2001: 18–24) is concerned with bolstering 'The Peace, Security, Democracy and Political Governance Initiatives', which resulted in major development of the pan-African peace and security institutions and instruments. Likewise, Chapter 12 of the MDGs Report (UN 2005: 183) is wholly devoted to 'Countries Affected by Conflicts', and it was also noted in the Millennium Declaration that peace, security and disarmament are fundamental for human well-being and eradicating poverty in all its forms (UN 2000).

Peace and security have become the common thread, informing the strategic thinking cutting across the core values of both NEPAD and MDGs, also ostentatiously part of a new development conception concerned with human development-cum-human security issues. In other words, the negative consequences of violent conflict on human security and its potential for exacerbating poverty cannot be ignored. I elaborate these in Table 10.2 in order to explain these complex relationships and their relevance to Africa both in terms of regional specificity (NEPAD) and universal human security attainment (MDGs).

Clearly Table 10.2 shows that the praxis (or theory of practice) informing NEPAD and the MDGs has a strong association with the core values of universal human security. They share a similar emphasis on the dimensions pertaining to general and policy objectives, scope and policy goals. In addition, although NEPAD has clear objectives, it is not as elaborate as the MDGs with their clear and measurable targets.

Some differences exist, however, in relation to some human security dimensions, such as values (NEPAD is Africa specific, whereas MDGs adopted more general universal values, i.e. one size fits all). International finance institutions' (particularly the World Bank and the IMF) global financial-cum-development governance frameworks heavily inform MDG values, placing a stronger emphasis on the institutions privileged by liberal peace advocates, such as civil society, the market, free trade, the private sector, property rights, growth, etc. NEPAD has devoted the whole of Chapter IV to appealing to the African people with an implicit contrast of individual versus collective (or African versus neoliberal) human security perspectives.

Despite their noble endeavours, neither NEPAD nor the MDGs are on course to achieving their targets. The latest MDG assessment (UN 2007c: 4, 5) reports that

the number of extremely poor people in sub-Saharan Africa has leveled off, and the poverty rate has declined by nearly six percentage points since 2000 ... in sub-Saharan Africa, the proportion of people living in extreme poverty fell from 46.8 per cent in 1990 to 41.1 per cent in 2004. Most of this progress has been achieved since 2000. The number of people living on less than $1 a day is also beginning to level off, despite rapid population growth. The per capita income of seven sub-Saharan African countries grew by more than 3.5 per cent a year between 2000 and 2005; another 23 had growth rates of more than 2 per cent a year over this period, providing a degree of optimism for the future.

Nevertheless, 'the region is not on track to reach the Goal of reducing poverty by half by 2015' (ibid.: 4).

The brighter image of poverty in Africa levelling off should, however, be tempered against the fact that growth has occurred in a few well-performing countries, while LDCs and war-stricken countries (with the exception of Angola and Sudan given their new-found oil wealth) are not really catching up with the good performers, such as South Africa and Ghana.

In contrast to the MDGs, NEPAD has not developed a comprehensive assessment framework to measure its achievements in any systematic manner, although some narrative reports about financial resources being committed and expended in various economic sectors are made available. For instance, the

TABLE 10.2 The human security dimensions of NEPAD and MDGs

No.	Human security dimension*	NEPAD	MDGs
1	*Original definitions* Human security aims at enabling people to exercise choices offered by human development, allowing these choices to be made safely and freely, while also guaranteeing that the opportunities brought today by development will not disappear tomorrow (UNDP 2004).	Peace, security, democracy, good governance, human rights and sound economic management are conditions for sustainable development.	Provide a framework for strengthening governance, promoting human rights, engaging civil society and promoting the private sector as a basis for MDG-based poverty reduction strategies.
2	*Values* Security, stability, sustainability of well-being.	Poverty eradication, sustainable development with growth, peace and security.	Poverty reduction, economic growth, rule of law, peace and security.
3	*General objectives* Prevention – going beyond coping mechanisms to avoiding poverty and potential conflict and preparing for disasters.	Poverty eradication, economic growth, conflict prevention, post-conflict development.	Linchpin to the quest for a more secure and peaceful world, bringing essential services to all the population, quickly, equitably and lastingly.
4	*Orientation* Even growth with equity does not provide protection for those hitherto excluded.	Sustainable development with growth, with special emphasis on protecting the vulnerable.	Economic growth, private sector, with special emphasis on the role of the market.
5	*Scope* Deals with root causes of potential insecurity (poverty, inequality, etc.). Identifies and prepares for recessions, conflicts, emergencies and the darker events of society.	Identifies poverty and inequality as major causes of insecurity and potentially conflict.	Identifies poverty and inequality as major causes of insecurity and potentially conflict.
6	*Timescale* Combines short-term measures to deal with risk and long-term preventive efforts.	Relatively short-term measures to deal with risk and weak in long-term preventive efforts.	Relatively short-term measures (2015) and weak in long-term preventive efforts.
7	*View of role of people* Protection and empowerment of people.	Protection and empowerment by appealing to the African peoples.	Make core investments in infrastructure and human capital that enable people to

	Human Security	NEPAD	MDGs
			join the global economy. Empowering the poor to make use of the infrastructure and human capital.
8 *View of society*	Emphasis on the individual and perceives large units as discriminatory.	Emphasis on people.	Emphasis on the individual.
9 *Measurements*	No Human Security Index in existence; subjective satisfaction and feeling of being secure.	African leaders established the NEPAD Peer Review Mechanism (NPRM) with indicators for periodic and regular measurement of progress per country.	Identified clear measurable targets for all eight MDGs goals.
10 *Policy objectives*	Actions to secure what is safeguarded, and prevent spiralling down, which might cause conflicts or crises (human-made and natural ones).	Eradicate poverty in Africa and place African countries, both individually and collectively, on a path of sustainable growth and development and thus halt the marginalization of Africa in the globalization process; and promote the role of women in all activities.	MDG-based poverty reduction strategy for scaling up public investment, capacity-building, domestic development mobilization and Official Development Assistance.
11 *Policy goals*	Promotion of human survival and daily life and avoidance of indignities that can result in injury, insult and contempt (Sen 2002).	Achieve and sustain an average gross domestic product (GDP) growth rate of over 7 per cent per annum for the next fifteen years; and ensure that the continent achieves the agreed International Development Goals (IDGs).	Promotion of human survival and poverty reduction for protection against want, hunger and disease.
12 *Policy example*	Preventing and coping with a sudden growing pandemic of HIV/AIDs, malaria, in addition to improvements in the provision of health, education, food security and water.	Wide, varied and comprehensive human security sectors from the social sector to infrastructure and the production sectors.	Concentrates on a human security conception based on improving the social sector and economic growth.

Note: * These dimensions are adapted from Tadjbakhsh and Chenoy (2007: 107–8), with a few minor paraphrasings or additions

Source: The poverty/human security dimensions have been compiled by the author from NEPAD and MDGs official sources

Namibia Economic Policy Research Unit (NEPRU 2006: 1) reported that NEPAD aid totalling over US$530 million has already been used in the development of roads, communications and energy networks, while projects worth around US$490 million were under consideration during 2005. In the same vein, Firmino G. Mucavele, the chief executive officer of NEPAD, reported (ibid.) to the African heads of state that about US$2.2 billion has been mobilized for implementing various projects within the NEPAD process. The report is rather thin on facts to support its claims, however, and in no way matches the report (UN 2007c) on the progress made thus far in achieving the MDGs.

The major failures of African countries to achieve NEPAD and the MDGs include the following: 1) undelivered commitments by international development agencies and organizations; 2) failure of the WTO negotiations to yield any concessions for Africa and developing countries vis-à-vis protectionist agricultural subsidies paid by EU and US governments to their farmers; 3) low level of harnessing science and technology; 4) conflict and political instability; 5) climate change has affected agricultural productivity, contributed to resource scarcity and fuelled conflicts among diverse natural resource users in Africa's land-based economies – to mention but a few factors.

Evidently, conflict and political instability and increased incidence of environmental conflicts because of climate change draw our attention to the human security dimension of both NEPAD and the MDGs, with the sad implication that the current levels of poverty and failure to meet their goals make sombre reading in terms of the nexus between poverty and human security.

In the following section, I explain the implications of the current debate on liberal peace for poverty and human security in Africa, given the demonstrated failure of MDGs to achieve their set targets.

The liberal peace connection

There is no gainsaying that dominant paradigms define the dominant trends in the academic debate, research and methodologies as well as policy orientation and practice. Currently, neoliberalism in its various manifestations informs the dominant peace paradigm, better known as the liberal peace. The resurrection of the liberal peace debate as a major academic and policy discourse in peace-building and the most favoured poverty reduction and human security arrangement is not exceptional. As the explanation of the relevance of the praxis (or theory of practice) of human security dimensions to NEPAD and MGDs illustrates, concerns with the neoliberal dispensation are evident in the values, objectives and policy orientation espoused by these agendas. Hence, it is not difficult to establish the relationship between liberal peace on the one hand and poverty reduction and human security strategies on the other. I begin by offering a synoptic view of the liberal peace and its relationship with peace-building on the one hand and poverty and human security on the other.

In short, the origins of the liberal peace, according to M. Fischer (2000: 2), are liberal, thus echoing the core values of the dominant paradigm in that:

liberalism aims at the freedom of the individual from oppression, especially from the rulers, and enshrines this freedom in a number of rights that must be respected under almost all circumstances: the right to life or immunity from violence, the right to assemble freely, to speak one's mind, to move about and choose one's abode, to acquire and dispose of property, to engage in arts, crafts, and commerce without hindrance, to profess and practice one's chosen faith, to educate one's children as one sees fit, etc.

Clearly these liberal values are consistent with a particular notion of human security enshrined in the theories of freedom, right and justice, a contention often viewed as at odds with collective notions of ownership of the means of production or social justice understood as a means for expansive state-enforced redistribution of wealth. Two important, yet comprehensively integrated, perspectives persist: one is concerned with trade and the free market, as echoed by Katherine Barbieri's (2005: 1–2) contention that 'the liberal employed arguments about the virtues of trade that included an explanation of how economic interdependence creates incentives for cooperation, reduces misconceptions, and fosters formal and informal mechanisms conducive to resolving conflicts of interest that might arise between states'. The second perspective focuses more on politics. This is succinctly presented by John Macmillan (1998), who contends that 'liberal states, founded on such individual rights as equality before the law, free speech and other civil liberties, private property, and elected representation are fundamentally against war. Thus, the very existence of liberal states makes for the liberal peace. And so peace and democracy are two faces of the same coin.'

In their response to the recent conflicts in Africa, the Balkans and central Asia, Newman and Richmond lament, 'the liberal peace is generally agreed to be the objective of peace processes. This means that any outcome should ostensibly be democratic, incorporate free and globalized markets, and aspire to human rights protection and the rule of law, justice, and economic development' (Newman and Richmond 2006). In a recent publication, Richmond attempted to relate these aspects of the liberal peace to human security, with special relevance to what he calls civil peace. Richmond argues that,

The discourse on humanitarianism and human security has become an important indicator of the involvement of International Organizations (IOs), agencies, and non-state actors in their contribution to the civil peace. This contribution is very important with regard to the development of the constitutional and institutional aspects of the liberal peace project. Furthermore, such actors, with access, reach, and legitimacy, are crucial in the evolving peacebuilding consensus. This has allowed intervention upon a humanitarian basis to forge its own legitimacy regardless of the norm of non-intervention. Furthermore this has created an apparent normative requirement for such action in the event of conflicts and crises on the part of the international community as part of its commitment to the liberal peace. (Richmond 2006: 8–9)

Using the language of the political economy of post-conflict reconstruction, Richmond explains the direct and indirect relations between the liberal peace and human security. In the specific case of Africa, the liberal peace is portrayed as a peace with two dimensions: economic liberalization supported by political liberalization and vice versa. Economic and political liberalization combined are, therefore, proposed as the tenets of the dominant peace-building paradigm and its positive effects attributed beyond peace to poverty reduction and human security.

Elsewhere I argue that, despite its noble objectives, the conception of the liberal peace on the African continent has suffered a serious blind spot inherent in the liberalism and the liberalization processes it proposed. This blind spot relates mainly to the fact that neoliberalism privileged the liberal over the social. Concerns with the liberal attributes recounted by Doyle and subsequently by several academics and policy-makers do not by themselves provide human security, even if it is narrowly defined as fundamental human needs, such as those elaborated in the introduction to this chapter.

The evidence available supports the argument that there is a tension inherent in the liberal peace, which is neoliberal in content and purpose. While Africans have attained considerable success in terms of the liberal aspects of the liberal peace (i.e. democracy, human rights and some modicum of the rule of law), these are decoupled from the social and economic conditions in which they live. The poverty indicators and low HDI implications for human security conditions, as presented in the opening pages of this chapter, illustrate that the liberal peace-building processes in post-conflict states are yet to improve the social conditions of the African poor.

In other words, the market-driven beneficiaries, private sector and free market operators, with sufficient financial resources to contest elections and patronize the post-conflict states, are the very criminal elements that benefited from the political economy of war and exacerbated conflict.

Evidently, global financial governance (the World Bank and the IMF) have promoted policies that have neglected the 'social conditions of citizens' and systematically undermined the African states' capacity to provide minimal social welfare support for the poor. In other words, economic liberalization conditionality associated with the liberal peace has not been helpful in furthering broader human security and even less so in attaining minimal poverty reduction. Cooper (2005) comments, 'At the global level, neoliberal globalization has fostered a particular kind of peace that is simultaneously weakening states and fostering the free movement of goods, has created conditions under which local conflict entrepreneurs have been able to utilize flexible worldwide trading networks to generate global revenues from local predation.'

The neglect of social conditions in the liberal peace has resulted in serious negative consequences for the development–conflict trajectory. It invites a problematic notion of peace dependent on what is known in the liberal peace literature as 'double finding', reinvented in this section to mean that while development contributes to peaceful coexistence and interdependence, it can also be an arena of conflict over scare resources. In both cases conflict undermines the very basis of development (human security) and exacerbates poverty.

Wilkin (2002: 633) laments,

> as capital and states, in their diverse types, are restructured in an era of neo-liberal global governance, it is not altogether surprising that the security and development agendas should become merged. Indeed, from the point of view of neoliberal global governance, it is a necessary fact that the nascent national, regional and global state security (NRGSS) apparatus should turn its attentions to the social crises that currently devastate the world system.

Unfortunately, the major policy directives to which African states have turned (NEPAD and MDGs) have fallen short of responding to these social crises originating in underdevelopment. The evidence supporting this statement is found elsewhere in the work of several peace and security human experts who have been able to corroborate strong evidence explaining the linkages between underdevelopment and insecurity or conflict. Therefore it is not difficult to infer that the dominant paradigm informing the transition from conflict to peace or post-conflict development in Africa and elsewhere is inseparable from the liberal peace and its preferred development agenda, which is neoliberal in form and content.

Unfortunately, and as has been explained earlier in the introductory sections, Africa's human security indicators are devoid of the ethos and core values required to engage the social crises that have engulfed the continent. These social crises and their outcomes can be directly traced to the development–security nexus. This is particularly so in post-conflict states where the development paradigm and the policy directives governing the transition from conflict to peace are liberal-peace-ridden and have ostensibly failed to establish the necessary linkages between the developmental and the liberal as mutually reinforcing elements of the human security endeavour.

My critique of the failure of the liberal peace on human security grounds in Africa is supported by, for instance, Rosato's (2003: 599) claim that

> one potential explanation of the liberal peace is that the democratic peace is in fact an imperial peace based on American power. This claim rests on two observations. First, the democratic peace is essentially a post-World War II

phenomenon restricted to the Americas and Western Europe. Second, the United States has been the dominant power in both these regions since World War II and has placed an overriding emphasis on regional peace.

Hence, the simple logic that democracies do not go to war with each other is both historically and geographically limited and therefore flawed if uncritically applied to Africa and other developing countries. Moreover, the social conditions prevailing in Africa make the possibility of obtaining a liberal peace without a human security face a difficult bargain to sell.

In short, when related to the poor results of regional (NEPAD) and global (MDGs) aims, projects aiming at poverty reduction as an important aspect of human security should by necessity lead to us questioning whether the core values of the liberal peace are consistent with the universal human security considerations ushered in by these noble agendas. There is therefore a need for a better understanding of the factors that appear to be detrimental to the attainment of the human security dimensions implicit in the global quest to reduce poverty – let alone to eradicate it.

Conclusion

The poverty–human security link in Africa is both absorbing and challenging. It is absorbing because the prevailing social conditions in peaceful countries are as precarious as in those that have just emerged from the shadow of conflict. Likewise, it is challenging because the conditions internal to Africa are not fully understood by the global players who, with all good intentions, attempt their level best to aid the last frontier of development.

The liberal peace debate is pertinent in that it is the most preferred strategy for poverty alleviation and development and their symmetrical other: human security. The material I have provided and analysed in this chapter and its accompanying tables allows examination of the core values of human security and their corresponding relevance in Africa's major development endeavours: the home-grown NEPAD and the human security universal ideal enshrined in MDGs. In both respects, I have attempted to explain why the liberal peace ideal is uninformed by African reality.

This conclusion is by no means anti-liberal or unappreciative of the linkages developed between democracy and peace. By and large, this perspective is supported by the fact that, although African exceptionalism should not dominate our thinking about the way forward, poverty and human insecurity should be treated not as exceptionally African but as a discourse that requires more African input than we have ever thought possible. In the circumstances, the democratic and human rights gains of the liberal peace cannot be swept away as irrelevant. They can potentially provide the building blocks for human security if the social conditions of the poor are given the same level of importance.

11 | Africa and globalization

JIM WHITMAN

When considering Africa and globalization, the temptations of crude generalization are clear. First, there is 'Africa the country' – a perception that some of the worst problems that beset many African states (and sub-Saharan ones in particular) are not, as elsewhere, best understood individually, and in terms of configurations of historically conditioned political, economic and social circumstances, but instead can be regarded as manifestations of a generally shared malaise. This perception is not only long-standing and pervasive, but in important ways it has also been self-validating, even in the face of contradictory evidence. So, for example, '[throughout the 1970s and 1980s], international financial markets ... perceived most of Africa as a "basket case" region. [During that period], donors, international organisations, investors and even African governments did not believe that private [capital] flows to Africa were significant or increasing' (Bhinda et al. 1999). And the problem persists:

> Given the extent of coverage of wars, famine and political instability in Africa, it might seem odd that investors would even consider business there. While the risks of expropriation, corruption and regulatory changes – let alone security risks and the threat of political instability and civil unrest – are high, they can be overstated. 'There is a widely-held picture that Africa is a complete basket case,' says Tara O'Connell of Kroll Worldwide. 'So many of the images we are surrounded by suggest that it's impossible to make money anywhere on the continent, which is completely untrue.'[1]

The vast increase in the quantity, variety and reliability of information on a near-instantaneous basis which is routinely cited as a key feature of globalization has not necessarily improved matters, since wars, disasters and political corruption routinely dominate the news media worldwide, with the effect of reinforcing 'Africa the country' stereotypes.

Globalization is itself open to depictions that reduce it to observable effects, abstracting what is most significant about it politically, socially and environmentally; and sidelining considerations of power, agency and causation. So it is that advocates of economic globalization are fond of the 'a rising tide lifts all boats' metaphor, which, in addition to the above, leaves out of consideration the numerous and inescapable human dislocations and injustices that are inevitably part of the process.

To site Africa within a globalized and still globalizing arena is to risk the kind of generalizations that obscure national differences, competing if not contradictory impulses, uneven outcomes and hard choices – and at times the absence of choice. Yet African governments and leaders in both public and private enterprises are not only keenly aware of globalizing pressures and opportunities; they also see in Africa-wide organization, stability and cooperation possibilities for managing these currents.

This is made plain by the African Union (AU) project, but also in concerted efforts by African leaders to bring peace and stability to the continent as a necessary precondition for its economic development (for a useful summary of which, see Cilliers and Sturman 2002). Indeed, in the preamble to the AU Constitutive Act, African heads of state declare themselves 'conscious of the fact that the scourge of conflicts in Africa constitutes a major impediment to the socio-economic development of the continent and of the need to promote peace, security and stability as a prerequisite for the implementation of our development and integration strategy'.[2] Still more significant are the close linkages between the principles and goals of the African Union and the New Partnership for Africa's Development (NEPAD). One of the most striking features of the NEPAD declaration is the emphasis given to the legal, political and social conditions required for sustained, continent-wide development. The following is indicative:

> It is now generally acknowledged that development is impossible in the absence of true democracy, respect for human rights, peace and good governance. With the *New Partnership for Africa's Development*, Africa undertakes to respect the global standards of democracy, which core components include political pluralism, allowing for the existence of several political parties and workers' unions, fair, open, free and democratic elections periodically organised to enable the public to choose their leaders freely. (AU 2001: Article 79)

And in language that would not be out of place in the primary AU documents, the NEPAD declaration asserts that in order to achieve their development objectives, 'African leaders will take joint responsibility for ... promoting and protecting democracy and human rights in their respective countries and regions, by developing clear standards of accountability, transparency and participatory governance at the national and sub-national levels' (ibid.: Article 49). What makes the forging of a stable, coherent and law-based Africa a matter of such pressing urgency is plain enough in one of the objectives of the AU Constitutive Act: 'establish[ing] the necessary conditions which enable the continent to play its rightful role in the global economy and in international negotiations' (Article 3i). As part of engaging the rest of the world in Africa's development, the AU is an assertion of the primacy of the state – but crucially, of the state in conformity with the larger, non-African state system, one increasingly coming under the sway of global rather than national or regional norms. The larger, systemic stability and coherence of the continent – in perception as well as fact – are central to individual African countries and their prospects: compare the perception of Africa and African politics, currently under the shadow of the violence and human suffering in Darfur, with the perception of Europe and European politics after the vicious and destructive war in the former Yugoslavia.

But securing the fundamentals of governance for the African continent and for the nations that comprise it will not obviate the difficulties that all states must confront in grappling with the complexities of globalization – and indeed, doing so will almost certainly hasten the number, frequency and speed of their arrival.

Globalization

Globalization has been defined as 'a reconfiguration of social geography marked by the growth of transplanetary and supraterritorial connections between people' (Scholte 2005: 8). As with any other generic term – 'war', 'peace' and 'capitalism', for example – we can in some contexts most usefully think of globalization as an aggregate; and in other contexts by focusing on one or a number of effects. Clearly, not every sectoral consideration – say, 'globalization and the environment' or 'globalization and cultural plurality' – will include every element in the following list (which is itself far from exhaustive), but we can at least get a sense of the most common characteristics that make 'globalization' a meaningful (if imprecise) term: the shrinkage of time and space (a mainstay of sociological and geographical discourse on globalization); movement of peoples and ideas across or through borders and boundaries, both physical and cultural; an increase in the span of access to common goods and services; knowledge supplanting production as the basis for economic prosperity; a blurring of the distinction between 'high' and 'low' politics; the emergence of new centres of allegiance, competence and authority; and new forms of complex interdependence – not only between states, but also between sub-state actors of various kinds. At the same time, globalization is not unilinear; irresistible; unambiguously good or bad; or easy to comprehend from a single viewpoint – political, economic, sociological. Globalizing dynamics are not a force of nature but qualitative, relational matters, brought about by human activity, directly or cumulatively.

Globalization has rapidly developed from an observable phenomenon to become a key feature of the human condition, at least in the sense that no nation and few individuals have not felt its impacts for better or for worse. Leaving aside the kinds of cost–benefit analyses open to many developed states and their citizens, it is plain that the condition of many millions of individuals and many governments leaves them powerless in the face of globalizing dynamics initiated and sustained at a considerable remove from them. A good deal of the anti-globalization literature documents the anguish and anger at the exclusion and impoverishment that is too often the result (Held and McGrew 2007). Of course, political contention over the effects of globalization is not confined to the developing world: not only are there 'winners and losers' between states, but also within them; and the questions 'whose interests?' and 'whose values?' hover over every important globalization negotiation and debate. But while states remain quite capable of subverting human security either at large or in particular locations as the price of narrower and/or more immediate gains, they are themselves often in a quandary over globalizing dynamics, not all of which they deliberately set in motion. There are three reasons for this.

First, states are both senders and receivers of globalizing dynamics, so although states continue to pursue their interests through all the familiar channels of international politics, the international system itself operates within a globalized arena – hence international negotiations to secure the environmental sustainability of the planet.

Second, all states struggle to mediate the effects of globalization, to minimize costs and undesirable effects and to distribute the benefits. Anti-globalization protests embracing quite disparate national and transnational interests are evidence of this (Munck 2005; Starr 2000).

Third, regulatory challenges of all kinds are set against an ever-expanding arena of interested parties, empowered actors and countervailing interests – hedge funds and transnational corporations not least (Morgenson 1998; Korten 1995), but also numerous and remarkably diverse groups of coalitions, affiliations and campaigns gathered under the term 'global civil society'.[3] The broad-based international lobby that helped to bring an end to apartheid in South Africa is certainly a instance of the way in which globalization can facilitate positive political change.

It is possible to see in these developments a general diminution of state authority and reach – a 'retreat of the state' (Strange 1996), and the prospects for 'governance without government' (Rosenau and Czempiel 1992). And it is certainly a striking feature of our time that globalization has empowered a great many non-state actors; and that by employing the levers of government alone, states cannot entirely secure such important matters as the value of a national currency, or control expanding or shrinking markets, or ensure adequate imports of key commodities. But change should not be mistaken for transformation. Newly empowered actors of every kind rely on the structure, order and stability that the international system provides; and in the absence of the political authority, legitimacy and accountability of states – and the mechanisms and procedures of international politics and international law – how else might humanity grapple with the emergence of issues that are now truly global in their extent and seriousness? Our most reliable and accountable means of bringing order and decency to human affairs under globalized conditions remain states and the international system. Of course, states are also highly competitive; and the sovereign equality of all states does nothing to make them equal in terms of their power to shape the conditions under which competition takes place.

As Susan Strange expressed the matter, 'Those who have structural power are recognizable because they are able to affect the range of options within which others can choose what to do. It may seem that others choose freely, but the risks and penalties of going outside that range of options are so punitive that they are not seriously considered' (Strange 1997: 136). This is the position in which most African states find themselves. African leaders are keenly aware that states' ability to mitigate unfavourable variables and to capitalize on positive ones is crucially conditioned by the quality of their governance; their infrastructural capacity to confront such pressures on equitable terms; and the state of human development within their borders. Globalizing pressures have intensified this awareness – and it is reflected in the concerns that informed both the AU and NEPAD.

When we speak of the increasing globalization of the world, what is fundamentally at issue is an extremely rapid and pervasive surmounting of all forms of barriers to human relatedness – physical, cultural and political. Advocates of globalization see in this an increase in interdependence, which will ultimately be for the good of international peace and security. Whatever the longer-term prospect, it remains the case that power differentials in the world mean that some human groups, be they states, corporations or the sum of tourists from developed-world states, are better placed to act and better equipped to avoid being acted upon if they so choose. For example, developed states are able to insulate particular sectors of their productive industries from poor trade conditions through subsidies of various kinds and favourable regulatory regimes. In addition, considerable freedom of movement (as well as some cushioning against shocks) accrues to states with strong currencies and extensive foreign exchange holdings. The following, from the OECD *African Economic Outlook 2006–2007*, is indicative:

> [The] drop [in cotton prices] illustrates the problems encountered by some
> of the poorest sub-Saharan countries in the context of trade distortions. West
> and Central African countries produce low-cost, high-grade cotton, but face
> unattractive world prices, which have been dampened by the provision of
> substantial subsidies from developed countries in recent years. An additional
> burden for the cotton-producing countries [in these regions] has been the
> appreciation of the Euro against the dollar since 2000.[4]

So for the powerful, the dissolution of barriers and restrictions and the increasing permeability of borders bring a considerable increase in opportunity without concomitant costs and risks. Of course, the traffic is not entirely one-way, as entire industries in the developed world lose out to considerably cheaper foreign competition; and immigration has become a contentious political issue, as it was during the first phase of nineteenth- and early-twentieth-century globalization (O'Rourke and Williamson 1999).

For many African states, globalizing dynamics do not present a short menu

189

of difficult choices, but merely hard realities. Such is the case with the African brain drain: some 30 per cent of Africa's university-trained professionals work abroad, affecting such fundamentals as healthcare, scientific research and public administration. As always, there are 'pull' as well as 'push' factors involved – and the former include developed-world dependence: according to Dr Peter Ngaita, director of the African Medical and Research Foundation in Nairobi, 'The [UK] National Health Service only trains 70 per cent of the doctors it needs, so where does that other 30 per cent come from? In the US they don't even train 50 per cent of the nurses they need. The health worker in this world is a precious commodity' (McVeigh 2006). Yet at the same time, such is the pervasiveness of globalization that further, quite complex interdependencies are also created by the African diaspora – and these are remarkably difficult to untangle and all but impossible to categorize as wholly positive or negative. The most recent UNCTAD report on least-developed nations notes that:

> Remittances have increased dramatically in recent years, totalling an estimated $167 billion in 2005, according to World Bank estimates. They have grown faster than foreign direct investment and official development assistance over the past decade, doubling in several countries and increasing by close to 10 per cent per annum between 2001 and 2005. Their major role in receiving countries is to stimulate consumption and investment in those countries, help relax foreign exchange constraints and contribute to poverty alleviation. Their contribution to development depends on their macroeconomic impact and how they are used in receiving countries. There is evidence that they are more directed to consumption than investment, which perhaps explains why no link between them and long-term growth has been found. (UNCTAD 2007: 142)

If globalization makes a fundamental strengthening of African states and the African state system more urgent, it also makes it more difficult and more complex: the hard choices and trade-offs that routinely feature as part of globalizing processes everywhere can be particularly stark in situations where human security is fragile and immediate needs can crowd out more measured and longer-term considerations. To this one can add critical deficiencies in governance which the AU constitutive document acknowledges forthrightly. Since sub-Saharan Africa is the poorest region of the world, even its best-placed states struggle to leverage development through the opportunities offered by globalization; and the weakest find themselves additionally burdened by globalization's less desirable pressures. It is these particulars which best allow us to site the prospects for Africa and African states within a globalized world.

African states, globalization and development

The central issue facing the majority of African states with respect to globalizing forces is less one of 'catch-up' than one of not being overwhelmed. The most serious danger is that the considerable resources of the continent will be 'sold too cheaply' – that is, for the minimalist demands that arise from impoverishment and poor infrastructural capacity, rather than to advance their competitive standing and to secure longer-term goals. The exceptions – such as Egyptian companies' extensive foreign acquisitions and booming foreign direct investment (Wallis 2006) – remind us not to make a caricature out of a characterization. But for much of sub-Saharan Africa, the following list of the hindrances to foreign direct investment in Africa could also stand as a catalogue of their deficiencies which apply to the organizational challenges of globalization more generally:

> The constraining factors include: low resources mobilization; high degree of uncertainty; poor governance; corruption, and low human capital development; unfavourable regulatory environment and poor infrastructure, small country sizes; high dependence on primary commodities exports and increased competition; poor image abroad; shortage of foreign exchange and the burden of huge domestic and foreign debt; and underdeveloped capital markets, their high volatility, and home bias by foreign investors. (Anyanwu 2006: 42)

When several of these factors combine with other severe weaknesses, and with the demands and/or opportunities of globalization, the losses are substantial – and the impacts multiple. To choose but one example, 'Perhaps 25 of the 44 sub-Saharan nations face crippling electricity shortages [in 2007], a power crisis that some experts call unprecedented. The causes are manifold: strong economic growth in some places, economic collapse in others, war, poor planning, population booms, high oil prices and drought have combined to leave both industry and residents short of power when many need it most' (Wines 2007). And these critical infrastructural shortcomings beset the whole of sub-Saharan Africa:

> The gravity of this year's shortage is all the more apparent considering how little electricity sub-Saharan Africa has to begin with. Excluding South Africa, whose economy and power consumption dwarf other nations', the region's remaining 700 million citizens have access to roughly as much electricity as do the 38 million citizens of Poland. [...] Moreover, some grids are so poorly maintained that electricity suppliers get paid for as little as 60 percent of the power they generate. The rest is either stolen or lost in ill-maintained networks. (ibid.)

This single example also illustrates the kinds of tension that exist between the demands for fundamental human development and capital- and energy-intensive industries: 'Much [of the electricity] goes to industry: a single aluminum smelter near Mozambique's capital, Maputo, gobbles four times as much power as the entire rest of Mozambique. On average [...] fewer than one in four sub-Saharan Africans are hooked to national electricity grids' (ibid.).

This and similar difficulties are likely to cripple African nations' ability to maximize the benefits of the current commodities boom, despite their considerable endowment of the most sought-after resources. And although an enthusiastic welcome has been extended to China's very considerable investments on the continent, there is also a good deal of ambivalence, since Africans are keenly aware that there is nothing altruistic in China's intentions. In any event, Africa has recently found itself the big loser to China in one of the continent's key export markets, textiles:

> The textile and clothing industry, one of the engines China used to fuel its own economic expansion in the 1980s, had been particularly hard hit in Africa. For decades, African countries exported large quantities of clothes and textiles to developed countries under a trade agreement designed to protect European and US markets from competition from China and others, while encouraging exports from the world's poorest nations. But the trade provision, the Multi-Fibre Agreement, expired in January 2000, putting these countries in direct competition with China. (Polgreen and French 2007)

The level and extent of Chinese investment in Africa is breathtaking, and it has also advanced considerable loans and debt relief. Perhaps its boldest venture is a US$5 billion loan to Congo, with which it promises to build 3,200 kilometres of rail lines and roads, thirty-one hospitals and two new universities (French 2007). In what might be regarded as a tactic to win African states away from Western states and the IMF, however, Chinese investments in Africa '... come with no conditionality related to governance, fiscal probity or other of the concerns that now drive western donors' (Lyman 2005: 2). Expressed bluntly by Denys Uwimana of the Rwandan embassy in China, 'China's aid comes with no strings attached' (Lovgren 2007).

There is considerable risk in this, principally the possibility of reinforcing all of the worst fixtures and practices of poor governance in so many African states, which is at the root of so much impoverishment, disenfranchisement and suffering. As one analyst expressed it: 'The question then is does China want to be seen in Africa as the defender of rogue states, the more aggressive seeker of Africa's natural resources, without regard to transparency, development and stability there? Is there room for developing some rules of the road, some common objectives, some ways in which Chinese economic gains for Africa (and itself) can come side by side with building more stability and democracy there?' (Lyman 2005). To these questions we might also add whether the African leaders who have pledged themselves to the normative standards and practical goals of the AU and NEPAD will be willing to forgo them with the right incentives?

In Zimbabwe, Robert Mugabe has now subordinated human security to regime preservation. In a country in which there is now 'little left to plunder', the UN estimated that a quarter of the population would be facing malnutrition by the time of the 2008 election. The backdrop to Mugabe's fulminations against Western conspirators is US food donations to 1.4 million Zimbabweans (Africa

Monitor: Southern Africa 2007: 4). What is dispiriting in this is the incapacity and unwillingness of southern Africa's budding security community (Schoeman 2002: 1–26) to grapple more directly with the implosion of Zimbabwe. Neither the Southern African Development Community (SADC) nor the African Union have seen fit to condemn, let alone engage in any but the most ineffectual ways with, the political crisis or looming humanitarian disaster there. Meanwhile, the political and practical strains on the AU occasioned by the continuing disaster in Darfur and by a resurgence of violence in Somalia have sorely tested the credibility of the AU/NEPAD normative project.

Individual states and entire regions of Africa are variously enmeshed in globalized configurations of interests that have played a part in initiating and sustaining patterns of violent conflict (Bourne 2007); and certainly China's importation of Sudanese oil and its concurrent supply of weapons to that country is a case in point (Human Rights Watch 2003). But responsibility for conflict prevention, mediation, the application of sanctions and even intervention are matters which all African states have pledged themselves to undertake, as circumstances (and especially the worst circumstances) dictate: the AU Peace and Security Council has as one of its Principles (4j) 'the right of the Union to intervene in a member State pursuant to a decision of the Assembly in respect of grave circumstances, namely war crimes, genocide and crimes against humanity, in accordance with Article 4(h) of the Constitutive Act'.[5] Quite aside from the humanitarian consequences of state collapse and/or violent conflict, the failure of African states actively to engage with matters on this scale undermines the credibility that the AU and NEPAD were in part crafted to establish and maintain. The peace and security of African states and regions are an essential, as they are in other parts of the world; and the pressures on state security are not entirely a matter of internal weaknesses of various kinds: the importance of oil and other commodities for the world political economy will almost certainly continue to bring unwelcome attention and pressures as well as opportunities to many African states. It is of note that the fourteen-nation SADC recently took the decision that none of its members would be willing to host the United States' new African Command (Africom).[6]

But it would be seriously misleading to abstract national security from human security – and given Africa's Human Development Index[7] ratings, the link is particularly stark and immediate. In 2007, halfway through the period set for achieving the UN's Millennium Development Goals, there is no nation in sub-Saharan Africa on track to meet them (UN 2007b). The scale of the task in meeting the goals is admittedly daunting – some 30 per cent of children in sub-Saharan Africa do not attend school, as opposed to 12 per cent globally; and in much the same way that globalizing pressures can force hard choices, so too does poor infrastructure and stretched treasury resources. For example, 'Malawi had cut the proportion of spending on water and sanitation [with poor hygiene, sanitation and unsafe drinking water accounting for 90 per cent of diarrhoeal deaths] at the same time as it had increased investment in health and education' (Elliott 2007). Yet the aggregate picture can obscure significant progress in many fields – and in many countries. Also in Malawi, a voucher scheme for fertilizers and seeds has doubled agricultural productivity in a single year; and many countries, including Kenya, Tanzania and Uganda, have abolished fees for primary schools.[8]

But incremental progress in key areas of human betterment in Africa is bedevilled by the decimation created by the multiple impacts of HIV/AIDS.

> With less than 11 per cent of the total global population, the continent has more than 70 per cent of all HIV/AIDS-related cases in the world. As well as a harrowing catalogue of lives lost, the implications of this human tragedy reach into the structure of economies, the capacity of institutions, the integrity of communities and the viability of families. In the extreme, the survival of some states may even be called into question. (Poku and Sandkjaer 2007: 127)

Something of the scale, the multiple impacts and the temporal dimension of this devastating disease can be gleaned from the fact that there are more than 12 million AIDS orphans in Africa; and that the continent is the only part of the world that has seen a rise in tuberculosis.

The most striking way in which globalization is related to HIV/AIDS in Africa (and developing countries in other parts of the world) is through the Trade-Related Aspects of Intellectual Property (TRIPS), agreed through the World Trade Organization. The effect of this was to protect the pharmaceutical patents of developed-world corporations against cheaper generic copies which could more readily be made available in poorer regions of the world. In this case, largely through non-governmental, transnational cooperation, sufficient opprobrium attached to companies trying to restrict cheap alternatives to antiretrovirals for AIDS that they backed down.

The International AIDS Vaccine Initiative[9] is now in its second decade – using, extending and strengthening existing global networks to combat the single largest cause of death in Africa. Of course, the spread of AIDS around the world illustrates the ways in which globalization opens channels for quite complex interactions of human and natural systems – both difficult to predict and to govern (Whitman 2005) – as avian flu may yet demonstrate. It is also notable that opposed interests in matters that are global in their extent – in the case of HIV/AIDS, protecting intellectual property as a source of profitability versus human solidarity – are both facilitated by the same, enhanced means of communication and dissemination of information. This does not dissolve differences in power and resources, but it does open the way for goodwill, progressive politics and creative thinking to find a voice and make a difference. In this light, the advance of human rights over several decades can be regarded as a part-outcome of globalization, and also as an agent of the globalization of norms governing power relationships of all kinds (Clark 2001) – norms that all African states have now formally embraced.

But many of the most important avenues of communication and exchange brought about by globalization – and certainly those that enable states and peoples actively to participate in shaping its forces – are not cost free. Access to telecommunications (and the Internet in particular) is a key infrastructural (and human capital) requirement for full and active participation in the world political economy. Unsurprisingly, there is a 'digital divide', with a recent world-wide survey revealing that 'Many sub-Saharan African states do not register in the figures at all: only South Africa, Sudan, Senegal and Gabon make it on to the list, with household broadband penetration running from 1.79 per cent in South Africa [...] to just 0.05 per cent in Sudan [...]' (Wray 2007). The gap between North Africa (with Morocco at nearly 7 per cent) and sub-Saharan Africa is also notable. There is some promise that mobile operators can now provide tele-communications access extensively and quickly where it is most sorely needed but, much like development assistance without conditionalities, the weakness or absence of regulatory bodies is likely to prove an eventual drawback. In any event, human development does not begin with telecommunications; and meanwhile, globalization and its many manifestations will not pause for African nations and peoples to secure the requisites for full participation.

Conclusion

Whatever the prospects for the 'African Renaissance' first championed by Thabo Mbeki nearly a decade ago, it is plain that it will need to be created within an encompassing and intensifying global arena. And although the many dynamics of globalization present Africa and its states with many opportunities, the best and largest of these require a level of development that – even if the Millennium Development Goals can be achieved – will effectively only bring the continent up to the starting line. At the same time, however, African governments have a great deal with which to negotiate – natural resources not least, but also the promise of markets for the developed world's goods. So it is not merely for humanitarian reasons that debt relief for African nations has featured so highly on the international political agenda in recent years.[10]

But the capacity to deal with globalization – which includes a full reckoning of the most important achievable goals, nationally and regionally – has its centre of gravity in African states themselves. Of course, this is a matter of the standards of good governance to which the leaders of all African states have subscribed, but it is also a matter of following that through by holding each other to account and not mistaking acquiescence for solidarity. Almost a decade ago the then deputy president of South Africa, Thabo Mbeki, spelled out the first requirement for the African Renaissance he and millions of others hope to bring about:

The question must therefore arise: What is it which makes up that genuine lib-eration? The first of these elements is that we must bring to an end the practices as a result of which many throughout the world have the view that as Africans, we are incapable of establishing and maintaining systems of good governance. Our own practical experiences tell us that military governments do not represent the system of good governance which we seek. (Mbeki 1998)

But in 2007, long after the inauguration of the AU and NEPAD, and with Mbeki serving his second term as president, we witness

... the election of Zimbabwe to chair the UN commission on sustainable development . [...] In putting forward Francis Nhema, Zimbabwe's environment minister, for the chair, African governments have inflicted on themselves [...] an astonishing blow. The commission [...] is the UN's main forum for addressing the relationship between development and the environment. Africa's turn to fill its chair – which rotates among regions – offered an opportunity to occupy the moral high ground.[11]

Despite every incremental advance and the platform African states have created for themselves to consolidate and direct their considerable assets and strengths, the *Financial Times* was incredulous, as was everyone who hopes to move world perceptions beyond the simplistic and damaging 'Africa the country' stereotypes: 'The timing of the UN debacle is [also] unfortunate [because] it sends a bad signal as talks start to re-capitalise the African Development Bank and replen-ish funds for the World Bank's International Development Association. Even if the issues are separate, Africa has scored a spectacular own goal.'[12] One is reminded forcefully of Benjamin Franklin's injunction at the signing of the US Declaration of Independence: 'We must all hang together, or assuredly we shall all hang separately.'

There remains hope that a new generation of African leaders, unburdened by misplaced loyalties and focused on trying to balance the demands brought about by globalization with the urgency of human development needs, will secure the fundamentals of good governance not only within their states, but also between them. And African states have something to offer a globalized and still-globalizing world: the splendour and variety of their cultures are a resource of alternative forms of social relations and ways of life in a world now intensively urbanized and in many regards flattened out by the feverish con-sumerism that globalization has enabled. A true African Renaissance might not only mediate globalization on behalf of African peoples, but also act positively to humanize the globalizing forces the developed world has often thoughtlessly set in train.

12 | Conclusion: future of peace and conflict in Africa

DAVID J. FRANCIS

Based on the critical issues outlined in this book, what is the future of peace and conflict in Africa? The contributions in this book have critically outlined the multiplicity and complexity of the problems, the challenges and the opportunities for peace and conflict in Africa. A generic theme that unites all the contributions is the view that Africa will no longer witness the generalized chaos manifested by perennial political instability, bloody civil wars and brutal armed conflicts which became the defining feature of the continent between 1990 and 2002. This cautious optimism is based on several factors. First, considerable effort is now being made to invest in conflict analysis by a range of national and international actors as well as conflict and development intervention agencies in an attempt to understand the root causes of conflicts as well as the possibilities for peace. This investment in conflict analysis is informed by the fact that previous dominant intervention activities and strategies have been framed by simplistic and pigeonholing interpretations of wars and armed conflicts, as well as the reasons for underdevelopment and economic crises. The result of this kind of response in conflict situations in Africa has been not only inappropriate solutions but also the usual 'quick fix, short-term and exit strategy' orientation of the international interventions. As discussed by Mohamed Salih and Tony Karbo, there is an emerging consensus within the security–development nexus debate that investment in conflict analysis that incorporates an appreciation of the opportunities for peace is an important contribution to the understanding of peace and conflict in Africa.

Second, based on Africa's emerging global relevance, and in particular the threat to international peace and security posed by wars, insecurity, extreme poverty and underdevelopment on the continent, there has been an increase in the international community's efforts to manage, stabilize and resolve ongoing wars and armed conflicts, though with varying degrees of success. These international engagements have taken two dominant forms: military-security interventions through peacekeeping deployments, and socio-economic, development and financial support through large-scale donor support by development cooperation partners, global governance institutions and IFIs. To complement the international efforts, we have seen the emergence of what has been described as 'assertive regionalism' in peace and security in Africa, with the deployment of regional peacekeeping and conflict stabilization interventions in West Africa

(ECOWAS and ECOMOG), southern Africa (SADC and SADC-AAF), the Horn of Africa (IGAD) and the African Union. These 'home-grown' African peacekeeping and conflict management intervention experiments, albeit with varying degrees of success, have attracted the support of the extra-regional actors such as the EU peacekeeping and peace support operations in the Ituri region of DR Congo (Operation Artemis) and Chad as well as NATO's first out-of-mission-facility support to the African Union Mission peacekeeping operation in Darfur. What is evidently emerging is the fact that issues of peace and conflict in Africa are inextricably linked to international peace and security, and hence it is in the 'common interest' of the international community to support African-led national and regional initiatives to manage and resolve conflicts as well as build the peace.

Third, though the imposition of the liberal peace project in Africa has largely led to the neglect of indigenous resources and institutions for peacemaking, conflict management and resolution and peace-building in transition societies, Jannie Malan, Tony Karbo, Isaac Albert and Tim Murithi have argued that some effort is now being made to incorporate and utilize the continent's 'rich reservoir' of traditional institutions, sociocultural resources and approaches to building the peace and addressing issues of justice and reconciliation in bitterly divided communities, as well as in countries emerging from violent civil war. The examples of the *gacaca* system of justice and reconciliation in Rwanda and the use of *Mato Oput* peace-building in northern Uganda give an indication of the potential relevance and application of African traditional resources and indigenous approaches to modern conflicts.

Fourth, according to the UNDP Human Development Index (2007), the majority of African countries are ranked in the Low Human Development category, and several international reports indicate that Africa is the only continent that will not achieve any of the MDG targets by 2015. These rather depressing socio-economic and development indicators mask the significant economic and development revival taking place on the continent, despite the considerable problems and challenges posed by rapid globalization. The Human Development Index (2007) also acknowledges that three African countries are ranked In the Medium Human Development category: Tunisia (91), Cape Verde (102) and Algeria (104). In addition, the continent registered 5.6 per cent annual GDP growth in 2006. These developments may be modest and easily dismissed as insignificant, but they demonstrate that something meaningful is happening in Africa along the path of modest economic growth and development revival. All of these factors potentially support the difficult and complex challenges of peace and conflict on the continent.

Finally, and beyond the generalized image of weak, fragile, failed and collapsed states in Africa, about one-third of the countries on the continent can be modestly described as strong, viable and modern states, at different levels of state formation and nation-building, bearing in mind that the majority of the states in Africa are still relatively new – about five decades old in comparison with the European states, which are more than four centuries old. In addition, the 'third wave of democratization' in Africa has had both positive and negative impacts, to the extent that more than two-thirds of the countries on the continent are in the process of building a viable and vibrant democratic culture and democratic 'associational life', particularly in transition societies. The democratic route and democratization process in Africa are, however, still fraught with dangers and reversals, as demonstrated by the post-election violence between December 2007 and February 2008 in one of Africa's politically and economically stable countries, Kenya. But the Kenyan democratic reversal, like other reversals on the continent, only reinforces the trajectory of advancement and reversal that has come to define contemporary Africa.

Conclusion

Notes

1 Introduction

1 It is important to recognize that this dominant international media presentation of Africa in the twenty-first century simpy builds on early foundations provided by the colonial contact and interaction with the continent and its putative Westernizing, civilizing and Christianizing project (the 'white man's burden'), and the role of nineteenth- and twentieth-century explorers, travellers, natural scientists, geographers and anthropologists. Edward Said's *Orientalism* (1978) and Frantz Fanon's *Wretched of the Earth: Black Skin, White Mask* (1967) have variously criticized the simplified, infantile and objectified portrayal of the 'Orient', which had justified domination of subject peoples and territories and created an inferiority complex. These dominant and stereotypical presentations of Africa have been challenged by a range of post-structural approaches and post-colonial scholars who try to present an alternative view and interpretation of the continent based on an 'African-focused history' from an African perspective and based on African realisms and conditions. See Asante (1988); Mudimbe (1994); Diop (1974); Lefkowitz (1997); Bernal (1987).

2 This 'Africa as a country' is often seen in descriptions by non-Africans and increasingly Africans in the West. For example, someone who has been on holiday to a single African country will describe or refer to the trip as being to Africa rather than to a single country, such as Kenya or Egypt.

3 The Bank report defines resource curse as 'a situation in which a country has an export-driven natural resources sector that generates large revenues for the state but leads, paradoxically, to economic stagnation and political instability. It is normally used to describe the negative development outcomes associated with non-renewable extractive resources (petroleum and other minerals)' (p. xix).

4 But these official statistics often discount the role of traditional birth attendants or culturally skilled local midwives because they do not fulfil the official Western-based health service delivery criteria.

5 The World Bank Africa Data & Statistics, <http://web.worldbank.org/; http://devdata.worldbank.org/external/CPProfile>.

6 These countries are Sudan (1), Somalia (3), Zimbabwe (4), Chad (5), Côte d'Ivoire (6), DR Congo (7), Guinea (9) and Central African Republic (10). See <www.fundforpeace.org/web/index>.

7 The seven countries are Somalia (179), Chad (172), Sudan (172), DR Congo (168), Guinea (168), Equatorial Guinea (168) and Central African Republic (162). See <www.transparency.org/surveys/#cpi>. It is important to note that these counties are also ranked in the Low Human Development Index category of the HDI between 1990 and 2007, thereby establishing the link between corruption, bad governance, underdevelopment and state failure.

8 <www.pcr.uu.se/database/countries.php?regionSelect=1-Africa>.

9 See also Commission for Africa (2005: 2); UN (2007c).

10 These so-called philanthropic engagements with Africa include the 2006 launch of RED mobile phones to aid Africa by the U2 Irish rock star Bono, the opening of a multimillion-dollar school for girls in South Africa by the American talk show host Oprah Winfrey, and the

adoption of a Malawian boy by the pop star Madonna, which generated a controversial media circus. See Ray (2008).

11 About AFRICOM, <www.africom. mil/AboutAFRICOM.asp>.

12 For literature on modernization and dependency schools of thought on African politics, see Kambhampati (2006); Berstein (1971: 141–60); Nash (1984); Apter (1987); Huntington (1965: 386–430; Rostow (1960); Presbish (1950); Frank (1969); Amin (1976); Rodney (1972); Chazan et al. (1999: 14–32).

13 See Clapham (1985); Callaghy (1984); Sandbrook (1985); Jackson and Rosberg (1982); Rothchild and Chazan (1988).

14 For a critique of Chabal and Daloz's thesis, see Southall and Melber (2006: xv–xxv).

2 African approaches to peace and conflict resolution

1 For more on the concept of *ubuntu* in conflict resolution and indigenous approaches, see Murithi (2006).

2 This discussion on the Tiv has been drawn from work by Yakubu (1995: 4–13).

3 This discussion is taken from Dent (1994: 2–4).

4 For his efforts Martin Dent was honoured by the Tiv Traditional Council with a chieftaincy title, *A-Sor-tar-U-Tiv*, which literally means Peacemaker of Tivland, in 1994.

5 All citations on Somaliland are drawn from Yusuf and Le Mare (2005: 160–65).

6 For more on the five stages of conflict resolution based on *ubuntu*, see Tutu (1999) and Murithi (2006: 9–35).

7 On the merits of cultural norms and collective wisdom, see Surowiecki (2005).

4 The mainstreaming of conflict analysis in Africa

1 This chapter expands on an earlier essay by the author entitled 'Contemporary conflict analysis in perspective', to be found in Lind and Sturman (2002: 1–50). It also builds on the work that the author has developed over the last couple of years with Ulf Engel and Doug Bond on the African Union's Continental Early Warning System, to be published in 2009 as an Ashgate volume entitled *Africa's New Peace and Security Architecture*.

2 Hobsbawm found that 187 million people had been direct and indirect victims of two global wars and a myriad of revolutions and counter-revolutions in the twentieth century. See Hobsbawm (1994).

3 This author found that while 33 million people perished in actual battle, the combined estimate of direct and indirect casualties stood at 203 million for the first eighty-seven years of the twentieth century; Rummel (1995, 1997). Moreover, as A. P. Schmid and A. J. Jongman point out, while 'the storybook of war is one of a clash of two hierarchically structured organisations of officers and soldiers fighting and killing each other for the defence and interests of their states', the fact is that 'war as a clash of two armed forces is not the biggest problem of collective violence. Rather genocide, politicide ("mass killings for political reasons") and democide are the chief killers' (Schmid and Jongman 1998).

4 Charlayne Hunter-Gault in an interview with AllAfrica.com entitled 'Africa: "new news" from Africa – looking beyond death, disease, disaster and despair', 6 October 2006.

5 Ayoob reminds us that, to a large extent, violence in the post-colonial world is partly explained by the pace at which state-building had to be undertaken and the fact that it takes place in a 'dramatically changed international environment' (Ayoob 1995: xiii, 23).

6 To paraphrase the title of a fascinating volume dedicated to the topic (Siverson and Midlarski 1990).

7 In this respect see *inter alia* the excellent collection of essays on interstate war in Bremer and Cusak (1995). A good

example regarding the causes of interstate war can be found in Vasquez (1993).

8 The increase in the total magnitude of violent conflict from the 1950s to the early 1990s, the main component of which was a long-term rise (1950 to late 1980s) in violent conflict within societies, is well documented. According to Gurr et al. (2000: 8), 'societal conflicts', or non-international disputes, represented roughly three times the magnitude of interstate war during most of the last half-century, increasing sixfold between the 1950s and the early 1990s.

9 His argument relates to the fact that concentrating on *Big Wars* alone could prevent us from understanding why and how small wars develop into system-altering conflicts; Bruce Bueno de Mesquita in Siverson and Midlarski (1990: 161).

10 In this regard, see Creveld (1991); K. Holsti (1996); Kaldor (1999). The concept of 'wars of the third kind' was originally developed by Edward Rice (1988). Owing to the more recent and up-to-date analysis provided by Professor Holsti (1996) we will base our discussion on his approach to the concept. Mary Kaldor believes that currently used terms to describe contemporary armed conflict, such as privatized or informal wars, do not fully grasp the complexity of contemporary armed conflict; the term 'post-modern' war may equally be as appropriate as 'new war' (Kaldor 1999: 2). Both Mary Kaldor and Kalevi Holsti build heavily on Van Creveld's thesis of the 'transformation of war'. In this respect Holsti considers Van Creveld to be 'among the first to recognize that the Clausewitzian eighteenth- and nineteenth-century concept of war – which I have called "institutionalized war" – is not only fast fading but is inappropriate as both an analytical and a policy guide to those who must think about and respond to violence that concerns ideology and/or the nature of communities rather than state interests' (Holsti, K. 1996: 36).

11 Anderson (1999). Kenneth Bush's Peace and Conflict Impact Assessment (PCIA) methodology developed for the International Development Research Centre (IDRC) in Canada is also paradigmatic of these concerns, PCIA's main objective being to give development and peace-building interventions a tool to enhance their awareness of how their interventions may create negative effects. In this regard, see Bush (1998).

12 An often cited definition of conflict sensitivity is that contained in a resource pack produced by a consortium of organizations (International Alert et al. 2004). Conflict sensitivity is defined as the capacity of an organization to: understand the (conflict) context in which it operates; understand the interaction between its operations and the (conflict) context; and, finally, act upon the understanding of this interaction in order to avoid negative impacts and maximize positive impacts on the (conflict) context.

13 See Bush (1998) as well as his later 'Peace and Conflict Impact Assessment (PCIA) five years on: the commodification of an idea', in Austin et al. (2001).

14 We should also note that, for the World Bank, these variables must be considered in terms of the ways in which they affect not only conflict but also poverty, a task for which the use of a scale of intensity ranging through *warning*, *increased escalation* and *de-escalation* is recommended (World Bank 2005: 7, 8).

15 As noted by this author, 'stakeholder analysis is intended to help understand conflict-ridden relationships and alliances between the stakeholders, as well as the central conflict issues' (Leonhardt 2001: 19).

16 Jung et al. (1996: 61). In this respect Jung et al. point out that 'since the end of the Cold War, the slogan "ethnic conflict" does not only appear more and more often in the media, but also in the discourse of social science' (ibid.: 60–61).

17 Lake and Rothchild (1998). The

instrumentalist approach is used by, *inter alia*, Glazer and Moynihan (1975); Rothchild (1986); and Brass (1985).

18 Lake and Rothchild (1998). The primordialist approach is developed by, among others: Isaacs (1975); Kaplan (1993); and A. D. Smith (1986).

19 Anthony D. Smith, 'The sources of ethnic nationalism', in Michael Brown (ed.), *Ethnic Conflict and International Security*, Princeton, NJ: Princeton University Press, 1993, as cited in Sisk (1996: 120).

20 Lake and Rothchild (1998). The instrumentalist approach is used by, *inter alia*, Glazer and Moynihan (1975); Rothchild (1986); and Brass (1985).

21 Jabri (1996). See also Jung et al. (1996: 61).

22 Gurr (1996: 63). In this regard Peter Worsley considers that 'cultural traits are not absolutes or simply intellectual categories, but are invoked to provide identities which legitimise claims to rights. They are strategies or weapons in competitions over scarce social goods' (cited in Eriksen 1993). This is also the position of the instrumentalists, as defined by Timothy Sisk: 'Instrumentalists often view ethnic conflict as less a matter of incompatible identities and more a consequence of (a) differential rates and patterns of modernisation between groups and (b) competition over economic and environmental resources in situations where relations among groups vary according to wealth and social status. In other words, ethnicity is often a guise for the pursuit of essentially economic interests' (Sisk 1996: 12).

23 Gurr (1970). See also Oberschall (1969: 5–23). For a case-study application, see Birrel (1972: 317–43).

24 Gurr (1970: 24). Relative deprivation as conceptualized by Ted Robert Gurr arises when an individual does not attain what he thinks is justifiably due to him. It is a mechanism that produces frustration of sufficient intensity to motivate

people to engage in political protest and violence. Accordingly, Ted Gurr states that 'the greater the deprivation an individual perceives relative to his expectations the greater his discontent; the more widespread and intense is discontent among the members of a society, the more likely and severe is civil strife'.

25 According to Dennis J. D. Sandole, James Davies modifies the 'hierarchy of needs' developed by Abraham Maslow, considering that it is the frustration of substantive (physical, social-affectional, self-esteem and self-actualization) or implemental needs (security, knowledge and power) which can facilitate the transition from manifest conflict processes to aggressive manifest conflict processes (Sandole 1993: 14).

26 For an in-depth discussion of structuration theory and its application to conflict, see Jabri, 'A structuration theory of conflict', in Jabri (1996: 54–90).

27 Brown (1996b: 574). See also Schmid (1998).

28 For an in-depth discussion of the development of the level-of-analysis problem in international relations, refer to, *inter alia*, Buzan (1995); Singer (1961); Moul (1973: 494–513). For an application of this framework in the discussion of the leading theories of international conflict, refer to, among others, Levy (1996); Sandole (1993).

29 Waltz (1959). After publication, the shift from 'images of international relations' to 'levels of analysis' was essentially a result of Singer (1960).

30 In Waltz's own words, 'Where are the major causes of war to be found? The answers are bewildering in their variety and in their contradictory qualities. To make this variety manageable, the answers can be ordered under the following three headings: within man, within the structure of the separate states, within the state system' (Waltz 1959: 12).

31 Ibid.: 160, 225. See also 'Introduction', in Midlarksy (1993: xiii–xv).

32 In this respect Ronald Fisher posits that 'it follows that the central unit of analysis in protracted social conflict is the *identity group* [sic], defined in ethnic, racial, religious, linguistic, or other terms, for it is through the identity group that compelling human needs are expressed in social and often in political terms. Furthermore, communal identity itself is dependent upon the satisfaction of basic needs for security, recognition, and distributive justice' (Fisher 1997: 5).

33 Kriesberg (1982: 68). This author adds that 'we are primarily concerned with understanding how conflict groups become conscious of themselves as groups, come to perceive that they have grievances, and formulate goals that would lessen their dissatisfaction at the apparent expense of another party'.

34 An updated version of this book can be found in Kriesberg (1998).

35 In this respect, see, *inter alia*, Vasquez (1993: ch. 5).

36 Levy (1996: 5). For an in-depth discussion of this issue refer to Jervis (1976). Also Nicholson (1992b).

37 As Kriesberg points out, 'continuously organised conflict groups enjoy a mobilisation advantage over emergent conflict parties, as is the case between governments and protesters or revolutionaries' (Kriesberg 1998: 92).

38 Ibid.: 172. This same point is highlighted by Gurr (1970: 35) and also Berkowitz (1969: 42–6).

39 In this respect see Miall et al. (1999: 70). Also the original development of this in Azar (1990b: 7–12).

40 In this respect see, *inter alia*, Zartman (1995).

41 See Migdal (1996) and Ayoob (1996). Also Cohen et al. (1981); Tilly (1985).

42 Van de Goor et al. (1996: 9). See also R. Jackson (1990).

43 Brown (1996b: 18–20). As regards the vast topic of conflict and development, see, *inter alia*, and as an introduction,

Huntington (1968, 1971). Also Gurr (1970) and Newman (1991).

44 Edward Azar considered two main models of international linkage: economic dependency (limiting the autonomy of the state, distorting the patterns of economic development and therefore exacerbating denial of the access needs of communal groups) and political-military client relationships with strong states (where patrons provide protection for the client state in return for the latter's loyalty, which may result in the client state pursuing both domestic and foreign policies that are disjointed from or contradictory to the needs of its own public). In this respect see Azar (1990b: 11, 12).

6 Context of security in Africa

1 For one, the physical map of Africa contrasts such sprawling giants as Sudan, the Democratic Republic of Congo and Algeria with the mini-states of Djibouti and the Gambia. The Gambia, for example, could fit into Sudan 240 times! Substantial diversity was and is also apparent in population size. Nigeria's population is now estimated at well over 130 million people, in contrast with places like Guinea and Botswana with less than 2 million.

2 President Thabo Mbeki, Address to the Joint Sitting of the National Assembly and the National Council on the New Partnership for Africa's Development, 31 October 2001.

3 At the 2002 Kananaskis summit G8 leaders declared, 'Each of us will decide, in accordance with our respective priorities and procedures, how we will allocate the additional money we have pledged. Assuming strong African policy commitments, and given recent assistance trends, we believe that in aggregate half or more of our new development assistance could be directed to African nations that govern justly, invest in their own people and promote economic freedom.'

4 Capital flows into Africa have

declined greatly in real terms since the early 1980s. In 2000 the real per capita inflows were less than a third of what they had been two decades earlier. Over the same period SSA share of total capital inflows to developing countries declined from more than 20 per cent to 10 per cent (UNCTAD 2001: 19).

5 Privatizations have played an important role in the integration of Africa's financial markets into the global system. The creation of stock exchanges to facilitate privatization and the fact that the shares of financial institutions have been a significant proportion of trading on most of these new exchanges have been important contributory factors.

6 Countries that benefited from MDRI: Benin, Burkina Faso, Cameroon, Ethiopia, Ghana, Madagascar, Malawi, Mali, Mauritania, Mozambique, Niger, Rwanda, Senegal, Tanzania, Uganda and Zambia.

7 When fully implemented the MDRI will provide a modest increase in development assistance through reflows.

7 Peace-building in Africa

1 Isaac Albert and Tim Murithi both discuss conceptions of peace and approaches to peace in Africa respectively. They argue convincingly that the idea of peace is not new on the continent and, like other cultures, peoples and traditions, Africa has drawn its understanding and practice of peace and peace-building from various religions, including Islam and Christianity.

2 In his explanation of endogenous methods of peace-building and conflict resolution of the Tiv people of Nigeria, Murithi narrates processes that seek short-term solutions without necessarily addressing the long-term impact on long-term relationships. The goal of this process was to evoke communal solidarity and responsibility.

3 Johan Galtung, one of the chief architects of the conflict resolution field, introduced the concepts of negative and positive peace. Negative peace simply focuses on halting direct, physical violence, while positive peace seeks to end indirect, structural and cultural violence, which are found in the economic, social and cultural structures of society. See Galtung (1969).

4 The land issue in Zimbabwe is one of the contentious issues in the current conflict. This began in 1954 when many native Zimbabweans were removed from the fertile land to be resettled in 'reserves'. The failure to address skewed distribution of land after the 1980 independence contributed to the 'land invasions' of the 1998 by land-hungry peasants and former liberation veterans.

5 The current Zimbabwean crisis has many faces. The war veterans play a leading role in this conflict because they were the proponents of a land resettlement programme that has resulted in almost all the white commercial farmers losing land to the Zimbabwean government through a compulsory land acquisition programme.

6 United Nations Secretary-General's Report on the Peacebuilding Fund, A/62/150, July 2007.

7 The United Nations Secretary-General formally announced this during his address to the Africa summit.

8 See the United Nations Security Council on the Peacebuilding Commission.

9 Following the inauguration of the AU in July 2002, in Durban, South Africa, the continental body promulgated a Protocol Relating to the Establishment of the Peace and Security of the African Union, at the 1st Ordinary Session of the Assembly of Heads of State and Government.

10 *Gacaca* is a traditional mechanism of conflict resolution among the Banyarwanda of Rwanda. This method is used to resolve conflict at the grassroots level through dialogue and a community justice system. It is an intricate system of custom, tradition, norm and usage.

11 *Mato oput* means reconciliation among the Acholi of northern Uganda. It is a detailed ceremony meant to reconcile conflicting parties.

12 Speech by Kofi Annan, former UN Secretary-General, 40th Anniversary of the UNECA, Addis Ababa, April 1998.

13 The Golden Tulip Declaration was signed by representatives of the various Liberian women's organizations in Accra, Ghana, on 15 March 2003. Women pledged to strategize on the inclusion of women in all structures in Liberia in the country's post-conflict peace-building process.

11 Africa and globalization

1 'Risky Business', Africa-Investor. com – News, 1 October 2004, <www.africa-investor.com/article.asp?id=1124>.

2 The Constitutive Act of the African Union, <www.africa-union.org/About_AU/AbConstitutive_Act.htm>.

3 See (from 2001) successive editions of the *Global Society Yearbook*, various publishers.

4 OECD, *African Economic Outlook, 2006–2007*, available at: <www.oecd.org/

document/22/0,2340,de_2649_201185_38561046-1-1-1-100.html>

5 *Protocol Relating to the Establishment of the Peace and Security Council of the African Union*, <www.africa-union.org/organs/orgThe_Peace_%20and_Security_Council.htm>.

6 'Opposition to Africom grows', *Africa Research Bulletin*, 44(8): 17208A–9A.

7 The Human Development Index features in the yearly *Human Development Report* published by the United Nations Development Programme, available at: <http://hdr.undp.org/en/>.

8 'Millennium Development Goals: halfway point', *Africa Reseach Bulletin*, 44(6): 17215A–B.

9 International AIDS Vaccine Initiative, available at: <www.iavi.org/>.

10 See the section on Africa under 'Policy issues' in the 2005 Gleneagles G8 Summit, available at: <www.g8.gov.uk/servlet/Front?pagename=OpenMarket/Xcelerate/ShowPage&c=Page&cid=10942 35520151>.

11 'Africa's own goal', Leading article, *Financial Times*, 16 May 2007.

12 Ibid.

Bibliography

Abdullah, I. (ed.) (2004) *Between Democracy and Terror: The Sierra Leone Civil War*, Dakar: CODESRIA.

Abgaje, Adigun (2004) 'Nigeria: prospects for the Fourth Republic', in E. Gyimah-Boadi (ed.), *Democratic Reform in Africa: The Quality of Progress*, Boulder, CO: Lynne Rienner.

Addison, T. (2005) *Post-Conflict Recovery, Does the Global Economy Work for Peace?*, Discussion Paper no. 2005/05, United Nations University, World Institute for Development Economics Research (WIDER), February.

Adewoye, O. (1987) 'Proverbs as vehicle of juristic thought among the Yoruba', *OAU Law Journal*, 3/4.

Africa Monitor: Southern Africa (2007) 'The price of nothing', September.

African Development Bank (2007) *Natural Resources for Sustainable Development in Africa*, Oxford: OUP.

African Studies Center (2007) *East Africa Living Encyclopedia*, University of Pennsylvania, <www.africa.upenn.edu/NEH/rwhistory.htm>, accessed 29 September 2007.

Ake, C. (1987) 'Sustaining development on the indigenous', Paper prepared for World Bank long-term perspectives study on Africa.

Albert, I. O. (1999) 'Ife-Modakeke crisis', in O. Otite and I. O. Albert (eds), *Community Conflicts in Nigeria: Management, Resolution and Transformation*, Ibadan: Spectrum Books.

— (2001) 'USAID/OTI intervention in Ife-Modakeke crisis', in I. O. Albert (ed.), *Building Peace, Advancing Democracy: Third Party Intervention in Nigeria's Conflicts*, Ibadan: PETRAF/John Archers Books.

— (ed.) (2007) *Local Approaches to Conflict Transformation*, Ibadan: CEPACS, University of Ibadan.

— (2008) 'From "Owo crisis" to "Dagbon dispute": lessons in the politicization of chieftaincy disputes in modern Nigeria and Ghana', *Round Table*, 97: 392.

Albert, I. O., T. Awe, G. Herault and W. Omitoogun (1995) *Informal Channels for Conflict Resolution in Ibadan, Nigeria*, Ibadan: IFRA.

Ali, T. and R. Mathews (2004) *Durable Peace: Challenges to Peace-building in Africa*, Toronto: University of Toronto Press.

Almond, G. A. and B. Powell (1966) *Comparative Politics: Developmental Approach*, Boston, MA: Little, Brown.

Amin, S. (1976) *Unequal Development*, NY: Monthly Review Press.

Anderson, M. (1999) *Do No Harm: How Aid Can Support Peace – or War*, London: Lynne Rienner.

Anderson, P. (1974) *Lineages of the Absolutist State*, London: Verso.

Annan, K. (2004) *An Agenda for Development*, New York: United Nations.

Anyanwu, J. C. (2006) 'Promoting investment in Africa,' *African Development Review*, 18(1).

Apter, D. (1987) *Re-thinking Development: Modernisation, Dependency and Post-modern Politics*, Beverly Hills, CA: Sage.

Arbom, L. and P. Wallensteen (2007) 'Armed conflict, 1989–2006', *Journal of Peace Research*, 44(5).

Aron, R. (2001) *The Opium of the Intellectuals*, New Brunswich, NJ: Transaction.

Asante, M. (1988) *Afrocentricity*, New Jersey: Africa World Press.

Assefa, H. (1993) *Peace and Reconciliation as a Paradigm: A philosophy of peace and its implications on conflict, govern-*

ance, and economic growth in Africa, Nairobi: Nairobi Peace Initiatives.

— (1999) 'The meaning of reconciliation', in *People Building Peace: 35 Inspiring Stories from Around the World*, European Centre for Conflict Prevention.

AU (2001) *The New Partnership for Africa's Development (NEPAD)*, Main document, Addis Ababa: African Union.

Austin, A., M. Fischer and N. Ropers (eds) (2001) *Berghof Handbook for Conflict Transformation*, Berlin: Berghof Centre for Constructive Conflict Management.

Ayittey, G. B. N. (1991) *Indigenous African Institutions*, New York: Transnational Publishers, Inc.

— (1999) *Africa in Chaos*, New York: St Martin's Griffin.

— (2005) *Africa Unchained: The blueprint for Africa's future*, New York: Palgrave Macmillan.

Ayoade, J. A. A. (1986) 'The African search for democracy: hopes and reality', in D. Ronen (ed.), *Democracy and Pluralism in Africa*, London: Hodder and Stoughton.

Ayoob, M. (1995) *The Third World Security Predicament: State Making, Regional Conflict and the International System*, London: Lynne Rienner.

— (1996) 'State-making, state-breaking and state failure', in L. van de Goor with K. Rupesinghe and P. Sciarone (eds), *Between Development and Destruction. An Enquiry into the Causes of Conflict in Post-Colonial States*, London and New York: Macmillan Press Ltd.

Azar, E. (1986) 'Protracted international conflicts: ten propositions', in E. Azar and J. Burton (eds), *International Conflict Resolution: Theory and Practice*, Boulder, CO: Lynne Rienner.

— (1990a) 'Protracted international conflicts: ten propositions', in J. Burton and F. Dukes (eds), *Conflict: Readings in Management and Resolution*, London: Macmillan Press Ltd.

— (1990b) *The Management of Protracted Social Conflict. Theory and Cases*, Darmouth Publishing Co.

Ball, N. (2005) 'The challenge of rebuilding war-torn societies', in C. Crocker, F. O. Hampson and P. Aall (eds), *Turbulent Peace: The Challenges of Managing International Conflict*, Washington, DC: USIP Press.

Bangura, Y. (2004) 'The political and cultural dynamics of the Sierra Leone civil war: a critique of Paul Richards', in I. Abdullah (ed.), *Between Democracy and Terror: The Sierra Leone Civil War (2004)*, Dakar: CODESRIA.

Barber, B. (1996) 'Foundationalism and democracy', in S. Benhabib (ed.), *Democracy and Difference: Contesting the boundaries of the political*, Princeton, NJ: Princeton University Press.

Barbieri, K (2005) *The Liberal Mission: Does Trade Promote Peace?*, Michigan: University of Michigan Press.

Barbolet, A., R. Goldwyn, H. Groenewald and A. Sherriff (eds) (2005) *The Utility and Dilemmas of Conflict Sensitivity*, Berghof Research Center for Constructive Conflict Management, April.

Barth, F. (1969) 'Pathan identity and its maintenance', in Fredrik Barth (ed.), *Ethnic Groups and Boundaries*, Boston, MA: Little, Brown.

Bascom, William R. (1984) *Yoruba of Southwestern Nigeria*, Waveland Press.

Bayart, J.-F., S. Ellis and B. Hibou (1999) *The Criminalization of the State in Africa*, Oxford: James Currey.

Bell, R. H. (2002) *Understanding African Philosophy: A Cross-cultural Approach to Classical and Contemporary Issues*, New York: Routledge.

Benhabib, S. (1996) 'Toward a deliberative model of democratic legitimacy', in S. Benhabib (ed.), *Democracy and Difference: Contesting the boundaries of the political*, Princeton, NJ: Princeton University Press.

Berdal, M. (1996) *Disarmament and Demobilisation after Civil Wars*, Adelphi

Paper 303, London: International Institute for Strategic Studies.

Berdal, M. and D. Malone (eds) (2000) *Greed and Grievance: Economic Agendas in Civil Wars*, Boulder, CO: Lynne Rienner.

Berkowitz, L. (1969) 'The frustration-aggression hypothesis revisited', in L. Berkowitz (ed.), *Roots of Aggression*, New York: Lieber-Atherton Inc.

Berman, B. (2004) 'Ethnicity, bureaucracy and democracy: the politics of trust', in B. Berman et al. (eds), *Ethnicity and Democracy in Africa*, Oxford: James Currey.

Berman, B. et al. (2004) 'Ethnicity and democracy in historical and comparative perspective', in B. Berman et al. (eds), *Ethnicity and Democracy in Africa*, Oxford: James Currey.

Bernal, M. (1987) *Black Athena*, North Carolina: Duke University Press.

Berstein, H. (1971) 'Modernisation theory and the sociological study of development', *Journal of Development Studies*, 7(2).

Bhinda, N., J. Leape, M. Martin and S. Griffith-Jones (1999) *Private Capital Flows to Africa: Perception and Reality*, The Hague: FONDAD.

Biko, S. (1984) 'Some African cultural concepts', *Frank Talk*, 1(4), reprinted in P. H. Coetzee and A. P. J. Roux (2000), *Philosophy from Africa: A Text with Readings*, Oxford: Oxford University Press.

Birch, A. (1993) *The Concepts and Theories of Modern Democracy*, London: Routledge.

Birrel, D. (1972) 'Relative deprivation as a factor in conflict in Northern Ireland', *Sociological Review*, 20(2): 317–43.

Bloomfield, D. (2006) *On Good Terms: Clarifying Reconciliation*, Berghof Report no. 14, <www.berghof-center.org>.

Boege, V. (2006) *Traditional Approaches to Conflict Transformation: Potentials and Limits*, Berlin: Berghof Research Centre for Constructive Conflict Management, July.

Boothby, D. (2001) 'The UNTAES experience: weapons buy-back in eastern Slovenia, Baranja and western Sirmium (Croatia)', in Faltas and Di Chiaro, *Journal of Peace Research*, 41 (4): 499–516.

Boraine, A. (2004) 'Transitional justice', in C. Villa-Vicencio and E. Doxtader, *Pieces of the Puzzle*, Rondebosch: Institute for Justice and Reconciliation.

Borris, E. R. (2002) 'Reconciliation in postconflict peacebuilding: lessons learned from South Africa', in J. Davies and E. Kaufman, *Second Track/Citizens' Diplomacy: Concepts and Techniques for Conflict Transformation*, Lanham, MD: Rowman and Littlefield.

Boulding, K. (1987) 'Peace through the evolutionary process', in R. Vayrynen (ed.), *The Quest for Peace: Transcending collective violence and war among societies, cultures and states*, New York: Sage Publications.

Bourne, M. (2007) *Arming Conflict: The Proliferation of Small Arms*, Basingstoke: Palgrave.

Boutros-Ghali, B. (1995) *Agenda for Peace*, 2nd edn, New York: United Nations.

Brahimi, L. (2000) *Report of the Panel on United Nations Peace Operations*, Manuscript, <www.un.org/peace/reports_operations/docs/full_report.htm/>.

Brass, P. (ed.) (1985) *Ethnic Groups and the State*, London: Croom-Helm.

Bratton, M. and E. Masunungure (2007) 'Popular reactions to state repression: Operation Murambatsvina in Zimbabwe', *African Affairs*, 106.

Bremer, S. A. and T. R. Cusak (1995) *The Process of War. Advancing the Scientific Study of War*, Amsterdam: Gordon and Breach.

Brenes, A. (1990) 'Educating for universal responsibility', *Peace Review*, Spring.

Broadman, H. G. (2007) *Africa's Silk Road: China and India's new economic frontier*, Washington, DC: World Bank.

Brock-Utne, B. (2001) 'Indigenous conflict resolution in Africa', University of

Oslo Seminar on Indigenous Solutions to Conflicts, 23–24 February, <http://africavenir.com/publications/occasionalpapers/BrockUtneTradConflictResolution.pdf>, accessed on 9 December 2007.

Brown, Michael E. (1996a) 'Introduction', in Michael E. Brown, *The International Dimensions of Internal Conflict*, CSIA Studies in International Security, Cambridge, MA and London: MIT Press.

— (1996b) 'The causes and regional dimensions of internal conflict', in Michael E. Brown, *The International Dimensions of Internal Conflict*, CSIA Studies in International Security, Cambridge, MA and London: MIT Press.

— (1996c) *The International Dimensions of Internal Conflict*, CSIA Studies in International Security, Cambridge, MA and London: MIT Press.

Bueno de Mesquita, B. (1986) 'The war trap revisited', *American Political Science Review*, 79(1): 156–77.

— (1987) 'A catch to Moul's catch, or why great powers act as expected by utility maximisers', *International Interactions*, 13(2).

Burton, J. (1990) *Conflict: Resolution and Prevention*, New York: St Martin's Press.

Burton, John W. (1987) *Resolving Deep-Rooted Conflict, a Handbook*, Boston, MA: University Press of America.

Bush, K. (1998) *A Measure of Peace: Peace and Conflict Impact Assessment (PCIA) of Development Projects in Conflict Zones*, Working Paper no. 1, Peacebuilding and Reconstruction Program Initiative and Evaluation Unit, Ottawa: International Development Research Centre, <www.idrc.ca/uploads/user-S/10757546941Working_Paper1.doc>.

Busia, K. A. (1967) *Africa in Search of Democracy*, New York: Praeger.

Buzan, B. (1991) *People, States, and Fear*, 2nd edn, Hemel Hempstead/ Boulder, CO: Harvester Wheatsheaf/ Lynne Rienner.

— (1995) 'The level of analysis problem in international relations reconsidered', in K. Booth and S. Smith (eds), *International Relations Theory Today*, Cambridge: Polity Press.

Byron, D. (2007) Address of Judge Dennis Byron, President of the International Criminal Tribunal for Rwanda, to the United Nations Security Council, 18 June 2007, <http://69.94.11.53/default.htm>, accessed 15 September 2007.

Callaghy, M. (1984) *The State–Society Struggle: Zaire in Comparative Perspective*, New York: Columbia University Press.

Cappelleti, M. (ed.) (1978) *Access to Justice*, vol. 4, Milan: Guifre.

Centre for the Study of Violence and Reconciliation (2007) *Justice in Perspective: A Website on Truth, Justice and Reconciliation in Transition*, <www.justiceinperspective.org.za/index.php?option=com_content&task=view&id=26&Itemid=62>, accessed 15 September 2007.

Chabal, P. (1998) 'A few considerations on democracy in Africa', *International Affairs*, 74(2).

— (2005) 'Violence, power and rationality: a political analysis of conflict in contemporary Africa', in P. Chabal, U. Engel and A.-M. Gentili, *Is Violence Inevitable in Africa? Theories of Conflict and Approaches to Conflict Prevention*, Leiden: Brill.

Chabal, P. and J.-P. Daloz (eds) (1999) *Africa Works: Disorder as Political Instrument*, Oxford: James Currey.

Chandler, D. (2004) 'The responsibility to protect? Imposing the liberal peace', *International Peacekeeping*, 11(1).

— (2006) *Empire in Denial: The Politics of State Building*, London: Pluto.

Charles, A., J. Kenny and T. Moss (2007) 'The trouble with the MDGs: confronting expectations of aid and development success', *World Development*, 35(5).

Charlton, R. (1983) 'Dehomogenising the study of African politics – the case of inter-state influence on regime formation and change', *Plural Societies*, 14(1/2).

Chazan, N., P. Lewis, R. Mortimer, D. Roth-child and S. Stedman (eds) (1999) *Politics and Society in Contemporary Africa*, 3rd edn, Boulder, CO: Lynne Rienner.

CHF International (2006) *Grassroots Conflict Assessment of the Somali Region*, Ethiopia, August.

Cilliers, J. (2000) 'Resource wars – a new type of insurgency', in J. Cilliers and C. Dietrich (eds), *Angola's War Economy. The Role of Oil and Diamonds*, South Africa: Institute for Security Studies.

Cilliers, J. and K. Sturman (2002) 'Commitments by African heads of state to peace, democracy, human rights and associated issues', ISS Paper 58, Institute of Strategic Studies, July.

Clapham, C. (ed.) (1982) *Private Patronage and Public Power*, London: Pinter.

— (1985) *Third World Politics: An Introduction*, Madison: University of Wisconsin Press.

— (1990) *Transformation and Continuity in Revolutionary Ethiopia*, 2nd edn, Cambridge: CUP.

— (1996) *Africa and the International System: The politics of state survival*, Cambridge: CUP.

— (ed.) (1998a) *African Guerrillas*, Oxford: James Currey.

— (1998b) 'Introduction: analysing African insurgencies', in C. Clapham (ed.), *African Guerrillas*, Oxford: James Currey.

Clark, A. M. (2001) *Diplomacy of Conscience: Amnesty International and Changing Human Rights Norms*, Princeton, NJ: Princeton University Press.

Clay, E. and O. Stokk (eds) (2002) *Food Aid and Human Security*, London: Frank Cass.

Clement, M. and T. Moss (2005) *What's Wrong with the Millennium Development Goals?*, Centre for Global Development brief, September.

Coelho, P. B. and A. Vines (1994) *Pilot Study on Demobilisation and Reintegration of Ex-Combatants in Mozambique*, Oxford: OUP.

Coetzee, P. H. and A. P. J. Roux (2000) *Philosophy from Africa: A Text with Readings*, Oxford: OUP.

Cohen, Y., B. R. Brown and A. F. K. Organski (1981) 'The paradoxical nature of state-making: the violent creation of order', *American Political Science Review*, 75(4).

Colletta, N., M. Kostner and I. Wiederhofer (1996) *The Transition from War to Peace in Sub-Saharan Africa*, Washington, DC: World Bank.

Collier, P. (1994) 'Demobilization and insecurity: a study in the economics of the transition from war to peace', *Journal of International Development*, 6(3): 343–51.

— (1999) 'Doing well out of war', Paper prepared for Conference on Economic Agendas in Civil Wars, London, 26–27 April 1999, World Bank 'Economics of Crime and Violence' project, Washington, DC, <www.worldbank.org/ research/conflict/papers/econagenda. htm>.

Collier, P. and A. Hoeffler (1998) *On Economic Causes of Civil War*, World Bank 'Economics of Crime and Violence' project, Washington, DC, January, <www.worldbank.org/research/conflict/ papers/cw-cause.htm>.

— (2000) *Greed and Grievance in Civil War*, Washington, DC: World Bank, <www.worldbank.org/research/conflict/ papers/greedgrievance_23oct.pdf>.

— (2001) *Greed and Grievance in Civil War*, World Bank 'Economics of Crime and Violence' project, Washington, DC, 4 January, <www.worldbank.org/ research/conflict/papers/greedand-grievance.htm>.

— (2004) *Greed and Grievance in Civil War*, Oxford Economic Papers 56.

Collier, P., L. Elliot, H. Hegre, A. Hoefller, M. Reyan-Querol and N. Sambanis (2003) *Breaking the Conflict Trap*, New York: World Bank and Oxford University Press.

Collier, P. et al. (2005) *Breaking the Conflict Trap: Civil War and Development Policy*, Washington, DC/Oxford: World Bank/ Oxford University.

Commission for Africa (2005) *Our Common Interest: Report of the Commission for Africa*, London.

Conciliation Resources (2002) *Protracted Conflict, Elusive Peace: Initiatives to End the Violence in Northern Uganda*, London: Accord.

Cooper, N. (2005) 'Picking out the pieces of the liberal peace: representations of conflict economics and implications for policy', *Security Dialogue*, 36(4).

Cox, G. (1986) *The Ways of Peace: A philosophy of peace as action*, New York: Paulist Press.

Creveld, V. (1991) *The Transformation of War*, New York: Free Press.

Crocker, C. et al. (2005) *Turbulent Peace: The Challenges of Managing International Conflict*, Washington, DC: USIP Press.

Crocker, D. A. (1998) *Transitional Justice and International Civil Society*, Working Paper no. 13, National Commission on Civic Renewal, University of Maryland.

Cusak, T. R. (1995) 'On the theoretical deficit in the study of war', in S. A. Bremer and T. R. Cusak (eds), *The Process of War. Advancing the Scientific Study of War*, Amsterdam: Gordon and Breach.

Dahl, R. A. (1989) *Democracy and Its Critics*, New Haven, CT: Yale University Press.

Darnolf, S. and L. Laakso (eds), *Twenty Years of Independence in Zimbabwe: From liberation to authoritarianism*, London: Palgrave Macmillan.

Davies, J. (1962) 'Toward a theory of revolution', *American Sociological Review*, 27.

Davies, J. and E. Kaufman (2002) *Second Track/Citizens' Diplomacy: Concepts and Techniques for Conflict Transformation*, Lanham, MD: Rowman and Littlefield.

Davies, J. C. (1973) 'Aggression, violence, revolution and war', in J. N. Knutson (ed.), *Handbook of Political Psychology: Contemporary Problems and Issues*, San Francisco, CA: Jossey-Bass.

Deng, F. M. and I. W. Zartman (eds) *Conflict Resolution in Africa*, Washington, DC: Brookings Institution Press.

Dent, M. (1994) 'Practical peacekeeping', Unpublished paper, Keele University.

Deutsch, K. W. (1974) *Politics and Government: How people decide their fate*, Boston, MA: Houghton Mifflin.

Development Cooperation Directorate (2006) *Final ODA Data for 2006*, Paris: OECD.

Dewey, J. (1955) *Democracy and Education: An introduction to the philosophy of education*, New York: Macmillan.

DfID (Department for International Development) (1997) *Eliminating World Poverty: A challenge for the 21st century*, London: TSO.

— (2002) *Conducting Conflict Assessments: Guidance Notes*, London: TSO.

Diamond, L. (2004) 'Promoting real reform in Africa', in E. Gyimah-Boadi (ed.), *Democratic Reform in Africa: The Quality of Progress*, Boulder, CO: Lynne Rienner.

Diop, C. A. (1974) *The African Origin of Civilisation: Myth or Reality*, Lawrence Hill Books.

Douma, P., G. Frerks and L. van de Goor (1999) *Major Findings of the Research Project 'Causes of Conflict in the Third World': Executive Summary*, Occasional Papers, Conflict Research Unit, Netherlands Institute of International Relations 'Clingendael'.

Dowden, R. (2007) 'Endgame in Zimbabwe', *Time*, 169(14).

Doyle, M. W. (1986) 'Liberalism and world politics', *American Political Science Review*, 80(4).

— (1997) 'Liberal internationalism: peace, war and democracy', excerpts from M. W. Doyle's *Ways of War and Peace*, New York: W. W. Norton, published by Nobelprize.org, 22 June 2004, <http://nobelprize.org/nobel_prizes/peace/articles/doyle/index.html#1>, accessed 10 December 2007.

— (2005) 'Three pillars of the liberal peace', *American Political Science Review*, 99(3).

Duffield, M. (2002) *Global Governance and the New Wars: The merging of security and development*, London: Zed Books.

— (2008), *Development, Security and Un-ending Wars*, Cambridge: Polity Press.

Dugan, Maire (1997) 'A nested theory of conflict', *Women in Leadership*, 1(1), Washington, DC: US Institute of Peace Press.

Easterly, W. (2007) 'How the Millennium Development Goals are unfair to Africa', *Global Economy and Development*, Working Paper 14, November.

Egwu, Samuel G. (2007) 'Beyond revival of old hatred: the state and conflict in Africa', in S. G. Best (ed.), *Introduction to Peace and Conflict Studies in West Africa*, Ibadan: Spectrum Books.

Elliott, L. (2007) 'Anti-poverty targets in Africa will not be met, UN warns', *Guardian*, 2 July.

Eriksen, T. H. (1993) *Ethnicity and Nationalism: Anthropological Perspectives*, London: Pluto Press.

Esteban, J. M. and D. Ray, 'On the measurement of polarisation', *Econometrica*, 62(4).

Evans, P. B. (1995) *Embedded Autonomy: States and Industrial Transformation*, Princeton, NJ: Princeton University Press.

Eze, C. P. (2008) *Don't Africa Me: 'Their' Geo-branding War. 'Our' Trade*, Tourism Wounds Expertz.

Failed States Index (2007), *Foreign Policy*, July/August, pp. 54–63.

Fairhead, J. (2000) 'The conflict over natural and environmental resources', in E. W. Wayne, F. Stewart and R. Vayrynen (eds), *The Origins of Humanitarian Emergencies: War and Displacement in Developing Countries*, Oxford: OUP.

Fanon, F. (1967) *Wretched of the Earth: Black Skin, White Mask*, New York: Grove Press.

Fatton, R. (1992) *Predatory Rule: State and Civil Society in Africa*, Boulder, CO: Lynne Rienner.

Ferguson, J. (1978) *War and Peace in World Religions*, Oxford: OUP.

Fetherston, A. B. (2000) *From Conflict Resolution to Transformative Peacebuilding: Reflections from Croatia*, Centre for Conflict Resolution Working Paper 4, Department of Peace Studies, University of Bradford, April.

Fischer, D. (1996) 'A global peace service', *Peace Review*, 8.

Fischer, M. (2000) *The Liberal Peace: Ethical, historical and philosophical aspects*, Discussion Paper no. 2000-07, Befler Center for Science and International Affairs, John Kennedy School for Government, Harvard University, April.

Fisher, R. (1997) *Interactive Conflict Resolution*, Syracuse, NY: Syracuse University Press.

Fisher, S. et al. (2000) *Working with Conflict – Skills and Strategies for Action*, London: Zed Books.

Fogarty, B. E. (2000) *War, Peace and the Social Order*, Boulder, CO: Westview Press.

Forum on Early Warning and Early Response (FEWER) (2001) *Conflict Analysis and Response Definition. Abridged Methodology*, London, April, <www.fewer.org/research/index.htm>.

Francis, D. (2001) *The Politics of Economic Regionalism: Sierra Leone in ECOWAS*, Aldershot: Ashgate.

— (2005) 'Introduction', in D. Francis (ed.), *Civil Militia: Africa's Intractable Security Menace?*, Aldershot: Ashgate.

— (2006a) 'Linking peace, security and

Bibliography

developmental regionalism: regional economic and security integration in Africa', *Journal of Peacebuilding and Development*, 2(3).

— (2006b) *Uniting Africa: Building Regional Peace and Security Systems*, Aldershot: Ashgate.

— (2007) 'Peace and conflict studies: an African overview of basic concepts', in S. G. Best (ed.), *Introduction to Peace and Conflict Studies in West Africa*, Ibadan: Spectrum Books.

Francis, D. et al. (2004) *Dangers of Co-Deployment: UN Cooperative Peacekeeping in Africa*, Aldershot: Ashgate.

Frank, A. G. (1969) *Capitalism and Underdevelopment in Latin America*, New York: Monthly Review Press.

French, H. W. (2007) 'The Chinese and Congo take a great leap of faith', *International Herald Tribune*, 21 September.

Friedman, S. (2004) 'South Africa: building democracy after apartheid', in E. Gyimah-Boadi (ed.), *Democratic Reform in Africa: The quality of progress*, Boulder, CO: Lynne Rienner.

Galtung, J. (1964a) 'A structural theory of aggression', *Journal of Peace Research*, 1(2): 95–119.

— (1964b) 'Editorial', *Journal of Peace Research*, 1(1): 1–4.

— (1969) 'Violence, peace and peace research', *Journal of Peace Research*, 10(3): 217–26.

— (1981) 'Social cosmology and the concept of peace', *Journal of Peace Research*, 18(2).

— (1990) 'Violence and peace', in P. Smoker et al. (eds), *A Reader in Social Studies*, New York: Pergamon Press, pp. 9–14.

Gasana, E., J.-B. Butera, D. Byanafashe and A. Kareikezi (1999) 'Rwanda', in A. Adedeji (ed.), *Comprehending and Mastering African Conflicts: The Search for Sustainable Peace and Good Governance*, London and New York: Zed Books.

Geertz, C. (1973) *The Interpretation of Cultures*, New York: Free Press.

Geisler, G. (2004) *Women and the Remaking of Politics in Southern Africa: Negotiating Autonomy, Incorporation and Representation*, Uppsala: Nordic Africa Institute.

Ghebremeskel, A. (2002) 'Regional approach to conflict management revisited: the Somali experience', *Online Journal of Peace and Conflict Resolution*, 4(2).

Gibson, J. L. and H. Macdonald (2001) *Truth – Yes, Reconciliation – Maybe: South Africans Judge the Truth and Reconciliation Process*, Research report, Rondebosch: Institute for Justice and Reconciliation.

Glazer, N. and D. P. Moynihan (1975) *Ethnicity: Theory and Experience*, Cambridge, MA: Harvard University Press.

Gleneagles G8 Summit (2005) *Africa: 'Policy issues'*, <www.g8.gov.uk/servlet/Front?pagename=OpenMarket/Xcelerate/ShowPage&c=Page&cid=1094235520151>.

Global Security (2005) 'Liberia: first civil war: 1989–96' <http://www.globalsecurity.org/military/world/war/liberia-1989.htm>.Goldberg, S. et al. (1985) *Dispute Resolution*, Boston, MA: Little, Brown.

Goldstone, R. (1996) 'Justice as a tool for peace-making: truth commissions and international criminal tribunals', *New York University Journal of International Law and Politics*, 28, extract reprinted in C. Heyns and K. Stefiszyn (2006), *Human Rights, Peace and Justice in Africa: A Reader*, Pretoria: Pretoria University Law Press.

Goodhand, J., T. Vaux and R. Walker (eds) (2001) *Guide to Conflict Assessment*, United Nations Development Programme/Department for International Development, 3rd draft, unpublished, September.

Govier, T. (1998) *Social Trust and Human*

Communities, Montreal: McGill-Queen's University Press.

Graybill, L. S. (2004) 'Pardon, punishment and amnesia: three African post-conflict methods', *Third World Quarterly*, 25, extract reprinted in C. Heyns and K. Stefiszyn (2006), *Human Rights, Peace and Justice in Africa: A Reader*, Pretoria: Pretoria University Law Press.

Green, W. (2007) 'Where investors fear to tread', *Time*, 170(1).

Grugel, J. (2002) *Democratization: A Critical Introduction*, New York: Palgrave.

Gurr, T. (1970) *Why Men Rebel*, Princeton, NJ: Princeton University Press.

— (1993) *Minorities at Risk: A Global View of Ethnopolitical Conflicts*, Washington, DC: United States Institute of Peace Press.

— (1996) 'Minorities, nationalists and ethnopolitical conflict', in C. A. Crocker and F. O. Hampson with P. Hall (eds), *Managing Global Chaos: Sources of and Responses to International Conflict*, Washington, DC: US Institute of Peace.

Gurr, T. R., M. G. Marshall and D. Khosla (2000) *Peace and Conflict 2001: A Global Survey of Armed Conflicts, Self-Determination Movements, and Democracy*, Center for International Development and Conflict Management (CIDCM), University of Maryland, <www.bsos.umd.edu/cidcm/peace.htm>.

Gyimah-Boadi, E. (ed.) (2004) *Democratic Reform in Africa: The Quality of Progress*, Boulder, CO: Lynne Rienner.

Habermas, J. (1996) 'Three normative models of democracy', in S. Benhabib (ed.), *Democracy and Difference: Contesting the boundaries of the political*, Princeton, NJ: Princeton University Press.

Habimana, A. (2001) 'What does "international justice" look like in post-genocide Rwanda?', Carnegie Council on Ethics and International Affairs – Human Rights Dialogue:

Human Rights in Times of Conflict: Humanitarian Intervention Series 2, no. 5, extract reprinted in C. Heyns and K. Stefiszyn (2006), *Human Rights, Peace and Justice in Africa: A Reader*, Pretoria: Pretoria University Law Press.

Harris, I. M. (1990) 'The goals of peace education', *Peace Review*, Spring.

Harrison, R. H. (1984) 'War and expected utility theory', *World Politics*, 40(1).

Harsch, E. (2005) 'Peace pact raises hope in Senegal', *Africa Renewal*, 19(1), <www.un.org/ecosocdev/geninfo/afrec/vol19no1/191senegal.htm>, accessed 9 September 2007.

Havermans, J. (1999a) 'Burundi: peace initiatives help stem the violence', in Mekenkamp et al. (1999).

— (1999b) 'Rwanda: Rwandan crisis lingers on', in Mekenkamp et al. (1999).

Haward and Baker (1997) 'Development and security: towards more conflict sensitive development policies and progress', *Haword Journal of Criminal Justice*, 44(5): 558–9.

Hegre, H., T. Ellingsen, S. Gates and N. Gleditsch (2001) 'Towards a democratic civil peace? Democracy, political change, and civil war, 1816–1992', *American Political Science Review*, 95(1): 33–48.

Held, D. and A. McGrew (2007) *Globalization/Anti-Globalization*, 2nd edn, Cambridge: Polity Press.

Helman, G. B. and S. R. Ratner (1997) 'Saving failed states', *Foreign Policy*, 89, Winter.

Hendricks, C. (2004) 'The burdens of the past and challenges of the present: coloured identity and the "Rainbow Nation"', in B. Berman et al. (eds), *Ethnicity and Democracy in Africa*, Oxford: James Currey.

Herbst, J. (2000) *States and Power in Africa: Comparative Lessons in Authority and Control*, Princeton, NJ: Princeton University Press.

Heyns, C. and K. Stefiszyn (eds) (2006) *Human Rights, Peace and Justice in*

Africa: A Reader, Pretoria: Pretoria University Law Press.

Hickman, L. A. and T. M. Alexander (eds) (2004) *The Essential Dewey: Pragmatism, education, democracy*, Bloomington: Indiana University Press.

History World (2007) 'History of Rwanda', <www.historyworld.net/wrldhis/PlainTextHistories.asp?historyid=ad24>, accessed 29 September 2007.

Hobbes, T. (1928) *Elements of Law*, ed. F. Tonnies, Cambridge: CUP.

— (1968) *Leviathan*, ed. C. B. Macpherson, Harmonsworth: Penguin.

Hobsbawm, E. (1994) *The Age of Extremes: The Short Twentieth Century, 1914–1991*, London: Michael Joseph.

Holsti, K. (1989a) 'Ecological and Clausewitzian approaches to the study of war: assessing the possibilities', Paper presented at the 30th Anniversary Convention of the International Studies Association, London.

— (1989b) 'Mirror, mirror on the wall, which are the fairest theories of all?', *International Studies Quarterly*, 33(3).

— (1991) *Peace and War: Armed Conflicts and International Order 1648–1989*, Cambridge: CUP.

— (1996) *The State, War, and the State of War*, Cambridge Studies in International Relations, Cambridge: CUP.

Holsti, O. (1990) 'Crisis nanagement', in B. Glad (ed.), *Psychological Dimensions of Conflict*, London: Sage.

Homer-Dixon, T. (1994) 'Environmental scarcities and violent conflict', *International Security*, 19(1): 5–40.

— (1998) 'Environmental scarcity and intergroup conflict', in M. T. Klare and Y. Chandrani (eds), *World Security: Challenges for a New Century*, New York: St Martin's Press, pp. 342–65.

Hoyweghen, S. (2005) *DRC's Natural Treasures: Source of Conflict or Key to Development?*, Report of the expert meeting, 23–24 November, Brussels, <www.globalwitness.org/reports/

show.php/en.00095.html> accessed 23 August 2006.

Human Rights Watch (2003) 'China's involvement in Sudan: arms and oil', <www.hrw.org/reports/2003/sudan1103/26.htm>.

Human Sciences Research Council (1985) *The South African Society: Realities and future prospects*, Main committee: HSRC investigation into intergroup relations, Pretoria: Human Sciences Research Council.

Hunt, J. T. (2006) *The Politics of Bones*, Toronto: McClelland and Stewart.

Hunter-Gault, C. (2006) *New News out of Africa: Uncovering the African Renaissance*, New York: OUP.

Huntington, S. (1965) 'Political development and political decay', *World Politics*, 17(3).

— (1968) *Political Order in Changing Societies*, New Haven, CT: Yale University Press.

— (1971) 'Civil violence and the process of development', in *Civil Violence and the International System*, Adelphi Paper no. 83, London: IISS.

Hyden, G. (2006) *African Politics in Comparative Perspective*, Trenton, NJ: CUP.

Idris, A. . (2005) *Conflict and Politics of Identity in Sudan*, Trenton, NJ: Palgrave Macmillan.

IGAD (2007) *The Conflict Early Warning and Response Mechanism (CEWARN) of IGAD*, <www.cewarn.org/>, accessed 6 September 2007.

IMF/World Bank (2004) *Heavily Indebted Poor Countries (HIPC) Initiative: Status of Implementation*, Washington, DC, 20 August.

Institute for Justice and Reconciliation (2002) *Annual Report 2002: Reconciliation: No future without it*, Cape Town: Institute for Justice and Reconciliation.

International Alert (1996) *Resource Pack for Conflict Transformation*, London.

International Alert, Saferworld, CECORE, APFO and CHA (2004) *Conflict-sensitive Approaches to Development, Humani-*

tarian Assistance and Peacebuilding, Colombo: Consortium of Humanitarian Agencies.

International Criminal Tribunal for Rwanda (2007) *International Criminal Tribunal for Rwanda: General Information*, <http://69.94.11.53/default.htm>, accessed 15 September 2007.

International Crisis Group (2006) *Beyond Victimhood: Women's Peacebuilding in Sudan, Congo, and Uganda*, Africa Report no. 112, 28 June.

Isaacs, H. (1975) *Idols of the Tribe: Group Identity and Political Change*, New York: Harper and Row.

Ishida, T. (1969) 'Beyond the traditional concepts of peace in different cultures', *Journal of Peace Research*, 2.

Jabri, V. (1996) *Discourses on Violence*, Manchester: Manchester University Press.

Jackson, H. R. (2000) *The Global Covenant: Human Conduct in a World of States*, London: OUP.

Jackson, R. (1990) *Quasi-States, Sovereignty, International Relations and the Third World*, Cambridge: CUP.

Jackson, R. and C. Rosberg (1970) *Personalised Rule in Black Africa: Prince, Autocrat, Prophet, Tyrant*, Berkeley: University of California Press.

— (1982) 'Why Africa's weak states persist: the empirical and juridical in statehood', *World Politics*, 35(1).

Jalata, A. (2005) *Oromia and Ethiopia: State formation and ethno-national conflict, 1868–2004*, Trenton, NJ: Red Sea Press.

James, M. (1991) *The Hope and Fears of Independence*, in D. Rimmer (ed.), *Africa 30 Years On*, London: James Currey.

— (2003) *Somalia and Somaliland: Strategies for Dialogue and Consensus on Governance and Democratic Transition*, Oslo: UNDP Governance Centre.

Jervis, R. (1976) *Perception and Misperception in International Politics*, Princeton, NJ: Princeton University Press.

Johnson, G. L. (1976) 'Conflicting concepts

of peace in contemporary peace studies', *International Studies*, 4(2).

Jordaan, W. and J. Jordaan (1997) *Man in Context*, Isando: Lexicon Publishers.

Joseph, R. (1987) *Democracy and Prebendal Politics in Nigeria: The Rise and Fall of the Second Republic*, Cambridge: CUP.

— (1997) 'The international community and armed conflict in Africa: post cold war dilemmas', in G. M Sorbo and P. Vale (eds), *Out of Conflict: From war to peace in Africa*, Uppsala: Nordiska Afrikainstitutet.

Jung, D., K. Schlite and J. Siegelberg (1996) 'Ongoing wars and their explanation', in L. van de Goor with K. Rupesinghe and P. Sciarone (eds), *Between Development and Destruction. An Enquiry into the Causes of Conflict in Post-Colonial States*, London and New York: Macmillan Press.

Kabia, J. (2008) 'Greed or grievance?: diamonds, rent-seeking and the recent civil war in Sierra Leone', in K. Omeje (ed.), *Extractive Economies and Conflicts in the Global South: Multi-Regional Perspectives on Rentier Politics*, Aldershot: Ashgate.

Kabongo, I. (1986) 'Democracy in Africa: hopes and prospects', in D. Ronen (ed.), *Democracy and Pluralism in Africa*, Boulder, CO: Lynne Rienner.

Kacoke Madit (2000) *The Quest for Peace in Northern Uganda*, London: Kacoke Madit, <www.km-net.org.uk>, accessed 11 December 2007.

Kaldor, M. (2006) *New and Old Wars. Organized Violence in a Global Era*, Cambridge: Polity Press.

Kambhampati, U. (2006) *Development and the Developing World*, Cambridge: Polity Press.

Kaplan, R. (1993) *Balkan Ghosts: A Journey through History*, New York: St Martin's Press.

Kaplan, R. D. (1994) 'The coming anarchy', *Atlantic Monthly*, 273(2).

Karl, T. L. (1997) *The Paradox of Plenty:*

Oil Boom and Petro-Politics, Berkeley: University of California Press.

Kaufmann, D. et al. (2007) *Governance Matters VI: Aggregate and Individual Governance Indicators 1996–2006*, World Bank, July.

Kayizzi-Mugerwa, S. (2001) 'Africa and the donor community: in search of a partnership for development', in L. Rikkila and K. Sehm-Patomaki (eds), *Democracy and Globalization, Promoting a North South Dialogue*, Helsinki: Department for International Development Cooperation, Ministry of Foreign Affairs.

— (ed.) (2003a) *Reforming Africa's Institutions: Ownership, incentives and capabilities*, Tokyo: United Nations University Press.

— (2003b) 'Introduction', in S. Kayizzi-Mugerwa (ed.), *Reforming Africa's Institutions: Ownership, incentives and capabilities*, Tokyo: United Nations University Press.

Keen, D. (1998) 'Economic functions of violence in civil wars', Adelphi Paper no. 320, International Institute for Strategic Studies, Oxford: OUP.

Khalil, M. (2000) 'Conflict resolution in Africa', *Journal of African Economies*, 9(3).

King, C. (1997) *Ending Civil Wars*, Adelphi Paper no. 308, London: International Institute for Strategic Studies.

Kingma, K. (1999) 'Post-war demobilisation and reintegration and peacebuilding', Report submitted to the International Conference and Expert-Group Meeting: The Contribution of Disarmament and Conversion to Conflict Prevention and Its Relevance for Development Cooperation, Bonn: Bonn International Centre for Conversion.

— (ed.) (2000) *Demobilisation in Sub-Saharan Africa: The Development and Security Impacts*, New York: St Martin's Press.

— (2001) 'Demobilisation and reintegration of ex-combatants in post-war and transition countries: trends and challenges of external support', Eschborn: GTZ.

— (2002) 'Demobilisation, reintegration and peacebuilding in Africa', in E. Newman and A. Schnabel (eds), *Recovering from Civil Conflict: Reconciliation, Peace and Development*, London: Frank Cass.

Kiss, E. (2000) 'Moral ambition within and beyond political constraints: reflections on restorative justice', in R. I. Rotberg and D. Thompson (2000).

Klare, M. T. (2001) 'The new geography of conflict', *Foreign Affairs*, May/June.

Knight, M. and A. Ozerdem (2004) 'Guns, camps and cash: disarmament, demobilization and reinsertion of former combatants in transitions from war to peace', *Journal of Peace Research*, 41(7).

Korpi, W. (1974) 'Conflict, power, and relative deprivation', *American Political Science Review*, 68(4): 1569–78, December.

Korten, D. C. (1995) *When Corporations Rule the World*, London: Earthscan.

Kpundeh, S. J. (2004) 'Corruption and corruption control', in E. Gyimah-Boadi (ed.), *Democratic Reform in Africa: The quality of progress*, Boulder, CO: Lynne Rienner.

Krause, K. and M. C. Williams (1997) *Critical Security Studies: Concepts and Cases*, London: University College.

Kriesberg, L. (1982) *Social Conflicts*, 2nd edn, New York: Prentice-Hall.

— (1998) *Constructive Conflicts. From Escalation to Resolution*, New York: Rowman and Littlefield.

Lake, D. and D. Rothchild (1998) 'Ethnic fears and global engagement: the international spread and management of global conflict', in D. A. Lake and D. Rothchild (eds), *The International Spread of Ethnic Conflict*, Princeton, NJ: Princeton University Press.

Le Billon, P. (2000) 'The political economy of resource wars', in J. Cilliers and C. Dietrich (eds), *Angola's War Economy. The Role of Oil and Diamonds*,

South Africa: Institute for Security Studies.

Lederach, J. P. (1978) *Preparing for Peace: Conflict Transformation across Cultures*, Syracuse, NY: Syracuse University Press.

— (1998) *Building Peace: Sustainable Reconciliation in Divided Societies*, Washington, DC: USIP Press.

— (1999) 'The challenge of the 21st century: just peace', in *People Building Peace: 35 Inspiring Stories from around the World*, Utrecht: European Centre for Conflict Prevention.

Lefkowitz, M. (1997) *Not Out of Africa: How Afrocentrism Has Become an Excuse to Teach Myth as History*, New York: Basic Books.

Lemarchand, R. (2007) 'Consociationalism and power sharing in Africa: Rwanda, Burundi, and the Democratic Republic of the Congo', *African Affairs*, 106(422).

Leonhardt, M. (2001) *Conflict Analysis for Project Planning and Management. A practical guideline*, Eschborn: Deutsche Gesellschaft für technische Zusammenarbeit (GTZ).

Levy, J. S. (1996) 'Contending theories of international conflict: a level-of-analysis approach', in C. A. Crocker and F. O. Hampson with P. Hall (eds), *Managing Global Chaos: Sources of and Reponses to International Conflict*, Washington, DC: US Institute of Peace.

Lewer, N. (2002) *Training Manual on Conflict Resolution*, Centre for Conflict Resolution, Department of Peace Studies, University of Bradford.

Lewis, P. (1996) 'Economic reform and political transition in Africa: the quest for a politics of development', *World Politics*, 49(1).

Lienert, I. (1998) 'Civil service reform in Africa: mixed results after 10 years', *Finance and Development*, 35(2).

Lind, J. and K. Sturman (eds) (2002) *Scarcity and Surfeit: The Ecology of Africa's Conflicts*, Pretoria: African Centre for Technology Studies and Institute for Security Studies.

Linklater, A. (1996) 'Rationalism', in S. Burchill et al. (eds), *Theories of International Relations*, London: Macmillan.

Llobera, J. R. (1999) *Recent Theories of Nationalism*, Working Paper no. 164, Barcelona: Institu de Ciencies Politique i Socials.

Lockwood, M. (2006) *The State They are In: An agenda for international action on poverty in Africa*, Bourton on Dunsmore: Practical Action Publishing.

Loper, J. (2006) 'What are values', <http://personaldevelopment.suite101.com/article.cfm/what_are_values>.

Lovgren, Stefan (2007) 'The big play for Africa: China elbows its way into a resource-rich continent', *US News and World Report*, 29 July.

Luckham, R. (2004) 'The international community and state reconstruction in war-torn societies', *Conflict, Security & Development*, 4(3): 481–507.

Lund, M. S. (1996) *Preventing Violent Conflicts: A Strategy for Preventive Diplomacy*, Washington, DC: US Institute of Peace Press.

Lutheran World Federation (2002) 'Interfaith peace summit: rediscovering indigenous conflict resolution practices', Geneva: Lutheran World Federation, <www.lutheranworld.org/News/LWI/EN/1088.EN.html>, accessed 17 August 2007.

Lyman, P. N. (2005) 'China's rising role in Africa', Council on Foreign Relations, 21 July, <www.cfr.org/publications/8436/chinas_rising_role_in_africa.html>.

Lyons, T. and A. I. Samatar (1995) 'Somalia, state collapse, multilateral intervention, and strategies for political reconstruction', Brookings Occasional Papers, Washington, DC: Brookings Institution.

Mackie, G. (2003) *Democracy Defended*, Cambridge: CUP.

Macmillan, J. (1998) *On Liberal Peace: Democracy, War and the International Order*, London: Tauris Academic.

Macquarrie, J. (1973) *The Concept of Peace*, London: SCM Press.

Magang, D. N. (1986) 'Democracy in Africa: The Case of Botswana', cited in D. R. Ronan (ed.), *Democracy and Pluralism in Africa*, Boulder, CO: Lynne Rienner.

Mahdavy, H. (1970) 'The patterns and problems of economic development in rentier states: the case of Iran', in M. A. Cook (ed.), *Studies in the Economic History of the Middle East*, Oxford: OUP.

Makoba, W. (1999) 'Rethinking current explanations of political changes in Sub-Saharan Africa', *Journal of Third World Studies*, XVI(2).

Malan, J. (1997) *Conflict Resolution Wisdom from Africa*, Durban: ACCORD.

Maley, W., C. Sampford and R. Thakur (2003) *From Civil Strife to Civil Society: Civil and military responsibilities in disrupted states*, Tokyo: United Nations University.

Malu, L. (2003) 'Collective peacekeeping in West Africa', *Peace & Conflict Monitor*, Special Report of the University for Peace, <www.monitor.upeace.org/archive.cfm?id_article=61>, accessed 6 September 2007.

Mamdani, M. (1996) *Citizen and Subject: Contemporary Africa and the Legacy of Late Colonialism*, Princeton, NJ: Princeton University Press.

— (1998) *When Does Reconciliation Turn into a Denial of Justice?*, Sam Molutshungu Memorial Lectures, Pretoria: Human Sciences Research Council Publishers, extract reprinted in C. Heyns and K. Stefiszyn (2006), *Human Rights, Peace and Justice in Africa: A Reader*, Pretoria: Pretoria University Law Press.

Management Systems International (2002) *Rwanda Conflict Vulnerability Assessment*, Washington, DC: Greater Horn of Africa Peace Building Project.

Mansfield, E. D. and J. Snyder (1995) 'Democratization and the danger of war', *International Security*, 20(1).

Maren, M. (1996) 'Somalia: whose failure', *Current History*, 95(202).

Marks, S. (2004) 'The dog that did not bark, or why Natal did not take off: ethnicity and democracy in South Africa – KwaZulu-Natal', in B. Berman et al. (eds), *Ethnicity and Democracy in Africa*, Oxford: James Currey.

Masina, N. (2000) 'Xhosa practices of Ubuntu for South Africa', in I. W. Zartman (ed.), *Traditional Cures for Modern Conflicts: African Conflict 'Medicine'*, Boulder, CO: Lynne Rienner.

Mayall, J. (1990) *Nationalism and International Relations*, Cambridge: CUP.

— (1991) 'The hope and fears of independence', in D. Rimmer (ed.), *Africa 30 Years On*, London: James Currey.

Mazula, B. (2004) 'Mozambique: the challenge of democratisation', in E. Gyimah-Boadi (ed.), *Democratic Reform in Africa: The Quality of Progress*, Boulder, CO: Lynne Rienner.

Mbeki, T. (1998) 'The African renaissance, South Africa and the world', Speech at the United Nations University, 9 April, <www.unu.edu/unupress/mbeki.html>.

— (2001) Address to the Joint Sitting of the National Assembly and the National Council on the New Partnership for Africa's Development, 31 October.

Mbeki, T., O. Obasanjo and A. Bouteflika (2001) *Millennium Partnership for the African Recovery Programme (MAP)*, A development blueprint for Africa, submitted at the Organization for African Unity (OAU) summit in Lusaka, Zambia, July.

Mbigi, L. and J. Maree (1995) *Ubuntu: The Spirit of African Transformation Management*, Randburg: Knowledge Resources Limited.

Mbiti, J. S. (1975) *The Prayers of African Religion*, London: SPCK.

McCandless, E. (2006) 'Peace-related concepts', Handout at the Curriculum Development Workshop on Peacebuilding and Conflict Transformation in Post-War Liberia, jointly organized by the Africa Centre, University of Bradford, and the Kofi Annan Institute for Conflict Transformation, University of Liberia, Monrovia, 1–5 May.

McCarran, H. and A. Varshney (2004) 'Violent conflict and the Millennium Development Goals: diagnosis and recommendations', Working Paper no. 19, Working Papers Series, Center on Globalization and Sustainable Development (CGSD), Earth Institute, Columbia University.

McVeigh, T. (2006) 'Nurse exodus leaves Kenya in crisis', *Observer*, 21 May.

Mekenkamp, M., P. van Tongeren and H. van de Veen (1999) *Searching for Peace in Africa: An Overview of Conflict Prevention and Management Activities*, Utrecht: European Platform for Conflict Prevention and Transformation, in cooperation with the African Centre for the Constructive Resolution of Disputes (ACCORD).

Mengisteab, K. and O. Yohannes (2005) *Anatomy of an African Tragedy: Political, economic, and foreign policy crisis in post-independence Eritrea*, Trenton, NJ: Red Sea Press.

Menkhaus, K. (2006/7) 'Governance without government in Somalia: spoilers, state building, and the politics of coping', *International Security*, 31(3).

Meredith, M. (2003) *Our Votes, Our Guns: Robert Mugabe and the tragedy of Zimbabwe*, New York: Public Affairs.

— (2005) *The Fate of Africa: From the hopes of freedom to the heart of despair; a history of fifty years of independence*, New York: Public Affairs.

Miall, H. (2004) *Conflict Transformation: A Multi-Dimensional Track*, Monograph of the Berghof Research Centre for Constructive Conflict Management, August, <www.berghof-handbook.net/uploads/download/miall_handbook.pdf>, accessed 16 October 2007.

Miall, H. with O. Ramsbotham and

T. Woodhouse (eds) (1999) *Contemporary Conflict Resolution*, Cambridge: Polity Press.

Midlarsky, M. I. (ed.) (1993) *Handbook of War Studies*, Michigan: University of Michigan Press (originally published by Unwin Hyman, 1989).

Migdal, J. (1988) *Strong Societies and Weak States: State–Society Relations and State Capabilities in the Third World*, Princeton, NJ: Princeton University Press.

— (1996) 'Integration and disintegration: an approach to society formation', in L. van de Goor with K. Rupesinghe and P. Sciarone (eds), *Between Development and Destruction. An Enquiry into the Causes of Conflict in Post-Colonial States*, London and New York: Macmillan Press.

Miguel, E., S. Satyanath and E. Sergenti (2004) 'Economic shocks and civil conflict: an instrumental variables approach', *Journal of Political Economy*, 112(41).

Miles, W. F. S. and D. A. Rochefort (1991) 'Nationalism versus ethnic identity in Sub-Saharan Africa', *American Political Science Review*, 85.

Mitchell, C. R. (1981) *The Structure of International Conflict*, London: Macmillan Press.

Mlambo, N. (2006) 'Evolution of peace and Security Council of the African Union and the African Standby Force', *Africa Insight*, 36(3/4).

Mokitimi, M. I. (1997) *The Voice of the People: Proverbs of the Basotho*, Ibadan: Daystar Press.

Molutsi, P. (2004) 'Botswana: the path to democracy and development', in E. Gyimah-Boadi (ed.), *Democratic Reform in Africa: The quality of progress*, Boulder, CO: Lynne Rienner.

Morgenson, G. (1998) 'Seeing a fund as too big to fail, New York Fed assists its bailout', *New York Times*, 24 September.

Morgenthau, H. J. (1960) *Politics among Nations: The Struggle for Power and Peace*, 3rd edn, New York: Knopf.

Bibliography

Moser, C. and A. Norton (2001) *To Claim Our Rights: Livelihood security, human rights and sustainable development*, London: Overseas Development Institute.

Mouffe, C. (1996) 'Democracy, power, and the "political"', in S. Benhabib (ed.), *Democracy and Difference: Contesting the boundaries of the political*, Princeton, NJ: Princeton University Press.

Moul, W. B. (1973) 'The level of analysis problem revisited', *Canadian Journal of Political Science*, 61(1).

Moundi, M. O. et al. (2007) *Getting In: Mediators' Entry into the Settlement of African Conflicts*, Washington, DC: USIP.

Moyo, S. (2004) 'The land and agrarian question in Zimbabwe', Paper presented at conference on 'The Agrarian Constraint and Poverty Reduction: Macroeconomic Lessons for Africa', Addis Ababa, 17–18 December, <www.sarpn.org.za/documents/d0001097/P1211->.

Mudimbe, V. (1994) *The Idea of Africa*, Bloomington: Indiana University Press.

Munck, R. (2005) *Globalization and Contestation: The New Great Countermovement*, London: Routledge.

Murithi, T. (ed.) (2000) *All Africa Conference on African Principles of Conflict Resolution and Reconciliation, November 8–12, 1999, United Nations Conference Centre – ECA, Addis Ababa, Ethiopia: Final Report*, Addis Ababa: Shebelle-Ethiopia Conference Services.

— (2006) 'Practical peacemaking wisdom from Africa: reflections on Ubuntu', *Journal of Pan-African Studies*, 1(4).

Mustapha, A. R. (2004) 'Ethnicity and the politics of democratisation in Nigeria', in B. Berman et al. (eds), *Ethnicity and Democracy in Africa*, Oxford: James Currey.

Mwagiru, M. (ed.) (2004) *African Regional Security in the Age of Globalization*, Nairobi: Heinrich Böll Foundation, Regional Office, East and Horn of Africa.

Nash, M. (1984) *Unfinished Agenda: The dynamics of modernisation in the developing world*, Boulder, CO: Westview Press.

Newman, E. and O. Richmond (2006) 'Introduction: obstacles to peace processes: understanding spoiling', in E. Newman and O. Richmond (eds), *Challenges to Peacebuilding: Managing spoilers during conflict resolution*, Tokyo: United Nations University Press.

Newman, S. (1991) 'Does modernisation breed ethnic conflict?', *World Politics*, 43(3).

Ngoie, G. T. and K. Omeje (2008) 'Rentier politics and low intensity conflicts in the DRC: the case of Kasai and Katanga provinces', in K. Omeje (ed.), *Extractive Economies and Conflicts in the Global South: Multi-Regional Perspectives on Rentier Politics*, Aldershot: Ashgate.

Nhema, A. (ed.) (2004) *The Quest for Peace in Africa: Transformations, Democracy and Public Policy*, Addis Ababa/Utrecht: OSREA/International Books.

Nicholson, M. (1987) 'The conceptual bases of the war trap', *Journal of Conflict Resolution*, 13(2).

— (1992a) 'International crisis: the warping of rationality', in *Rationality and the Analysis of International Conflict*, Cambridge Studies in International Relations, Cambridge: CUP.

— (1992b) *Rationality and the Analysis of International Conflict*, Cambridge Studies in International Relations, Cambridge: CUP.

Nkrumah, K. (1970) *Consciencism: Philosophy and ideology for de-colonization*, New York: Monthly Review Press.

Nnoli, O. (1995) *Ethnicity and Development in Nigeria*, Aldershot: Avebury.

Ntahobari, J. and B. Ndayiziga (2003) 'The role of Burundian women in the peaceful settlement of conflicts', in UNESCO, *Women and Peace in Africa: Case studies on traditional conflict resolution practices*, Paris: UNESCO.

Nyerere, J. K. (1971) *Ujamaa: Essays on Socialism*, Oxford: OUP.

Oberschall, A. R. (1969) 'Rising expectations and political turmoil', *Journal of Development Studies*, 6(1).

OECD (2006) 'FDI and Africa: context and opportunity', *OECD Review*.

Olaoba, O. B. (2000) *The Significance of Cross-examination in Yoruba Traditional Jurisprudence*, Ibadan: John Archers.

Olzak, S. (1986) 'A competition model of ethnic collective action in American cities 1877–1889', in S. Olzak and J. Nagel (eds), *Competitive Ethnic Relations*, Orlando, FL: Academic Press.

Omeje, K. (2006) *High Stakes and Stakeholders: Oil Conflict and Security in Nigeria*, Aldershot: Ashgate.

— (ed.) (2008) *Extractive Economies and Conflict in the Global South: Multiregional perspectives on rentier politics*, Aldershot: Ashgate.

Orjuela, C. (2004) 'Civil society in civil war, peace work and identity politics in Sri Lanka', PhD dissertation, Department of Peace and Development Research, University of Göteborg.

O'Rourke, H. and J. G. Williamson (1999) *Globalization and History: The Evolution of a Nineteenth-Century Economy*, Boston, MA: MIT Press.

Otite, O. and I. O. Albert (eds) (1999) *Community Conflicts in Nigeria: Management, Resolution and Transformation*, Ibadan: Spectrum Books.

Pain, D. (1997) *The Bending of Spears: Producing Consensus for Peace and Development in Northern Uganda*, London: International Alert and Kacoke Madit.

Paris, R. (2004) *At War's End: Building Peace after Civil Conflict*, Cambridge: CUP.

Parry, G. and M. Moran (1994) *Democracy and Democratization*, London: Routledge.

Peck, M. S. (1987) *The Different Drum: Community making and peace*, Simon and Schuster.

Perry, A. (2007) 'Africa's oil dreams', *Time*, 169(24).

Picciotto, R., F. Olonisakin and M. Clarke (2007) *Global Development and Human Security*, London: Transaction Publishers.

Pkalya, R. et al. (2004) *Indigenous Democracy: Traditional conflict resolution mechanisms*, East Africa: Intermediate Technology Development Group.

Poku, N. (1996) 'The construction of ethnic identities in contemporary Africa', in N. Renwick and J. Krause (eds), *Identities and International Relations*, London: Macmillan Press.

Poku, N. K. and B. Sandkjaer (2007) 'HIV/AIDS in the context of poverty: Africa's deadly predicament', in R. J. Ostergard, Jr (ed.), *HIV/AIDS and the Threat to National and International Security*, Basingstoke: Palgrave.

Poku, N., N. Renwick and J. G. Porto (2007) 'Human security and development in Africa', *International Affairs*, 83(6).

Polgreen, L. and H. W. French (2007) 'China's largess in Africa isn't free', *International Herald Tribune*, 20 August.

Porto, J. G. (2002) 'Contemporary conflict analysis in perspective', in J. Lind and K. Sturman (eds), *Scarcity and Surfeit: The Ecology of Africa's Conflicts*, Pretoria: African Centre for Technology Studies and Institute for Security Studies.

Powell, K. (2005) *From Promise to Practice? The African Union in Burundi and Darfur*, Monograph no. 119, South Africa: Institute for Security Studies (ISS), May, <www.iss.org.za/pubs/Monographs/No119/Chap6.htm>.

Presbish, R. (1950) *The Economic Development of Latin America and Its Principal Problems*, New York: United Nations.

Ramcharan, B. G. (2002) *Human Rights and Human Security*, The Hague: Martinus Nikhoff.

Ramsbotham, O., T. Woodhouse and H. Miall (2005) *Contemporary Conflict Resolution*, Cambridge: Polity Press.

Ray, C. (2008) 'The dangers of "Brand Aid"', *New African*, February, pp. 18–19.

Reardon, B. (1988) *Comprehensive Peace*

Education: Educating for global responsibility, New York: Teachers College Press.

Reno, W. (1995) Corruption and State Politics in Sierra Leone, Cambridge: CUP.

Republic of South Africa (1996) The Constitution of the Republic of South Africa, 1996, Cape Town: Constitutional Assembly.

Reychler, L. (2001) 'From conflict to sustainable peacebuilding: concepts and analytical tools', in L. Reychler and T. Paffenholz (eds), Peacebuilding: A Field Guide, Boulder, CO: Lynne Rienner.

Reynal-Querol, M. (2000) Religious Conflict and Growth: Theory and Evidence, Mimeo, London School of Economics and Political Science.

Rice, E. (1988) Wars of the Third Kind: Conflict in Underdeveloped Countries, Berkeley: University of California Press.

Richmond, O. (2006) 'Human security and the liberal peace: tensions and contradictions', Paper presented to the EKEM Workshop on International Peacekeeping and Peacemaking: Global and Regional Perspectives.

Rinehart, M. (2005), 'Toward a better concept of peace', <www.beyondintractability.org/essay/peace>, accessed 17 August 2007.

Rodney, W. (1972) How Europe Underdeveloped Africa, London: Bogle L'Ouverture.

Ronning, H. (2003) 'The media in Zimbabwe: the struggle between state and civil society', in S. Darnolf and L. Laakso (eds), Twenty Years of Independence in Zimbabwe: From liberation to authoritarianism, London: Palgrave Macmillan.

Rorty, R. (1996) 'Idealisations, foundations and social practices', in S. Benhabib (ed.), Democracy and Difference: Contesting the boundaries of the political, Princeton, NJ: Princeton University Press.

— (1999) Philosophy and Social Hope, London: Penguin.

— (2007) Philosophy as Cultural Politics, Cambridge: CUP.

Rosato, S. (2003) 'The flawed logic of democratic peace theory', American Political Science Review, 97(4).

Rosenau, J. N. and E.-O. Czempiel (eds) (1992) Governance without Government: Order and Change in World Politics, Cambridge: CUP.

Ross, M. (2003) 'The natural resource curse: how wealth can make you poor', in I. Bannon and P. Collier (eds), Natural Resources and Violent Conflict: Options and Actions, Washington, DC: World Bank.

Rosser, A. (2006) 'The political economy of the resource curse: a literature survey', IDS Working Paper 268, Sussex: Institute of Development Studies.

Rostow, W. W. (1960) The Stages of Economic Growth, Cambridge: CUP.

Rotberg, R. (2004) 'Strengthening African leadership', Foreign Affairs, 83(4).

Rotberg, R. I. and D. Thompson (eds) (2000) Truth v. Justice: The Morality of Truth Commission, Princeton, NJ: Princeton University Press.

Rothchild, D. (1986) 'Interethnic conflict and policy analysis in Africa', Ethnic and Racial Studies, 9(1).

Rothchild, D. and N. Chazan (eds) (1988) The Precarious Balance: State and Society in Africa, Boulder, CO: Westview Press.

Rothchild, D. and V. Olorunsola (eds) (1983) State vs Ethnic Claims: African Policy Dilemmas, Boulder, CO: Westview Press.

Rummel, R. J. (1995) 'Democracy, power, genocide, and mass murder', Journal of Conflict Resolution, 39(1).

— (1997) Statistics of Democide, Genocide and Mass Murder since 1990, Charlottesville: School of Law, Center for National Security Law, University of Virginia.

Rupesinghe, K. (1995) Conflict Resolution, New York: St Martin's Press.

— (1998) 'Negotiating peace in Sri Lanka:

efforts, failures and lessons', London: International Alert.

Rupesinghe, K. with S. N. Anderlini (1998) *Civil Wars, Civil Peace. An Introduction to Conflict Resolution*, London: Pluto Press.

Said, E. (1978) *Orientalism*, New York: Pantheon.

Salih, M. (1999) 'The Horn of Africa: human security in the new world order', in C. Thomas and P. Wilkin (eds), *Globalization, Human Security and the African Experience*, Boulder, CO: Lynne Rienner.

— (2006) 'Globalizing party politics in Africa: the influence of party-based democracy networks', in P. Burnell (ed.), *Globalising Democracy: Party politics in emerging democracies*, London: Routledge.

— (forthcoming) *A Critique of the Liberal Peace: The African Experience*.

Sandbrook, R. (1985) *The Politics of Africa's Economic Stagnation*, Cambridge: CUP.

Sandole, D. J. D. (1993) 'Paradigms, theories, and metaphors in conflict and conflict resolution: coherence or confusion?', in D. J. D. Sandole and H. van der Merwe (eds), *Conflict Resolution Theory and Practice. Integration and Application*, Manchester: Manchester University Press.

— (1999) *Capturing the Complexity of Conflict. Dealing with Violent Ethnic Conflicts of the Post-Cold War Era*, London and New York: Pinter.

Santho, S. (2000) 'Lesotho: lessons and challenges after a SADC intervention, 1998', in D. Philander (ed.), *Franco-South African Dialogue: Sustainable Security in Africa*, Monograph no. 50, South Africa: Institute for Security Studies (ISS), August.

Sarkin, J. (1999) 'The necessity and challenges of establishing a Truth and Reconciliation Commission in Rwanda', *Human Rights Quarterly*, 21.

Scheff, T. J. (1967) 'Toward a sociological model of consensus', *American Sociological Review*, 32.

Schelling, T. (1960) *The Strategy of Conflict*, Cambridge, MA: Harvard University Press.

Schmid, A. P. (1998) 'Causes of internal conflicts', in S. B. Anderlini (ed.), *Thesaurus and Glossary of Early Warning and Conflict Prevention Terms*, abridged edn, FEWER/Synthesis Foundation, <www.fewer.org/research/index.htm>.

Schmid, A. P. and A. J. Jongman (1998) 'Mapping dimensions of contemporary conflicts and human rights violations', in *World Conflict and Human Rights Map 1998*, The Netherlands: PIOOM – Interdisciplinary Research Programme on Causes of Human Rights Violations.

Schneiderman, W. (1993) 'Conflict resolution in Mozambique', in D. Smock (ed.), *Making War and Peace: Foreign intervention in Africa*, Washington, DC: United States Institute of Peace.

Schoeman, M. (2002) 'Imagining a community: the African Union as an emerging security community', *Strategic Review for Southern Africa*, XXIV(1).

Scholte, J. A. (2005) *Globalization: A Critical Introduction*, 2nd edn, Basingstoke: Palgrave.

Shehadi, K. S. (1993) *Ethnic Self-Determination and the Break-up of States*, Adelphi Paper 283, London: International Institute for Strategic Studies.

Shorter, A. (1975) *Prayer in the Religious Traditions of Africa*, Oxford: OUP.

SIDA (2004) *A Strategic Conflict Analysis for the Great Lakes Region*, Division for Eastern and Western Africa, March.

Singer, J. D. (1960) 'International conflict. Three levels of analysis', Review article, *World Politics*, 12(3): 453–61.

— (1961) 'The level of analysis problem in international relations', in K. Knorr and S. Verba (eds), *The International System. Theoretical Essays*, Princeton,

NJ: Princeton University Press. Reprinted by Greenwood Press, 1982.

— (1996) 'Armed conflict in the former colonial regions: from classification to explanation', in L. van de Goor with K. Rupesinghe and P. Sciarone (eds), *Between Development and Destruction. An Enquiry into the Causes of Conflict in Post-Colonial States*, London and New York: Macmillan Press.

Singer, J. D. and M. Small (1982) *Resort to Arms: International and Civil Wars: 1816–1980*, Beverly Hills, CA: Sage.

Sisk, T. D. (1996) *Power Sharing and International Mediation in Ethnic Conflicts*, Washington, DC: Carnegie Commission on Preventing Deadly Conflict, United States Institute of Peace.

Siverson, M. and M. I. Midlarski (eds) (1990) 'Big wars, little wars – a single theory?', *International Interactions*, 16(3).

Smith, A. D. (1986) *The Ethnic Origins of Nations*, New York: Basil Blackwell.

Smith, D. (2004) *Towards a Strategic Framework for Peacebuilding: Getting Their Act Together: Overview report of the Joint Utstein Study of Peacebuilding*, Evaluation Report 1/2004, Oslo: Royal Ministry of Foreign Affairs, <www.dep. no/filarkiv/210673/rapp104.pdf>.

Smith, D. J. (2006) *A Culture of Corruption: Everyday deception and popular discontent in Nigeria*, Princeton, NJ: Princeton University Press.

Smith, R. M. (2002) 'Modern citizenship', in E. F. Isin and B. S. Turner (eds), *Handbook of Citizenship Studies*, London: Sage.

Smock, D. R. (1997) 'Building on locally-based and traditional peace processes', <http://southsudanfriends. org/LocallyBasedPeace.html>, accessed 17 August 2007.

Sorbo, G. M. (1997) 'From Mogadishu to Kinshasha – concluding remarks', in G. M. Sorbo and P. Vale (eds), *Out of Conflict: From war to peace in Africa*, Uppsala: Nordiska Afrikainstitutet.

Sorbo, G. M. and P. Vale (eds) (1997) *Out of Conflict: From war to peace in Africa*, Uppsala: Nordiska Afrikainstitutet.

South African Government (1995) *The Promotion of National Unity and Reconciliation Act, No. 34 of 1995*, Cape Town: South African Parliament.

Southall, R. and H. Melber (2006) *Legacies of Power: Leadership Change and Former Presidents in African Politics*, Cape Town: HSRC Press.

Starr, A. (2000) *Naming the Enemy: Anticorporate Movements Confront Globalization*, London: Zed Books.

Stedman, J. (1991) *Peacemaking in Civil War: International Mediation in Zimbabwe, 1974–1980*, London: Lynne Rienner.

Stock, R. (2004) *Africa South of the Sahara: A Geographical Interpretation*, 2nd edn, London: Guilford Press.

Strange, S. (1996) *Retreat of the State: The Diffusion of Power in the World Political Economy*, Cambridge: CUP.

— (1997) 'An international economy perspective', in J. H. Dunning, *Governments, Globalization, and International Business*, Oxford: OUP.

Surowiecki, J. (2005) *The Wisdom of Crowds*, New York: Anchor Books.

Tadjbakhsh, S. and A. M. Chenoy (2007) *Human Security: Concepts and implications*, London: Routledge.

Taisier, A. and R. Mathews (2004) *Durable Peace: Challenges for Peacebuilding in Africa*, Toronto: University of Toronto Press.

Tellewoyan, Joseph K. (2000) 'The Liberian civil war', <www.liberia-leaf.org/reports/trials/war/war.htm>.

Thomas, C. and P. Wilkin (eds) (1999) *Globalization, Human Security and the African Experience*, Boulder, CO: Lynne Rienner.

Thompson, C. (2007) 'Senegal's President has won another term, but the youth are getting restless', *Time*, 169(14).

Thompson, W. R. (1990) 'The size of war, structural and geopolitical contexts, and theory building/testing', in R. M. Siverson and M. I. Midlarski (eds), *International Interactions*, 16(3).

Thomson, A. (2007) *An Introduction to African Politics*, London: Routledge.

Tilly, C. (1985) 'War-making and state-making as organised crime', in P. B. Evans, D. Rueschemeyer and T. Skocpol, *Bringing the State Back In*, Cambridge: CUP.

Tocqueville, A. (1956) *Democracy in America*, New York: New American Library of World Literature.

Transparency International (2007) *Global Corruption Report: Corruption in Judiciary Systems*, Cambridge: Cambridge University Press.

Tripp, A. M. (2004) 'Women's movements, customary law, and land rights in Africa: the case of Uganda', *African Studies Quarterly*, 7(4), <www.africa.ufl.edu/asq/v7/v7i4a1.pdf>.

Truth and Reconciliation Commission (1998) *Truth and Reconciliation Commission of South Africa Report*, vol. 1, Cape Town: Juta.

Tutu, D. M. (1998) 'Foreword by chairperson', in Truth and Reconciliation Commission (1998).

— (1999) *No Future without Forgiveness*, London: Rider.

UN (United Nations) (2000) *Millennium Declaration*, New York.

— (2001), *Report of the Panel of Experts on Illegal Exploitation of Natural Resources and Other Forms of Wealth of the Democratic Republic of Congo*, New York: United Nations Security Council, 12 April.

— (2005) *Investing in the Future: Practical Plan to Achieve the Millennium Development Goals*, London: Earthscan.

— (2007a) *Millennium Development*, New York.

— (2007b) *The Millennium Development Goals 2007*, <http://mdgs.un.org/unsd/mdg/Resources/Static/Products/Progress2007/UNSD_MDG_Report_2007e.pdf>.

— (2007c) *Africa and the Millennium Development Goals Update*.

UN Department of Public Information (2003) *Charter of the United Nations and Statute of the International Court of Justice*, New York: United Nations.

UN Economic Commission for Africa (2005) *African Governance Report 2005*, Addis Ababa: UNECA.

UN Millennium Project (2005) *Investing in Development: A Practical Plan to Achieve the Millennium Development Goals*, Main report, New York: United Nations.

UNCTAD (2000) 'FDI and Africa: context and opportunity', *UNCTAD Review*.

— (2005) *Statistical Profiles of the Least Developed Countries*, Geneva: United Nations Conference on Trade and Development.

— (2007) *The Least Developed Countries Report, 2007: Knowledge, Technical Learning and Innovation for Advancement*, <www.unctad.org/en/docs/ldc2007_en.pdf>.

UNDG-ECHA (2004) *Inter-agency framework for conflict analysis in transition situations*, November.

UNDP (United Nations Development Programme) (1994) *Human Development Report*, New York: OUP.

— (2004) *Poverty Trends and the Voices of the Poor*, Washington, DC: World Bank, Poverty Reduction and Economic Management Unit.

— (2006) *Human Development Index*, New York: United Nations Development Programme.

— (2007a) *Poverty Trends and the Voices of the Poor*, Washington, DC: World Bank, Poverty Reduction and Economic Management Unit.

— (2007b) *Human Development Report 2007/08*, New York: OUP.

UNESCO (2003) *Women and Peace in Africa: case studies on traditional conflict resolution practices*, Paris: UNESCO.

US Institute of Peace (USIP) (2004) 'Terrorism in the Horn of Africa',

Special Report 113, Washington, DC: USIP.

Uwazie, E. E. (2000) 'Social relations and peacekeeping among the Igbo', in I. W. Zartman (ed.), *Traditional Cures for Modern Conflict: African conflict 'medicine'*, Boulder, CO, and London: Lynne Rienner.

— (ed.) (2002) *Conflict Resolution and Peace Education in Africa*, New York: Lexington Books.

Uwazie, E. U., I. O. Albert and G. N. Uzogwe (eds) (1999) *Inter-Ethnic and Religious Conflict Resolution in Nigeria*, Lanham, MD: Lexington Books.

Van de Goor, L. with K. Rupesinghe and P. Sciarone (eds) (1996) *Between Development and Destruction. An Enquiry into the Causes of Conflict in Post-Colonial States*, London and New York: Macmillan Press.

Van den Berghe, P. (1981) *The Ethnic Phenomenon*, New York: Elsevier.

Van-Tongeren, P. et al. (eds) (2005) *People Building Peace II: Successful Stories of Civil Society*, Boulder, CO, and London; Lynne Rienner.

Vasquez, J. (1976) Assessment of quantitative international relations research in 'Statistical findings in international politics: a data-based assessment', *International Studies Quarterly*, 20(2).

— (1987) 'The steps to war: toward a scientific explanation of correlates of war findings', *World Politics*, 40.

— (1993) *The War Puzzle*, Cambridge Studies in International Relations, Cambridge: CUP.

Vaux, T., A. Mavela, J. Pereira and J. Stuttle (2006) *Strategic Conflict Assessment: Mozambique*, Department for International Development (DfID), April.

Villa-Vicencio, C. and W. Verwoerd (2000) *Looking Back, Reaching Forward: Reflections on the Truth and Reconciliation Commission of South Africa*, Cape Town: University of Cape Town Press.

Vlassenroot, K. (2003) 'Economies de guerre et entrepreneurs militaires', in P. Hassner and R. Marchal (eds), *Guerres et sociétés. Etat et violence après la guerre froide*, Paris: Karthala.

Vogt, M. A. (1997) 'Conflict resolution and peace-keeping – the Organisation of African Unity and the United Nations', in G. M. Sorbo and P. Vale (eds), *Out of Conflict: From war to peace in Africa*, Uppsala: Nordiska Afrikainstitutet.

Vraalsen, T. (1997) 'Thinking about peace and peace-making in Africa', in G. M. Sorbo and P. Vale (eds), *Out of Conflict: From war to peace in Africa*, Uppsala: Nordiska Afrikainstitutet.

Wade, A. (2001) *OMEGA Plan for Africa*, Presented at the Organization of African Unity (OAU) summit in Lusaka, Zambia, July.

Wagona, M. (1999) 'Rethinking current explanations of political changes in Sub-Saharan Africa,' *Journal of Third World Studies*, XVI(2).

Walker, R. (2004) 'Rwanda still searching for justice', <www.news.bbc.co.uk/2/hi/africa/3557753.stm>, accessed 18 September 2007.

Walker, R. B. J. (1989) 'History and structure in the theory of international studies', *Millennium*, 18(2).

Wallensteen, P. and M. Sollenberg (1999) 'Armed conflict, 1989–1998', *Journal of Peace Research*, 36(5).

Wallis, W. (2006) 'Egypt report, the economy: a break from the past?', *Financial Times*, 11 December.

Waltz, K. (1959) *Man, the State and War: A Theoretical Analysis*, New York and London: Columbia University Press.

Watts, M. J. (1999) 'Petro-violence: some thoughts on community, extraction and political ecology', Posted at the eScholarship Repository, University of California.

Weber, M. (1958) 'Wirtschaftund Gesellschaft', in H. Gerth and C. Wright Mills (eds), *From Max Weber: Essays in Sociology*, New York: OUP.

Wehr, P. (1979), *Conflict Regulation*, Boulder, CO: Westview Press.

Weiss-Fagen, P. (1995) *After the Conflict: A Review of Selected Sources on Rebuilding War-torn Societies*, Geneva: United Nations Institute for Disarmament Research.

Whitman, J. (2005) *The Limits of Global Governance*, London: Routledge.

Wierzynska, A. O. (2004) 'Consolidating democracy through transitional justice: Rwanda's Gacaca courts', *New York University Law Review*, 79, extract reprinted in C. Heyns and K. Stefiszyn (2006), *Human Rights, Peace and Justice in Africa: A Reader*, Pretoria: Pretoria University Law Press.

Wilkin, P. (2002) 'Global poverty and orthodox security', *Third World Quarterly*, 23(4).

Williams, A. (1998) 'Intellectuals and the crisis of democratization in Nigeria: towards a theory of postcolonial anomie', *Theory and Society*, 27(2).

Williams, P. (2004) *Understanding Peacekeeping*, Cambridge: Polity Press.

Wines, M. (2007) 'Energy shortage hampers development in Africa', *International Herald Tribune*, 29 July.

World Bank (1993) *Demobilization and Reintegration of Military Personnel: The Evidence from Seven Country Case Studies*, Africa Region Working Group on Demobilization and Reintegration of Military Personnel, Washington, DC: World Bank.

— (2000) *Private Sector and Infrastructure: Tourism in Senegal*, Washington, DC: World Bank.

— (2005) *Conflict Analysis Framework (CAF)*, Washington, DC: World Bank.

— (2006) *World Development Report: The State in a Changing World*, Oxford: OUP.

— (2007) *Global Monitoring Report 2007*, SecM2007-0094, Washington, DC: World Bank.

Wray, R. (2007) 'China overtaking US for fast internet access as Africa gets left behind', *Guardian*, 14 June.

Yakubu, D. M. (1995) 'Conflict resolution in traditional African societies and present day realities: the Tiv experience', Paper presented at a seminar organized by the Centre for Nigerian Cultural Studies, Ahmadu Bello University, Zaria, July.

Yates, D. (1996) *The Rentier State in Africa: Oil Rent Dependency and Neo-colonialism in the Republic of Gabon*, Trenton, NJ: African World Press.

Yusuf, H. and R. Le Mare (2005) 'Clan elders as conflict mediators: Somaliland', in P. Van Tongeren, B. Malin, M. Hellema and J. Verhoeven (eds), *People Building Peace II: Successful Stories of Civil Society*, London: Lynne Rienner.

Zartman, I. W. (1964) 'Les relations entres la France et l'Algérie', *Revue française de science politique*, 6: 1087–113.

— (1995) *Collapsed States: The Disintegration and Restoration of Legitimate Authority*, Boulder, CO: Lynne Rienner.

— (ed.) (2000) *Traditional Cures for Modern Conflicts: African Conflict 'Medicine'*, Boulder, CO: Lynne Rienner.

— (2001a) 'Conflict reduction: prevention, management and resolution', in F. M. Deng and I. W. Zartman (eds), *Conflict Resolution in Africa*, Washington, DC: Brookings Institution Press.

— (2001b) 'Negotiating internal conflicts: incentives and intractability', *International Negotiation Journal*, 6(3).

— (2005) *Cowardly Lions: Missed Opportunities to Prevent State Collapse and Deadly Conflict*, Boulder, CO: Lynne Rienner.

— (2007) 'The African states', in N. K. Poku and J. Senghor, *Towards Africa's Renewal*, London: Ashgate.

Websites

<http://news.bbc.co.uk/2/hi/africa/6492961.stm>, accessed 20 August 2007.

<http://repositories.cdlib.org/iis/bwep/WP99-1-Watts>, accessed 29 June 2002.

Bibliography

<www.bsos.umd.edu/cidcm/peace.htm>.
<www.clingendael.nl/cru/pdf/execsyn.
    pdf>.
<www.conflictsensitivity.org/resource_
    pack.html>.
<www.dfid.gov.uk/pubs/files/
    conflictassessmentguidance.pdf>.
<www.fundforpeace.org/web/index>.
<www.globalsecurity.org/military/world/
    war/liberia-1989.htm>.
<www.iss.org.za/pubs/Monographs/No119/
    Chap6.htm>.

<www.liberia-leaf.org/reports/trials/war/
    war.htm>.
<www.pcr.uu.se/database/countries.
    php?regionSelect=1-Africa>.
<www.transparency.org/surveys/#cpi>.
<www.trinstitute.org/ojpcr/4_2gheb.htm>,
    accessed 9 September 2007.
<www.un.org/ecosocdev/geninfo/afrec/
    vol19no1/191senegal.htm>, accessed
    9 September 2007.
<www.worldbank.org/research/conflict/
    papers/greedgrievance_23oct.pdf>.

Index